Faulkner has, for forty years, been canonized as a master of modern literature. Contemporary critical theory, however, calls into question the very terms of this claim – canon, mastery, literature. *Faulkner's Subject: A Cosmos No One Owns* seeks to offer a reading of William Faulkner for our time, and does so by rethinking his masterpieces through the lenses of current critical theory. The book attends equally to the power of his work and to the current theoretical issues that would call that power into question. Drawing on poststructuralist, psychoanalytic, ideological, and gender theory, Weinstein examines the harrowing process of "becoming oneself" at the heart of these novels. This self is always male, and it achieves subjective focus only through strategically mystifying or marginalizing women and blacks. The cosmos he called his own – the textual world he produced, of which he would be "sole owner and proprietor" – emerges as a cosmos no one owns, a verbal territory also generated (and biased) by the larger culture's discourses of gender and race. Like subjectivity itself, it is a cosmos no one owns.

CAMBRIDGE STUDIES IN AMERICAN LITERATURE AND CULTURE

Faulkner's Subject:
A Cosmos No One Owns

Cambridge Studies in American Literature and Culture
Editor
Eric Sundquist, *University of California, Los Angeles*

Advisory Board
Nina Baym, *University of Illinois, Champaign-Urbana*
Sacvan Bercovitch, *Harvard University*
Albert Gelpi, *Stanford University*
Myra Jehlen, *University of Pennsylvania*
Carolyn Porter, *University of California, Berkeley*
Robert Stepto, *Yale University*
Tony Tanner, *King's College, Cambridge University*

Books in the series
56. Philip Weinstein, *Faulkner's Subject: A Cosmos No One Owns*
55. Stephen Fender, *Sea Changes: British Emigration and American Literature*
54. Peter Stoneley, *Mark Twain and the Feminine Aesthetic*
53. Joel Porte, *In Respect to Egotism: Studies in American Romantic Writing*
52. Charles Swann, *Nathaniel Hawthorne: Tradition and Revolution*
51. Ronald Bush (ed.), *T. S. Eliot: The Modernist in History*
50. Russell B. Goodman, *American Philosophy and the Romantic Tradition*
49. Eric J. Sundquist (ed.), *Frederick Douglass: New Literary and Historical Essays*
48. Susan Stanford Friedman, *Penelope's Web: Gender, Modernity, H.D.'s Fiction*
47. Timothy Redman, *Ezra Pound and Italian Fascism*
46. Ezra Greenspan, *Walt Whitman and the American Reader*
45. Michael Oriard, *Sporting with the Gods: The Rhetoric of Play and Game in American Culture*
44. Stephen Fredman, *Poet's Prose: The Crisis in American Verse*, Second edition
43. David C. Miller, *Dark Eden: The Swamp in Nineteenth-Century American Culture*

Continued on page following the Index

Faulkner's Subject
A Cosmos No One Owns

PHILIP M. WEINSTEIN
Swarthmore College

CAMBRIDGE
UNIVERSITY PRESS

Published by the Press Syndicate of the University of Cambridge
The Pitt Building, Trumpington Street, Cambridge CB2 1RP
40 West 20th Street, New York, NY 10011-4211, USA
10 Stamford Road, Oakleigh, Victoria 3166, Australia

© Cambridge University Press 1992

First published 1992

Printed in the United States of America

Library of Congress Cataloging-in-Publication Data
Weinstein, Philip M.
Faulkner's subject : a cosmos no one owns / Philip M. Weinstein.
        p.   cm. — (Cambridge studies in American literature and culture.)
    Includes index.
    ISBN 0-521-39047-8 (hc)
    1. Faulkner, William, 1897–1962—Criticism and interpretation.
I. Title. II. Series.
PS3511.A86Z9855   1992
813'.52—dc20   91-45027
                                                                          CIP

A catalog record for this book is available from the British Library.

ISBN 0-521-39047-8 hardback

For Penny, Liz, and Katie

Beginning with *Sartoris* I discovered that my own little postage stamp of native soil was worth writing about and that I would never live long enough to exhaust it. . . . It opened up a gold mine of other people, so I created a cosmos of my own. I can move these people around like God, not only in space but in time too.

–Faulkner, Interview with Jean Stein

All that touches me comes to my consciousness – beginning with my name – from the outside world, passing through the mouths of others (from the mother, etc.), with their intonation, their affective tonality, and their values. . . . Just as the body is initially formed in the womb of the mother (in her body), so human consciousness awakens surrounded by the consciousness of others.

–Mikhail Bakhtin

I see arising . . . an attitude of retreat from sexism (male as well as female). . . . This process could be summarized as an *interiorization of the founding separation of the socio-symbolic contract,* as an introduction of its cutting edge into the very interior of every identity. . . . This in such a way that the habitual . . . attempt to fabricate a scapegoat victim . . . may be replaced by the analysis of the potentialities of *victim/executioner* which characterize each identity, each subject, each sex.

–Julia Kristeva, "Women's Time"

Contents

Preface   ix
Acknowledgments   xi
List of Abbreviations   xiii
Map   xiv

Introduction   1

1 Gender   11
   Meditations on the Other: Faulkner's Rendering of Women   12
   "If I could say Mother": Construing the Unsayable about
      Faulknerian Maternity   29

2 Race   42
   Marginalia: Faulkner's Black Lives   43
   "He come and spoke for me": Scripting Lucas Beauchamp's
      Three Lives   64

3 Subjectivity   82
   "Thinking I was I was not who was not was not who":
      The Vertigo of Faulknerian Identity   83
   Becoming Joe Christmas and Ike McCaslin   99

4 Culture: A Cosmos No One Owns   110

Conclusion   154

Bibliography   167
Index   177

Preface

Abiding commitment to a writer may continue indefinitely, yet styles of interpretation change – sometimes dramatically – in time. This book proposes a reading of Faulkner marked by both of these truths. The texts I examine have been received as canonical masterpieces for some forty years now, and I (a participant in that assessment) have long seen in Faulkner a supreme master of modern fiction. But current ideas about what it means to write and to read have transformed this notion of mastery and have led many of us to reconceive our sense of the subject-in-culture, of culture-in-the-subject. The cosmos Faulkner proudly called his own now appears (inasmuch as it is constituted in writing) a cosmos no one can own, an achievement to the hilt enabled by discursive practices not amenable to private ownership.

This study's commitment to Faulkner abides, then, but it is refracted through a set of contemporary lenses focused upon kindred issues. The core issue is the production of subjectivity itself, that problematic interior resource prior to all predications of ownership. How is Faulknerian subjectivity produced? Within what decentering economies does it come into being? What allegiances inflect it, what resistances enable it, what menaces endanger it? How, as a white male writer, does he produce the subjectivities of those two groups who most constitute his Other: women and blacks? In what ways does the altering rhetorical practice within Faulkner's career suggest a refocusing, a suturing of his writerly subjectivity? What readers, for what reasons, have established Faulkner's canonical status? What status does his work deserve if we call into question the basis of its traditional standing? Finally, inasmuch as readerly subjectivity is (like all subjectivity) produced through immersion in a culture's texts, how does Faulknerian subjectivity seek to act upon our own?

Although the assumptions behind these inquiries preclude the heroizing of Faulkner, they need not reduce him to a mere puppet of impersonal forces. Rather, my aim is to show that the project of "becoming William Faulkner" not only involves a set of reciprocating complicities too intricate to be the property of any single thrusting male will, but also that, despite his death thirty years ago, his "becoming" is still taking place. So long as it continues to do so, his remarkable texts will retain their mediated and uninsured immortality.

Acknowledgments

A lot of acknowledging is needed to account for the making of this little book. Its argument centers on the institutional practices that enable individual activity, and I have been richly nourished. An NEH Fellowship in 1982–3 allowed me to study critical theory in Paris, attending seminars by Derrida and Foucault and beginning the task of altering my critical assumptions and procedures. On return to my home institution, Swarthmore College, I began to teach courses on Faulkner and critical theory; and I vowed that if I wrote another book, it would address that topic.

This address began formally in the summer of 1985, at the Faulkner and Yoknapatawpha Conference at the University of Mississippi, on "Faulkner and Women." Since then I have given three more lectures at the Faulkner Conference, each of them the basis for a portion of a chapter in this book. Its genesis is inseparable from the support generously provided during those summers. To Evans Harrington, Doreen Fowler, and Ann Abadie, I express my gratitude.

The work at that conference led to further conferences – the International Faulkner Symposium in Bonn in 1987, the American Literature Association conference in San Diego in 1989 – where other portions of the argument were tried out in a lecture format. More important, I came to know Faulknerians who have transformed my sense of what it means to share a scholarly life focused upon this writer. André Bleikasten, John Matthews, Stephen Ross, and Warwick Wadlington have accompanied my book at every stage – listening, reading, arguing, encouraging – and each page in it implicitly or explicitly engages their thinking about Faulkner. David Minter and Patrick O'Donnell read portions of the manuscript as well, and Richard Ludwig carefully responded to the entire book in draft stage. Albert Gelpi and Eric Sundquist, editors of the Cambridge Series on American Literature and Culture, provided supportive and incisive commentary as the book was nearing completion. And my colleagues Peter Schmidt, Abbe Blum, and Mark Breitenberg gave portions of the manuscript acute readings at critical junctures. With respect to good advice I have benefited by an *embarras de richesses*.

In 1988 I received an ACLS Fellowship and a George J. Becker Grant from Swarthmore College to begin to bring this work to completion. Swarthmore's greatest contribution to the book, though, took place less through its generous leave policy than through the courses and seminars I have taught there for many years. Most of what I know practically about the meaning of dialogic comes from the intellectual challenge and camaraderie of Swarthmore students and colleagues.

My twin brother Arnold has read and commented on most of my work, I on his, and his response has served as a mirror in which I better recognize the unsaid of my say. My daughters Elizabeth and Katherine not only forgave the absence that my years in Faulkner's company meant for them, but they have sustained me throughout, by entering that space and by reminding me of the burgeoning realities outside it. To my wife Penny, without whom there would be no words, I owe more than words can say.

Abbreviations

AA   *Absalom, Absalom!: The Corrected Text.* New York: Random House, 1986.

AILD   *As I Lay Dying: The Corrected Text.* New York: Random House, 1987.

FU   *Faulkner in the University: Class Conferences at the University of Virginia, 1957–58.* Edited by Frederick L. Gwynn and Joseph L. Blotner. New York: Random House, 1965.

GDM   *Go Down, Moses.* New York: Random House, 1942.

SF   *The Sound and the Fury: The Corrected Text.* New York: Random House, 1987.

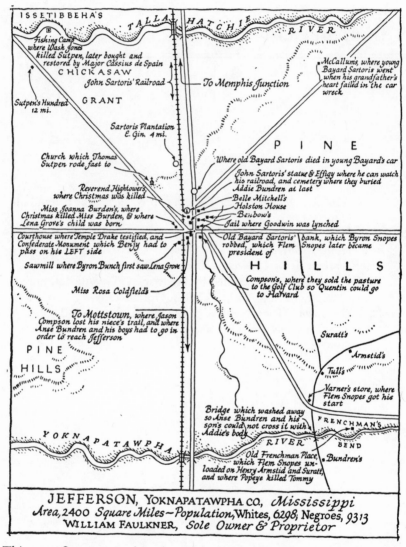

ISSETIBBEHA'S

TALLAHATCHIE RIVER

Fishing Camp
where Wash Jones
killed Sutpen, later bought and
restored by Major Cassius de Spain
CHICKASAW
John Sartoris' Railroad

To Memphis Junction

McCallum's, where young
Bayard Sartoris went
when his grandfather's
heart failed in the car
wreck

Sutpen's Hundred
12 mi.

GRANT

Sartoris Plantation
&. Gin. 4 mi.

PINE

Church which Thomas
Sutpen rode fast to

Where old Bayard Sartoris died in young Bayard's car

John Sartoris' statue & Effigy where he can watch
his railroad, and cemetery where they buried
Addie Bundren at last

Reverend Hightower's
where Christmas was killed

Belle Mitchell's
Holston House
Benbow's
Jail where Goodwin was lynched

Miss Joanna Burden's, where
Christmas killed Miss Burden, & where
Lena Grove's child was born

Courthouse where Temple Drake testified, and
Confederate Monument which Benjy had to
pass on his LEFT side

Old Bayard Sartoris' bank, which Byron Snopes
robbed, which Flem Snopes later became
president of

HILLS

Sawmill where Byron Bunch first saw Lena Grove

Compson's, where they sold the pasture
to the Golf Club so Quentin could go
to Harvard

Miss Rosa Coldfield's

To Mottstown, where Jason
Compson lost his niece's trail, and where
Anse Bundren and his boys had to go in
order to reach Jefferson

Suratt's

PINE

Armstid's

HILLS

Tull's

Varner's store, where
Flem Snopes got his
start

Bridge which washed away
so Anse Bundren and his
son's could not cross it with
Addie's body

FRENCHMAN'S

YOKNAPATAWPHA

RIVER   BEND

Old Frenchman Place,
which Flem Snopes un-
loaded on Henry Armstid and Suratt,
and where Popeye killed Tommy

Bundren's

JEFFERSON, YOKNAPATAWPHA CO., *Mississippi*
Area, 2400 *Square Miles—Population,* Whites, 6298; Negroes, 9313
WILLIAM FAULKNER, *Sole Owner & Proprietor*

This map first appeared in the 1936 edition, first printing, of *Absalom,
Absalom!* by William Faulkner, published by Random House.

Introduction

A cosmos of one's own: Faulkner conceived as early as the 1920s that his unfolding fictions would come together in the guise of a coherent world. As "sole owner and proprietor," his would be the gaze that brings into being such a world: *Be Yoknapatawpha!* is the vocative engendering the creation. Gary Stonum and Eric Sundquist, among others, have examined the pitfalls and betrayals attendant upon this generative masculine ideal; and Faulkner's commentators more broadly have remarked on the unevenness of the career, the inconsistencies within its unfolding, and the protracted sadness of its closing years.[1]

Like Balzac, but also like Sutpen, Faulkner would become a demigod, drawing upon given historical materials but designing them in such a way as to reveal no traces but his own – the writer's own subjective lineaments writ large in the lives and landscapes of his shaping. Such a masculine urge toward self-ratification appears everywhere in the novels themselves, aggressively in the dynastic ambitions of a Sartoris or McCaslin or Flem Snopes, but just as often defensively as the need for sanctuary (a stay against *"the maelstrom of unbearable reality"* [*AA* 186]), or as the intensifying narrative desire for completion: to say it all, now, in one inclusive, ten-thousand-word sentence that would close the circle of utterance. Say it now, while coherence – even if only an illusion of memory and desire, an artifact of discourses approaching obsolescence – is still intact, the abrasions of "Chinese and African and Aryan and Jew" (*GDM* 364) still at bay. "My last book will be the Doomsday Book, the

---

[1] "Apocrypha" (Faulkner's chosen word for the furthest reaches of his work: from the actual "into the apocryphal" [Stein 82]) has been read by Joseph Urgo as signaling, however unintentionally, the sense not of an orderly cosmos but of a transgressive space where authority is in crisis. Martin Kreiswirth has recently commented on the diachronic/dialogic impulse that generates Yoknapatawpha: "Faulkner is always breaking what Derrida calls 'the law of genre.'"

Golden Book of Yoknapatawpha County. Then I shall break the pencil and I'll have to stop" (Stein 82).

Faulkner's major novels are the ones in which this desire (imperial or beleaguered) for self-ratifying clashes most urgently with the differential forces – shaped by politics, race, and gender – that would unseat the coherence of the struggling male subject. In theme and form these novels enact the invasion of the unknown into the precincts of the familiar, and they suggest that such acts of self-constitution produce a selfhood not sutured but splintered – a subjectivity irreparably fissured, a cosmos no one owns. The goal of my study is to open up the dimensions of that invasion and to remap the terrain of a subjectivity requiring different terms for its reconstrual.[2] I attend therefore to the texts written between 1929 and 1942, the ones in which the pressures for and against the acknowledgment of human *being* (in the writer, his characters, and his readers in the act of response) are most agonistically in play.[3]

Put otherwise, Faulkner's supreme novels are those in which the project of subjective coherence is under maximal stress. As I read him, Faulkner was hurt into greatness. What Kristeva calls the "semiotic" – those gaps and discontinuities in discourse that betoken the subject's living struggle against the culture's grids of Symbolic meaning – drives the experimental novels and reveals a narratorial subjectivity profoundly at odds with its conventional options.[4] The self-ratifying he and his white male protagonists require collides with and shatters against the alterities that make up both his inner and his outer world – alterities that I shall

[2] This remapping involves the use of a variety of contemporary discourses for thinking about the fissured subject: Lacanian psychoanalysis, Althusserian reflection on the subject as constituted by ideology (a paradigm revised and further developed in Macherey, Eagleton, and Jameson), Derridean deconstruction, Foucauldian commentary on the subject as modeled by disciplinary practices, feminist critiques of the universalized male model of subjectivity (articulated by Kristeva and Irigaray, expounded by Gallop, Rose, and Moi), Bakhtin's location of the subject as a site of dialogic encounter, Bourdieu's reading of the subject as one who activates the culture's "habitus," and finally Smith's revisionary critique of the current theoretical dismissal of the subject as an inescapably mystified entity. I apologize for this slew of names at the outset, but insofar as they are going genuinely to be used in the following chapters, it seems wise to introduce them here.

[3] Wadlington's *Reading Faulknerian Tragedy* attends with great suppleness to this dimension of the work.

[4] Whenever Symbolic or Imaginary appears capitalized in this study, the meaning system at work is Lacanian. I elaborate at some length upon Lacan's terminology in Chapter 3, but I might briefly indicate here the range of meanings I intend. *Imaginary* refers to the dimension of experience that operates visually – through irrationally projected and introjected images in the spatial field – and that begins prior to entry into language. *Symbolic* refers to the dimension of experience that operates within the field of language – the learned networks of kinship and culture, of code and law – and that assumes centrality after the Oedipal crisis. Both these sense-making registers begin in early childhood, and they continue to inflect subjectivity in overlapping and conflicting ways throughout life.

examine most fully in the form of women and blacks. From the intensity of this collision come the precious texts.

My "own" criterion of value (my reason for preferring this handful of novels) registers a Modernist sensibility opened to a Postmodernist critique. Faulkner's brilliantly unruly early texts pass on to us (into us) the visceral assault of culture upon the subject. In their savage refusal to uplift – their continuous ironies – these novels creatively expose as unworkable the larger culture's ideological designs. Despite a current critical move to rebuke Modernism for the blindnesses preserved within this stance of "seeing through everything," I continue to locate Faulkner's most memorable achievement within such a stance of rebellious experimentation. Arguing for his Modernist texts as both the locus of his value and the gauge against which we can read the rest of the career, I seek to identify the implicit (and broadly shared) cultural discourses that, by enabling this cosmos, keep him from ever mastering it as "his own." The Postmodern dimension of this inquiry resides in my attempt to understand the necessary complicities – the cultural norms and linguistic resources, the positioning of the white male subject in relation to women and blacks – that permit subjective identity, that allow Faulkner to enter the field of discourse and become "Faulkner."

If these are the texts in which the author most risked his authority, they are also the ones in whose name, over time, he has most obtained his authority. *The Sound and the Fury, Light in August, Absalom, Absalom!*, and *Go Down, Moses* have enjoyed canonical status for some forty years now.[5] What larger cultural arrangements do they openly contest or implicitly endorse, such that we (the literary establishment) have institutionalized them, made them into Faulkner's "signature," even as, in their hazardous activities, they call the coherence of any signature into question? Why, especially, do we turn to *The Sound and the Fury* as not only Faulkner's "heart's darling" but ours too? I shall address these questions indirectly throughout the following chapters and explicitly in the conclusion, but my aim is less to puncture than to understand these novels' claims to canonicity. Indeed, *The Sound and the Fury* has been for me, ever since I encountered it in 1960, the supreme American novel of our century. This study is inconceivable without that prior affection, yet I could never have written it without assenting and responding to cumulative pressures (provoked by critical theory) upon such a protected icon of value. The sanctuary at stake in this book – the subjectivity under scrutiny – bears my name as much as Faulkner's.

---

[5] I omit *As I Lay Dying* from this scrutiny because so much of its representative quality is shared with *The Sound and the Fury*. My larger purpose is not to justify canonical exclusiveness but "repercussively" to interrogate Faulkner's practice within a limited (but not privileged) frame.

I propose to treat this double interrogation (of Faulkner's coherent subjectivity, of my own) not as embarrassing but as enabling. Assignments of literary value involve simultaneously the writer's work, the productive and the receptive cultures' aesthetic politics, and the reader's subjective positioning with respect to these economies. None of these orientations is simply given, all of them invite inquiry. I shall address the four novels identified above as among Faulkner's finest and as problematic sites on which the higher culture has registered its imprimatur. Further, I shall accord the form of *The Sound and the Fury* canonical status within my own study, for I propose, Faulkner-fashion, to treat these four novels as he came at the Compson materials: by approaching them (as a group) four different times and with four sets of competing questions. Such a dialogic strategy privileges difference itself, allowing each lens to produce what it produces as I revisit the same (but never the same) terrain. Faulkner is a supremely perspectival novelist – or a "repercussive" one – and it seems right to frame the theoretical issues that most call into question his "signature" within a dialogic form that virtually constitutes his "signature."

"Repercussive" I call him, and my book is likewise repercussive, always returning, though the place alters not just under a different set of lenses but in accord with the differing times of my visit. This diachronic dimension is, indeed, wrought into all writing. We would, like Faulkner, say it all in one monstrous sentence,[6] yet the fate of writing is that it proceeds in time and the mind alters during the time of the proceeding. "It is because writing is inaugural," Derrida writes, "that it is dangerous and anguishing. It does not know where it is going, no knowledge can keep it from the essential precipitation toward the meaning that it constitutes and that is, primarily, its future. There is thus no insurance against the risk of writing" ("Force" 11). This small scandal – the aleatory hallmark of all protracted writing – is what we seek to cover up as we revise, and I have sought in this book both to acknowledge the scandal and to make it productive. I *have* revised, but not with the illusion that my text can become seamless, its argument synchronically complete. So the chapters deliberately retain some of the flavor of their original impetus. I aim for dialogic interactions, not the authority of a magisterial synthesis. This is not a cosmos I can own.

I have claimed that the critical issues I explore in this book problematize Faulkner's "signature," and I mean by this more than the fact that his identity as a writer alters in time. It also alters according to the discursive options available to (and chosen by) him for pursuing it. No writer simply delivers into a neutral language his achieved identity: his self-engendered sense of "how it is" in here and out there. Perhaps the

---

[6] John Irwin candidly reveals this fantasy in the opening pages of *Doubling and Incest*, 9.

most far-reaching Western intellectual claim of our century is that between self and world there intervenes discourse, and that discourse in-
flects both self and world. Benjamin Lee Whorf writes:

> We dissect nature along lines laid down by our native languages. The
> categories and types that we isolate from the world of phenomena we do
> not find there because they stare every observer in the face; on the
> contrary, the world is presented in a kaleidoscopic flux of impressions
> which has to be organized in our minds – and this means largely by the
> linguistic systems in our minds. We cut nature up, organize into con-
> cepts, and ascribe significances as we do, largely because we are parties
> to an agreement to organize it in this way – an agreement that holds
> throughout our speech community and is codified in the patterns of our
> language. The agreement is, of course, an implicit and unstated one, *but
> its terms are absolutely obligatory;* we cannot talk at all except by subscrib-
> ing to the organization and classification of data to which the agreement
> subscribes. (213)

Implicit and obligatory, the agreement we are party to is most
efficacious in our ongoing ignorance of it. Like Molière's M. Jourdain
who can hardly believe that it is *prose* that he speaks, we daily participate
unawares in the most intricate arrangements the moment we draw upon
language. Foucault's epistemological work stems directly from this conviction and from a desire to revise – by exposing – its implications. "I
would like to show with precise examples," he writes in *The Archaeology
of Knowledge,* "that in analysing discourses themselves, one sees the
loosening of the embrace . . . of words and things, and the emergence of
a group of rules proper to discursive practices. These rules define not the
dumb existence of a reality, nor the canonical use of a vocabulary, but the
ordering of objects" (48–9). The words do not attach to the things; they
sketch out instead the language game in play, the discursive practice's
systemic way of ordering its objects.

The order arrived at, because it is produced in language, can only be
contestable. The unutterable truth is alone serene; it lives as inarticulable
doxa. But once it becomes encoded, enters language, it is available for
dispute. Orthodoxy is no more than the desperate battle to resist heterodoxy. As the homely analogy of the orthodontist makes clear, orthodoxy
seeks to *straighten* the doxa, and this effort (which is undertaken only
when things have gone crooked) can be both strenuous and painful.
Pierre Bourdieu writes: "Orthodoxy, straight, or rather *straightened,*
opinion, which aims, without ever entirely succeeding, at restoring the
primal state of innocence of doxa, exists only in the objective relationship
which opposes it to heterodoxy, that is, by reference to the choice –
haeresis, heresy – made possible by the existence of *competing possibles* and
to the explicit critique of the sum total of the alternatives not chosen that
the established order implies" (169).

To speak (or write) at all is to enter the Whorfian "agreement" wrought into the medium itself, but it is also to enter an inherently debatable arena, a world of "competing possibles," of discursive insistences that are always partial, always warding off unwanted alternatives. Faulknerian subjectivity – because, like all subjectivity, it is produced by entry into the politically charged turbulence of discourse itself[7] – cannot be conceived as a disinterested power solitarily authorizing a pristine cosmos. It emerges instead "as a way of being as it were at stake in the game from the outset" (Derrida, "Structure" 279). Faulkner becomes Faulkner by what he submits to exactly as much as by what he rejects. To use Derrida's terms again: without accepting the medium's authority there is no signification; without resisting it there is no force.

To be "in the game from the outset" does not mean remaining in it always in the same way. One of my chief purposes in this book is to chart Faulkner's changing mode of participation in his culture's "agreements." Between 1929 and 1942 a virtual revolution in his practice occurs, in which a Modernist aesthetic of shock emerges, transforms itself, and then yields to a more traditional one of recognition. He moves, formally, from the jagged invasions of *The Sound and the Fury* to the sonorous plenitude of *Go Down, Moses*. Whether the practice be iconoclastic or orthodox, it articulates "Faulkner" not as inaugurative native genius but as a set of individual performances and a certain way of activating or resisting the larger discourses – here gender and racial as well as avantgarde and traditional – furnished by his culture. To identify William Faulkner is to speak of an overdetermined site of interchanges in which come into play the writer's discrete performances, the discursive options (accepted, refused, or transformed) of his productive culture (America in the first half of our century), and the interpretive orientation of a reader responding in the receptive culture of the same country fifty years later. It all sounds not so much hopeless as dizzying.

It has not always seemed this complicated. Brooks, Vickery, Howe, and Warren could write with a certain confidence about an author whom they had brooded upon, sympathized with, and finally understood. "But the shift to this previously unknown narrator," Brooks claims in his introduction to *Light in August* (1968), "will seem like a trick only to the reader who has failed to sense the total meaning of the work" (xxv). I know of no astute Faulknerian in the past fifteen years who is

---

[7] The word "discourse" should be understood in a concrete and plural sense. Faulkner's career involves a changing relation to a range of discursive practices – the nymphs and fauns of *fin-de-siècle* late Victorianism, the ferocious stylistic experiments of international Modernism, the polysyllabic magniloquence of Southern oratory, the mean humor of Southwestern vernacular, among others.

willing to speak of "the total meaning of the work," and this not because
of timidity or laziness but because, in Derrida's words, "If totalization no
longer has any meaning, it is . . . because the nature of the field – that is,
language and a finite language – excludes totalization. This field is in
effect that of *play* . . . because instead of being too large, there is something missing from it: a center which arrests and grounds the play of
substitutions" ("Structure" 289).

The missing center is of course produced and posited in every reading
of Faulkner – I too will produce my center(s) in the course of these pages
– but this center is invented as a function of the argument(s) under way.
Faulkner centers differently according to who (read: what transpersonal
hermeneutic) is looking at him. He has been changing mightily in the
past twenty years (unlike his own heroic dead figures, his Sartorises and
McCaslins, whose images tend to stay put once they are interred), and I
have been changing with him. This book is possible because of these
changes. To discuss them, however briefly, is to see that a writer's identity (his, mine) is likewise not given but produced. How else could it alter
so much over time?

The Faulkner of my first love was a towering invention of the New
Critics: formally experimental, conservative in his values, detached above
and by means of his ever-present ironies, passionate yet not partisan,
aware of everything.[8] We competed with each other during the 1960s and
early 1970s to see who could celebrate him best, could point out how
much further his art penetrated into the nature of things than had yet
been conceded. The critic who both culminated this genre of commentary and inaugurated the next one is André Bleikasten. His full-length
reading (*Splendid* 1976) of *The Sound and the Fury* attended with great
suppleness to the complexity of Faulkner's formal achievement, but it
also began the process of inserting that achievement within a larger intellectual frame of Lacanian, structuralist, and poststructuralist values. Simultaneously with Bleikasten came John Irwin's intervention, in which
"Faulkner" joins the discourses of Nietzsche and Freud and emerges as a
latent structure lurking somewhere between his books rather than a set of
utterances contained within any of them. After Irwin, the opening of the
floodgates and the deluge.

A mere glance at the influential texts on Faulkner written since the
early 1980s shows that a writer centers according to the emphases of the

---

[8] Brooks and Vickery were probably the foremost shapers of Faulkner's image in the late
1950s and 1960s, though Sartre, Aiken, Cowley, Howe, and Warren – who wrote before
them – have remained distinctive voices for articulating Faulkner's form and value. By
1963 Millgate was able to consolidate these New Critical findings and propose a narrative
in which Faulkner's work appeared both selectively canonical and comprehensively
mapped.

culture doing the evaluating. The Faulkner for our decade is a writer about race (Sundquist, Snead), gender (Wittenberg, Gwin), language and voice (Matthews, Ross), the dynamics of reading (Wadlington, Morris), and ideology (Porter, Moreland). Without apology, this is the Faulkner addressed in the following chapters. Bleikasten, Matthews, Ross, and Wadlington have especially served for me as brothers in a many-peopled enterprise. Learning that subjective identity is a matter of affiliations rather than essences has allowed me to find my Faulkners by letting my Faulkner go. That is why the chapters that follow reengage the same books, also why the quarrels among the chapters are overt rather than concealed. Intentionally diachronic, striving to avoid the twin excesses of randomness and overpatterning, this study pursues a Faulkner whose own cultural immersion precludes heroism. But without these remarkable novels there would have been no study at all.

ेे

The "cosmos" Faulkner would own is articulable only within a language he cannot wholly own, and it bristles with figures unamenable to the lineaments of his own white male subjectivity. The first two chapters probe the writer's resources for articulating the Other within his world – its women and blacks – by examining his relation to his culture's larger discursive practices for saying/mystifying/scapegoating their differences. Chapter 1 focuses upon gender, both laterally, in the representation of women as *other* in the four novels under scrutiny, and vertically, as an attempt to unearth the discursive assumptions that generate a corrosive portrait like Mrs. Compson in *The Sound and the Fury*. In Chapter 2, I turn to Faulkner's rendering of race, and I begin by examining the marginalizing (as well as the fantasizing) that emerges in Faulkner's deployment of blacks upon his largely white canvas. This chapter concludes with another vertical exploration, this time into the three different scriptings of Lucas Beauchamp, from magazine stories to *Go Down, Moses* to *Intruder in the Dust*. Finally, they prepare the context for approaching (in the second half of the study) the problematics of subjectivity at the center of Faulkner's texts: the shaping of the white, male subject whose codes in turn command the figuring of both women and blacks.

Chapter 3 considers in two different ways the social construction of identity. I begin by exploring the privileged notion of individual identity within a Western liberal tradition. Then, through the use of conceptual terms provided by Lacan and Althusser, a critique is provided. Subjectivity emerges, in this later model, as simultaneously empowering and alienating, the interplay – within a single figure – of Imaginary affiliations and Symbolic insistences. Quentin Compson in *The Sound and the Fury* and a variety of figures in *Absalom, Absalom!* embody the cultural crossfire that is subjectivity within Faulkner's most experimental novels. The chapter concludes with a brief comparison of the processes of becoming Joe Christmas and Ike McCaslin in their respective novels. Continuing to draw upon Lacan and Althusser, but supplementing them with some other contemporary theorists of the "postindividualist subject," I propose a variety of signifying economies for thinking about the production of subjectivity. The striking shift in tone and procedure between these two novels about training-to-be-male reveals as well the other subjectivity that has decisively altered in the ten years between *Light in August* and *Go Down, Moses:* Faulkner's.

Chapter 4 broadens further to identify the ideological field of surveillance and contestation within which the Faulknerian voiced body moves and has its being.[9] I draw on Foucault and Bakhtin to chart the ways in which voice and body are figured according to the larger culture's norms regarding gender, class, and race. Faulkner's texts resist and absorb these assumptions in ways that change decisively between 1929 and 1942. This chapter probes the increasingly secure ideological alignment of Faulkner's work in terms, first, of his rendering of voice and body and, second, of the reader's transferential "contract" with the texts. By 1942, I argue, he had lost the capacity (or perhaps the desire) to dramatize through reader disorientation and immersion the traumatic entry of the individual subject into the culture's maturational field: a traumatic entry at the core of the great Modernist texts. At the level of the writing the hurt had ceased, the subject had sutured.[10]

The entry of the subject into the culture, the entry of the reader into the text: throughout my argument I maintain that the former is crucially figured in the latter. Each of these chapters attends to the experience of *reading* Faulkner, for if the subject's identity is always in process, then the act of reading powerfully activates that process. In reading we confirm/alter/rethink who we are; the suasions of the text seek to realign the traces of our minds. All writing is ideological inasmuch as it strategically offers to its reader models of being – models that normalize and marginalize according to determinate cultural criteria. I seek, therefore, to explore these texts at the intersection of representational tactics (the positioning of race and gender, the selective deployment of interiority) and readerly experience (the subject-shaping encounter with the novels themselves, the kinds of acknowledgment they propose or refuse).

Finally I want to ask why Faulkner has been so important to us, who

---

[9] "Ideology" serves as a master term in this study, and it receives more extensive definition in Chapters 2 through 4. I should say at the outset, however, that I take it to mean not false consciousness, but rather a set of beliefs and practices that propose coherent subjectivity by securing the individual's alignment within a repertory of socially propagated roles.

[10] I use the term "suture" in a specifically Lacanian way: "Suture . . . is the way in which the 'subject' at one and the same time separates itself from, or disavows, its construction in the field of the Other, and simultaneously erects itself in the garb of coherent 'subject'" (Smith 75).

the "we" is in this assertion, and what remains of any notion of coherent subjectivity if it can be endlessly reconfigured according to different signifying economies. Something still remains, or better: something new emerges. For subjectivity is a notion we cannot do without. Not the undivided subjectivity of liberal Western thought – the (white, male) autonomous self-knowing individual – but rather the subject in process, the subject in contestation. Beleaguered, charged with Imaginary desires, immersed from infancy within conflicting alignments of the Symbolic field, this subject is more likely to be a site of interior disturbance than a locus of concerted action. Who better than Faulkner has delineated the pathos and value of such a figure? How other than by first probing such disturbance can any demystified notion of concerted action – of subjective agency – once again be liberatingly conceived?

1

Gender

My study begins here, both conceptually and with respect to its own genetic history, with the following speculations about Faulkner's gender-coded habits of representation. "Subject," which seemed not so long ago a term of full value and the priority against which Faulkner's objectification of women was to be measured, has since become for me (as for most theoretically minded critics) a term of unpacifiable disturbance. I need it nevertheless, for the sense of an empowering interiority that we call subjectivity remains indispensable, however fissured we may show it to be. "No politics without identity," Jacqueline Rose maintains, "but no identity which takes itself at its word" (157). In like manner, no agency at all without recourse to the interiority of the subject, but at the same time no mystified sense of the subject as whole, sovereign, centered.

I begin laterally, by exploring Faulkner's strategies (conscious or unconscious) for representing female characters in the four canonical novels under scrutiny. I focus especially upon narrative positioning and the selective bestowal of subjectivity within these texts. This first inquiry into the *données* of Faulkner's canvas patently calls for a second one, keyed to other questions: why are these effects in place? what cluster of culturally shared assumptions about gender identity fuels such an uneven representational strategy? To answer these questions I turn inward and consider at length a single figure – Mrs. Compson of *The Sound and the Fury* – in order to suggest the lineaments of the ideological complex that underlies (and might explain the virulence of) this most antipathetic of Faulkner's female portraits. The issue, it has taken me twenty years to see, is not that Faulkner dislikes Mrs. Compson but why he does so: what in his cultural predisposition for thinking about women makes him find this figure so radically defective? At first Simone de Beauvoir, and later Julia Kristeva and Luce Irigaray, have helped me to recognize

11

Faulkner's optic in this matter – by enabling me to begin to change my own.[1]

MEDITATIONS ON THE OTHER: FAULKNER'S RENDERING OF WOMEN

"Sir," asked the undergraduate (gender unknown) at the University of Virginia, "do you find it easier to create a female character in literature or a male character?" "It's much more fun to try to write about women," Faulkner replied, "because I think women are marvelous, they're wonderful, and I know very little about them" (*FU* 45). In the debate about Faulkner's portrayal of women, this remark has been often cited (by Cleanth Brooks among others)[2] as evidence, amply supported by the books themselves, that Faulkner's fictional women are as richly portrayed as his men. Most of Faulkner's gender-conscious readers of today would disagree, and the terms of Faulkner's statement are indeed unthinkable if applied to men. What male author would speak of men as "marvelous . . . wonderful . . . I know very little about them"? Taking Faulkner at his word (though his tongue may have been near his cheek), I

---

[1] In the few years since I first conceived this chapter, feminist commentary on Faulkner has dramatically increased in variety and sophistication. Judith Wittenberg, Doreen Fowler, Judith Sensibar, and Linda Kauffman, among others, have shed light on the representation of women characters struggling within the Faulknerian male Symbolic; and Minrose Gwin has recently published the first full-length study of these issues. This is not the place adequately to assess such work, but Gwin's study – the most ambitious on this topic to have yet appeared – does require a few words. Her most provocative claims center upon "the process of women as the space of disruption in Faulkner's texts" (16), and she draws usefully on Cixous's sense of character-as-construction to develop an argument that the female emerges in Faulkner's great texts as a site for enacting "the rebellious unconscious of patriarchy" (16). This focus upon women less as characters than as a site of disturbance within the patriarchal leanings of Faulkner's texts is suggestive and will prove productive. To my mind, however, the limitation of Gwin's work inheres in its uncritical adhesion to Cixousian ecstasy as an all-resolving mode of transcendence – "spending" without check, "playing" without any attempt to understand – as she seeks to rewrite Caddy's subjectivity within the terms of such an emancipatory discourse: "When she [Caddy] speaks, she speaks of giving and of desire, of a *jouissance* which is as multiple as female orgasm" (52). Perhaps, but I also keep hearing the voice of a woman so caught up in the punitive sexual ideology of her culture that she sees herself as doomed: *"I died last year I told you I had . . . I know I'm dead I tell you"* (*SF* 153). A discourse composed of heady patches of Cixous, with interspersed phrases from Irigaray and Kristeva, sounds to me less like Faulkner's Caddy than like a 1980s French feminist rewriting of her. Gwin's commentary is recurrently stimulating, but I wish that it heeded better Ann Jones's reminder that the body (because it is always culturally mediated) can be no simple source of pure *jouissance* – that women live their bodies in complex, anxious, and satisfying ways – and that a polarized model of woman as difference/multiple orgasm/*jouissance* versus man as identity/castration/patriarchal imprisonment simply furthers the either–or binarisms that many of us are trying conceptually to free ourselves from.

[2] Cleanth Brooks, Introduction to *Faulkner's Women,* by Sally R. Page, xi–xii.

hope to identify what it means for Faulkner's women to be "marvelous" or "wonderful": not in the moral sense of how they are evaluated, but in the narrative sense of how they are deployed in the fiction. Marvels and wonders are objects one marvels and wonders at. They exist in a different relation to the narrative voice from that of understandable phenomena. More precisely, they exist as the nonsubjective *other:* noteworthy, remarkable, but continuously isolated within their own domain.[3]

In Quentin's section of *The Sound and the Fury* there are two significant encounters with unknown characters, one with a group of boys interested in fishing, the other with a little girl whom he calls "sister." The vignettes are of roughly equal length, but Quentin experiences them in quite different ways:

> The trout hung, delicate and motionless among the wavering shadows. Three boys with fishing poles came onto the bridge and we leaned on the rail and looked down at the trout. They knew the fish. He was a neighborhood character.
>
> "They've been trying to catch that trout for twenty-five years. There's a store in Boston offers a twenty-five dollar fishing rod to anybody that can catch him."
>
> "Why don't you all catch him, then? Wouldn't you like to have a twenty-five dollar fishing rod?"
>
> "Yes," they said. They leaned on the rail, looking down at the trout. "I sure would," one said.
>
> "I wouldn't take the rod," the second said. "I'd take the money instead."
>
> "Maybe they wouldn't do that," the first said. "I bet he'd make you take the rod."
>
> "Then I'd sell it."
>
> "You couldn't get twenty-five dollars for it."
>
> "I'd take what I could get, then. I can catch just as many fish with this

---

[3] The concept of "the other" is an important counterterm in most philosophic discussions of the subject from Hegel through Sartre. Contemporary (post-Saussurean) psychoanalytic theory (as articulated by Lacan), approaching the subject by way of a massive concern both with "others" and with the "Other" of the Symbolic system itself, generally argues that conscious subjectivity is inescapably mystified. For my purposes, the most useful formulation of "women as the other" is Simone de Beauvoir's: "Now, what peculiarly signalizes the situation of woman is that she – a free and autonomous being like all human creatures – nevertheless finds herself living in a world where men compel her to assume the status of the Other. They propose to stabilize her as object and to doom her to immanence since her transcendence is to be overshadowed and forever transcended by another ego [the man's] . . . which is essential and sovereign" (xxix). The crucial terms here are immanence and transcendence: woman, by being defined extrinsically, by being known only as the object of the male gaze, loses the intrinsic, moment-by-moment freedom of her own subjective self-awareness. In place of this unpredictable transcendence, she assumes her identity from without – as a foreclosed immanence, a completed text whose terms are imposed by the male.

pole as I could with a twenty-five dollar one." Then they talked about
what they would do with twenty-five dollars. They all talked at once,
their voices insistent and contradictory and impatient, making of unre-
ality a possibility, then a probability, then an incontrovertible fact, as
people will when their desires become words. (134)

This scene is clearly located in space and time and understanding: by a
bridge, with three boys and a trout, full of localizing details – the Boston
store, the bet, the fishing rods. The boys chatter at length (they share a
discursive practice, however fantastic), and Quentin enters into what they
are saying, into both their motives and their delusion. He is at home in
this scene; he understands the language game being played. Some fifteen
pages later he wanders into a bakery and encounters "sister." He buys
some cake and buns and they walk outside together:

> "You'd better take your bread on home, hadn't you?"
> She looked at me. She chewed quietly and steadily; at regular intervals
> a small distension passed smoothly down her throat. I opened my pack-
> age and gave her one of the buns. "Goodbye," I said.
> I went on. Then I looked back. She was behind me. "Do you live
> down this way?" She said nothing. She walked beside me, under my
> elbow sort of, eating. We went on. . . . She swallowed the last of the
> cake, then she began on the bun, watching me across it. "Goodbye," I
> said. I turned into the street and went on, but I went to the next corner
> before I stopped.
> "Which way do you live?" I said. "This way?" I pointed down the
> street. She just looked at me. "Do you live over that way? I bet you live
> close to the station, where the trains are. Don't you?" She just looked at
> me, serene and secret and chewing. (148)

This scene is as eery as the one with the boys is reassuring. The setting
seems both to shift and to remain the same – to move away from this girl
and yet, as in a dream, continuously to come upon her. Quentin cannot
establish a relation to her, cannot discover who she is, who her family is,
or even what tongue she speaks. Indeed, her tongue is doing something
more eloquent than speaking: it is participating in the methodical pul-
verization of the food – cake, bun, ice cream – that she never ceases to
put into her mouth. She is *other* throughout this scene – a silent body, all
of whose engulfing motions are intently observed, as though they had an
unspeakable connection with Quentin's own fantasy life. As indeed they
do. She is as conventionally unplaced in a foregrounded social setting as
she is scandalously implicated in Quentin's incestuous memories and
desires. As such, as a solitary female "marvelously" attached to the psychic stresses of her observer yet deprived of the component parts of her
own subjective setting – her friends, her voice, her fears, her desires –
"sister" serves as a model for the three Compson brothers' rendering of

their sister Caddy, as well as an indication of Faulkner's broader narrative stance toward his "wonderful" women.

Within the context of "sister" we can make more sense of Faulkner's often cited reason for not making Caddy a narrator: "because Caddy was still to me too beautiful and too moving to reduce her to telling what was going on, that it would be more passionate to see her through somebody else's eyes, I thought" (*FU* 1). Like "sister," a Caddy wholly presented through male optics is a Caddy wholly available to male emphases. She is "more passionate" because more focused: there is no leakage here, nothing expressed that is not relevant to the sibling crises through which she is perceived. (Artistically focused, yes, but not therefore domesticated: Caddy can encounter the male-generated narrative meant to contain her only in the form of disaster; the fallout from this encounter never ceases to poison her siblings.) Her "passionate" attraction lodges in the male-generated mystery of her perceived body, not the sympathetic articulation of her mind. Had Faulkner entered her mind and allowed *that* movement of thought and feeling to pace his own narrative, Caddy would have become more diffused, more tangentially implicated – through the promiscuous impetus of stream of consciousness itself – in the lives of other figures, as well as more present in her own life. In becoming a character whose narrative reality was not entirely a function of the love and hatred of her three brothers – a character whose subjectivity might in part elude the obsessive male gaze – she might have become less "beautiful," less tragic, and more free.[4]

The contrast between "sister" and the three boys fishing reveals another narrative principle commanded by gender. The female is essentially alone, whereas the male is granted the privilege of same-sex company. Caddy, her daughter Quentin, and "sister" are of course surrounded by males – they move through a male world as through a gauntlet – but this is a context that stifles rather than enables the female at the center. Deprived of female "correspondents," these figures are defined by, and at the mercy of, the brothers, fathers, uncles, and lovers who surround them, fear them, adore them, *speak* them. By contrast, the three boys going fishing and swimming speak freely and within a common language; they engage in common activities. The narrative's mode of encountering them does not automatically put their gender identity under

---

[4] Sartre explains succinctly this movement of (male) subjective consciousness through which the freedom of the other is foreclosed: "Thus at one and the same time I have regained my being-for-itself through my consciousness (of) myself as a perpetual center of infinite possibilities, and I have transformed the Other's possibilities into dead-possibilities by affecting them all with the character of '*not-lived-by-me*' – that is as simply given" (205).

pressure or at stake. There is no sense (while reading this episode) of male bodies or minds as sources of mystery. In like manner, Quentin and his father are free to talk casually to each other throughout *The Sound and the Fury*. That they disagree is beside the point. They share a common language (learned, philosophical: the male-restricted currency of high culture). They ratify each other's identity through argument.

Mrs. Compson is not similarly empowered. The words that pour forth unceasingly from her are the long-dead detritus of a culture's truisms rather than the living index of its doubt or its despair. She is a receptacle of the Symbolic petrified into inanity. Her words may meet with rebellion or acquiescence, it hardly matters; no one is going to engage them in dialogue. Who, indeed, would she talk to rather than at? Like the other "wonderful" women in *The Sound and the Fury*, she is essentially on display – unaware of the ideas that empower the book she lives in, dramatized not through any dialogic and self-risking interchanges with others but, rather, through her unremitting impact upon them.

The exception to this norm of gender representation is of course Dilsey. The narrative manages to render her as other and interrelated at the same time. It can do so because blackness is not only not proposed as problematic in *The Sound and the Fury*, it permits narrative escape from white problems of sexuality and gender both. (Insofar as this is so, it helps to explain Faulkner's unstinting focus upon Dilsey's social behavior, her words and gestures within Compson precincts.) The aristocratic retainer model looms large in this arrangement: a healthy (normative) black family devotes their daily energies to taking care of an unsalvageable white one, and nothing appears amiss to anyone involved.

Because the two bloods are innocently imagined as separate, the two families can be innocently imagined as together. It takes the scent of miscegenation to rouse Faulkner's racial anxieties. Dilsey (as well as Roskus, Frony, Versh, T. P., Luster) is fully contained within her role as black servant/helper/advisor/mother to the Compsons. Those three white brothers and their white author see in her only a loving (and immovable) domestic presence. Free of Nancy's aggressive sexuality, untainted as well by the scandalous possession of Clytie's Sutpen blood or the menacing possibility of Molly's liaison with Zack Edmonds, Dilsey is, so to speak, a portrait conceived in innocence. She is constructed to fulfill a white fantasy of a black woman at ease and functioning within a patriarchal world. Hers is a voice whose range and effectiveness (with white and black, male and female) are purchased by both an exclusion of private fear or desire and a willingness to leave Southern race relations unthought. (On matters of fear and desire, or the problematics of race, she can say nothing, though this silence becomes eloquent once the reasons for it begin to be probed.) Given the price paid, it is all the more remarkable that so much remains, and that her voice is – especially for white male readers nurtured in memory or fantasy by such a black woman – one of the most compelling in all of Faulkner's fiction.[5]

ॐ

"Joe Christmas is the most solitary character in American fiction, the most extreme phase conceivable of American loneliness" (253). For over thirty years these words of Alfred Kazin have seemed persuasive, but scrutiny of *Light in August* from the perspective of narrative strategy would as easily show that the most solitary figure is Lena Grove. Not that she is "lonely"; one of the reasons we have persistently gone to the Faulkner males as figures of isolation – Bayard, Benjy, Quentin, Darl, Joe Christmas, Sutpen, Ike – is that in them loneliness is thematized and tirelessly proclaimed. The narrative voice repeatedly emphasizes their predicament. But this move on the part of the narrative, which socializes their isolation by inviting the reader imaginatively to share it, is denied to the women. Conceived as gregarious beings, the women are not often portrayed as lonely. Yet they are solitary inasmuch as the narrative neither proposes a discourse that might articulate their subjective self-understanding nor dramatizes their sharing their inner lives in each other's company.

Consider the opening of *Light in August*. The first six pages are a tour de force that establishes, for the duration of the novel, Lena's "marvelous" quality. Her refrain of a "fur piece," her summarized past in which childhood, adolescence, pregnancy, and departure are all related without either demur or a word of dialogue with others, her lyrical meditation that "if he is going all the way to Jefferson, I will be riding within the hearing of Lucas Burch before his seeing. He will hear the wagon but he won't know. So there will be one within his hearing before his seeing" (9) – all these Lena notations are interwoven into poetic third-personal descriptions of the "evocation of *far*," of "something moving forever and without progress across an urn" (7). The result is a lyrical celebration of Lena Grove as a "wonderful" creature who communes with herself, who imperturbably sustains the vicissitudes of her life, and who moves with more than human grace and tranquillity across a height-

---

[5] The ways in which a Southern white male Imaginary constructs experience receives sustained attention in Chapter 3. But this is an instance, early on, where Faulkner's Imaginary bond with the black mammy emerges before us in all its strengths and weaknesses. Having shared something of that Imaginary for decades (I grew up in the South, nursed by a black woman whom I think of every time I reread this novel), I can testify to the intimacy of Faulkner's portrait of Dilsey. That this portrait radiates the white writer's creative trust in the black woman's nurturing groundedness – her essential stability – means, however, that it cannot touch upon crucial dimensions of Dilsey's subjective complexity: her unforeclosed relation to herself that must exceed the filial terms of his fixed and race-governed affection for her.

ened landscape. She carries very little genealogical baggage. These six pages eloquently tell us that she inhabits her own space, that there is no one like her.

There is no one like her, but Armstid and Winterbottom (whom she meets up with on page 9) appear as almost exactly like each other. Their setting is matter-of-fact rather than poetic, their activity is the quotidian one of arranging (in an insistently offhand way) the sale of a cultivator, and their medium is talk. They understand each other perfectly. The transaction they are embarked upon is part of the immemorial business of country life; and the unhurried, articulable rhythm of such communal activities carries (more than anything else) this novel's powerful sense of traditional values – values lodged within a male frame of shared assumptions.

In the next eighteen pages Armstid takes Lena home and we witness a dialogue that follows quite different premises from the one between him and Winterbottom. Mrs. Armstid and Lena engage in a comic ballet of cross-statements, the two of them speaking out of opposed and inarticulable centers:

> Mrs. Armstid watches the lowered face. Her hands are on her hips and she watches the younger woman with an expression of cold and impersonal contempt. "And you believe that he will be there when you get there. Granted that he ever was there at all. That he will hear you are in the same town with him, and still be there when the sun sets."
>
> Lena's lowered face is grave, quiet. Her hand has ceased now. It lies quite still on her lap, as if it had died there. Her voice is quiet, tranquil, stubborn. "I reckon a family ought to all be together when a chap comes. Specially the first one. I reckon the Lord will see to that." (22–3)

Interchanges such as this suggest not only that Lena protects what she is carrying in her womb. An invisible membrane seems to intervene between her and her interlocutors, permitting her to draw inward upon hidden resources and effortlessly to ward off the attempts of others to penetrate her space. The comic effect of this exchange, based upon incompatible assumptions, is exactly the reverse of the comic effect of the following:

> The others had not stopped work, yet there was not a man in the shed who was not again watching the stranger in his soiled city clothes. . . . The foreman looked at him, briefly, his gaze as cold as the other's. "Is he going to do it in them clothes?"
>
> "That's his business," the superintendent said. "I'm not hiring his clothes."
>
> "Well, whatever he wears suits me if it suits you and him," the foreman said. "All right, mister," he said. "Go down yonder and get a scoop and help them fellows move that sawdust."
>
> The newcomer turned without a word. The others watched him go

down to the sawdust pile and vanish and reappear with a shovel and go
to work. The foreman and the superintendent were talking at the door.
They parted and the foreman returned. "His name is Christmas," he
said.
　　"His name is what?" one said.
　　"Christmas."
　　"Is he a foreigner?"
　　"Did you ever hear of a white man named Christmas?" the foreman
said.
　　"I never heard of nobody a-tall named it," he said. (34–5)

As in the earlier dialogue between Armstid and Winterbottom, this
comic interchange is premised upon a common understanding. The
shared dislike of and acquiescence in work, the common awareness of
what clothes one wears for this job, the general conviction that "Christmas" is not a name befitting a white man: these settled matters of norm
and eccentricity constitute a minimal social space, an economy of mutual
assumptions within which jokes may be uttered and understood. Joe
Christmas may be lonely, but he is, by way of contrast, nicely placed in a
scene like this one. Because the novel proliferates its male scenes of
camaraderie, showing us in relaxed detail how the menfolk of Jefferson
talk to each other, Joe's social ostracism is precisely identified. We know
what he is not like. Further, the novel tirelessly tells us, through symbolic
parallels, what he is like. He is like McEachern and Hines in their unbending misogyny, like Grimm in his impatience with natural process,
like Burch in his being on the run, like Hightower in his latent homosexuality. The point is that Faulkner knows so richly what is normal, abnormal, and in between in male behavior that his novel teems with analogues
and foils to Christmas's descent into murder and self-immolation. His
loneliness is illuminated at every stage.

　　Lena, by contrast, is like no one else. Comparisons with the Virgin or
with the Magdalene only emphasize the point; her arena is less social than
"marvelous." Here is the scene of crisis with Lucas Burch:

> She did not speak at all. She just lay there, propped on the pillows,
> watching him with her sober eyes in which there was nothing at all –
> joy, surprise, reproach, love – while over his face passed shock, as-
> tonishment, outrage, and then downright terror. . . . She watched him
> holding his eyes up to hers like two beasts about to break, as if he knew
> that when they broke this time he would never catch them, turn them
> again, and that he himself would be lost. She could almost watch his
> mind casting this way and that, ceaseless, harried, terrified, seeking
> words which his voice, his tongue, could speak. "If it aint Lena. Yes,
> sir. So you got my message. Soon as I got here. . . ." His voice died
> somewhere behind his desperate eyes. Yet still she could watch his mind
> darting and darting as without pity, without anything at all, she

watched him with her grave, unwinking, unbearable gaze, watched him
fumble and flee and tack. (473–4)

Burch is as clearly understood – his expressions, his gestures, his
language, his motives – as Lena is mysterious. Her "unbearable" gaze
suggests an absolute register beyond the bounds of social life, and we do
not meet that word again until Joe Christmas also transcends the communal boundaries, lying castrated and bullet-riddled upon Hightower's
kitchen floor: "For a long moment he looked up at them with peaceful
and unfathomable and unbearable eyes" (513). Although she is easily
approachable, Lena remains beyond relationship, a "wonderful" figure
whose psyche is never reduced to articulation. Her all-portending
blankness reminds us of Judith in *Absalom, Absalom!* and of Lion in "The
Bear": likewise figures of inexpressible significance, representations of
the other. It is no more surprising that Burch runs from her than that
Bunch, when last seen, is still trying, hopefully but without much confidence, to discover access to her.

Another way of indicating *Light in August*'s narrative comfort with its
males is to point out how often it pairs them. Males are connected
throughout the novel, linked either legitimately or scandalously. The
females seem to hover on the edge of these male pairings. For example,
there are Hightower and Byron, Hightower and his grandfather, Hightower and the black male servant whom the townspeople beat, Hightower and Christmas whom they kill. What chance does Mrs. Hightower
have in this structure of intimate or obsessive male pairings? Likewise,
there is Mrs. Hines kept from her husband by his passionate preference
for his grandson, Mrs. McEachern kept from her husband by *his* passionate preference for his adopted son, Joanna Burden kept from her own
family history by its relentless four-generational focus on males
(Nathaniel and Calvin, Nathaniel and Calvin: Joanna's mother is not even
named). And finally there is the suggestive homosexual pairing of Christmas and Burch, sleeping in the same cabin, a couple whose violence is
peaceful and predictable compared with the heterosexual explosions in
the big house. In these instances the novel finds its way into the one male
by silhouetting him against the other male, hearing them talk to each
other, establishing their narrative history, and domesticating them both
through these comparisons.[6]

---

[6] In a passage relevant to Faulkner's narrative practice, de Beauvoir posits that the incapacity to render woman as a subject is intimately allied to the incapacity to render women
as a group: "For the male it is always another male who is the fellow being, the other
who is also the same, with whom reciprocal relations are established. The duality that
appears within societies under one form or another opposes a group of men to a group of
men; women constitute a part of the property which each of these groups possesses and
which is a medium of exchange between them. . . . To the precise degree in which

Women in *Light in August* are granted no such satisfying narrative space. Either they are given a top-heavy masculine history, like Joanna; or they are given a casually summarized history, like Lena; or they are cursed with their husband's history, like Mrs. Hines and Mrs. McEachern; or they are so absorbed into the economy of male institutions as to have no personal history at all – like Bobbie the prostitute or that poor little girl Alice who vanished from the orphanage in the middle of the night: "Vanished, no trace of her left, not even a garment, the very bed in which she had slept already occupied by a new boy. He never did know where she went to" (150).

❧

> That was why it did not matter to either of them which one did the talking, since it was not the talking alone which did it, performed and accomplished the overpassing, but some happy marriage of speaking and hearing wherein each before the demand, the requirement, forgave condoned and forgot the faulting of the other . . . in order to overpass to love, where there might be paradox and inconsistency but nothing fault nor false. (395)

This passage has been justly celebrated as intimating *Absalom, Absalom!*'s response to the irreversible doom embodied in Sutpen's design. That response is narrative: the Sutpen saga may be made bearable only by being interrogated, probed, pondered, and finally – crucially – spoken. Sutpen himself speaks rarely and without "feedback" reflexivity. Even when he rehearses his earlier history with Grandfather Compson, "he was not talking about himself. He was telling a story" (308). Incapable of probing himself or dialogically discovering his repressed motives through verbal encounter with another, Sutpen must be reclaimed through the imaginative narration of others. What is less often observed is that such narration, in order to "overpass to love," must be shared, and that only males are allowed to share it.

Mr. Compson talks to Quentin, whereas Rosa talks "through" him. Chapter 5, the most lyrical in the novel and the one that establishes Rosa unforgettably, is told in uninterruptible Rosa-ese.[7] Fifty pages of ital-

woman is regarded as the absolute Other – that is to say, whatever her powers, as the inessential – it is to that degree impossible to consider her as another subject" (71). Something like this irremediable marginality explains the isolation of the women in *Light in August,* especially those like Mrs. Armstid, Mrs. McEachern, and Mrs. Hines, whose every thought, feeling, and gesture are constrained by a male code of expectations and requirements.

7 Rosa Coldfield has been the occasion for the most spirited feminist commentary so far written on Faulkner. Matthews's rigorous attention to the nuances of her narrative (*Play* 122–34) has set the stage for readings that open up rather than pass judgment upon her rhetorical extravagance. See Wittenberg ("Gender"), Kaufmann, O'Donnell, and Gwin, for commentaries on Rosa's vocal performance as one that exposes "the repressive assumptions of all narrative and all theory which fails to hear its own unconscious voices" (Gwin 76).

icized intensity pass through Quentin, pass through the reader. It is neither processed through intermittent response nor pondered interrogatively. The first chapter as well gives us an inexplicably urgent Rosa, a woman whom Quentin can only assent to ("*Yessum'*, Quentin said. *Only she dont mean that*, he thought. *It's because she wants it told*" [7]). The demur must be silent. Rosa cannot be questioned, nor does she herself choose to raise questions other than rhetorically. But this condemns her to being rendered throughout *Absalom, Absalom!* as a recurrently questionable figure, an unconsciously eloquent witness, often eloquent because unconscious. Because she talks through others, it is hard to avoid (in some measure) reading through her. She does not enter into dialogue. There is no likelihood that Quentin or Shreve will mistake each other's voice for hers, as they do for Mr. Compson's ("Don't say it's just me that sounds like your old man" . . . "*Maybe we are both Father*" [326]). They neither say nor think this about Rosa's voice because, in its "marvelous" uninterruptibility, that voice verges on a state of feeling all too cheaply associated with the female: hysteria.

The hysteric, as Clément and Cixous usefully remind us, is one "whose body is transformed into a theatre for forgotten scenes, [and who] relives the past, bearing witness to a lost childhood that survives in suffering" (5). In this sense Rosa's voice, focused upon a past she can neither assimilate nor forget, eloquently testifies to the intolerably repressive gender arrangements of her culture. At the same time, she pays the price of her deformation. For the rhetorical brilliance of Chapter 5 – Rosa's extraordinary memories and feelings, still vibrant – does not disguise the fact that Faulkner has inserted her into a narrative scene in which she alone is the significant hearer of her own speech. Sutpen and Bon both dead, Ellen and Judith likewise, Rosa rehearses the pathos of her unacted life in a performance of which Quentin can only be the spectator. Her utterance may be said to court hysteria, then, because it does not attend to its audience as a participant, cannot address reflexively its own status as a narrative. Rosa never solicits a response from Quentin, never says "maybe," never punctuates her discourse (as Mr. Compson does his) with phrases such as "I can imagine them as they rode" (133). She is too full – or is it too hungry? – to ponder.[8]

Being aware of oneself as a teller and interacting dialogically with another person, however, signal the radical unpredictability of the pre-

[8] Assessing Rosa's narrative may be more difficult than I have suggested. For one thing, Rosa does speak to Quentin ("They will have told you . . .") recurrently, though not with any capacity to learn from his otherness. For another, the male-engendered dialogue she is kept from is not without its own problems. Although Moreland shares my sense of Rosa's nonrelational discourse – "she like Sutpen talking '*to no sane mortal listening* . . .'"(89) – he joins Gwin in faulting Mr. Compson's narrative as sterile, all-knowing, and dismissive of accents (women's, blacks') different from his own.

sent narrative moment in *Absalom, Absalom!* Deprived of this openness, Rosa's discourse is precariously poised between the telling and the told, the still-emerging present and the already-completed past. We read it as both subjective and objective; it carries her spontaneous feeling yet remains impenetrable to the words of others in the foregrounded time of 1909. Her narrative is positioned by Faulkner to receive their living speculations only as an object receives them, unresponsively, rather than as a subject does, dialogically altering in relation to what she hears. (This occulted relationship obtains within the text, not outside it. We as readers are free to hear in Rosa's passion and pathos a subjective elaboration/indictment of an entire culture's strategies for female containment.)

Rosa is not the only woman caught between the extremes of vatic speech and silence. Judith Sutpen is given almost no voice in this novel, but when she does speak (as in passing on Bon's letter to Grandmother Compson), her words are gnomic in their intensity and resonance.[9] In related fashion, Eulalia Bon hardly opens her mouth in *Absalom, Absalom!*, yet others imagine her as (all during Charles Bon's childhood) "a kind of busted water pipe of incomprehensible fury and fierce yearning and vindictiveness and jealous rage" (373). If Eulalia's state of male-imposed frustration is akin to hysteria, Rosa's aunt is nearer to it yet, a "grim virago fury of female affront" (64) who descends upon Jefferson society with her incoherent invitations to Sutpen's wedding. And there are women more vocally eccentric than these: the octoroon who weeps rather than speaks, Wash Jones's granddaughter who is given a total of one and a half broken lines to say (just before she is decapitated), and Sutpen's daughter Clytie whose role in the novel is as significant as her voice is irrelevant. Indeed, these are all major figures – even Milly Jones plays her part in Sutpen's downfall – but their importance is symbolic and objective: symbolic insofar as they are counters in a male design, objective insofar as they are approached from without, as objects. Few characters speak to these women; none speaks with them. Deprived of an intersubjective frame within which they might think their spontaneous thoughts and speak their unpredictable words, they are all representations of the other, beyond relationship.

By contrast, how easily the men can be imagined talking to each other. Sutpen may be Faulkner's isolated demigod, but he nevertheless accommodates fairly easily to a number of narrative situations: in a hammock

---

9 The closest Judith comes to being spoken to is Bon's letter to her: an occasion when she is both solicited and absent. The eventless period between Bon's murder and Sutpen's return is shared by Rosa, Judith, and Clytie; but Faulkner goes out of his way to insist that there is neither purpose nor discourse among them: "we were three strangers" (195). With the pointed exception of Rosa's dreams, all plots and projects in this novel are either patriarchal or marplot revenges. They depend on the male for their direction, and Sutpen has not yet returned.

talking with Wash Jones, by a campfire with Grandfather Compson, later in a law office with Grandfather Compson. Henry and Bon are tirelessly envisaged together – *their* departure from Sutpen's Hundred, not Bon and Judith's, constitutes the elopement in this novel[10] – and the novel may be said to reach its crescendo of inventiveness as it seeks to imagine Bon and Sutpen together (that, rather than Bon and Judith together, becomes the charged scenario, the relationship most worth exploring).[11]

Quentin and his father achieve a satisfying narrational relationship; Quentin and Shreve achieve a sublime one. It is sublime because each accepts the other as a subject, not an object, and between subjects capable of forgiving, condoning, and forgetting the faultings of each other – capable therefore of responding creatively to each other's differences – there arises the possibility of a "marriage of speaking and hearing." In *Absalom, Absalom!* this marriage seems limited to males.

I might close this "between men" analysis by noting that the most famous passage from the novel imagines genealogical descent as a fantasy of purely male making:

> *Yes, we are both Father. Or maybe Father and I are both Shreve, maybe it took Father and me both to make Shreve or Shreve and me both to make Father or maybe Thomas Sutpen to make all of us.* (326–7)

From male to male, an orgy of males; yet this descent reveals in its figures what it cannot manage to dignify with a name: the place of the female. The passage depends on a figurative setting to deliver its thematic descent, and that setting is memorably constituted by ripples, pools, feeding, and umbilical water cords. The females kept out of the Symbolic dynasty – and for that reason causing the collapse of the dynasty – reappear, namelessly, as the space of potential nurture, the space where the phallic pebble falls. Were the women named, could the male narrators see that none of these circular pairings will fructify without the legitimized recognition of the female, then "the old ineradicable rhythm" might lead to regeneration rather than the barren repercussion of unchanging male names.

≈

There is no Caddy nor Lena nor Rosa in *Go Down, Moses,* and what women there are – with the minor exception of Miss Worsham in

---

[10] I owe this insight to Elizabeth W. Weinstein's senior thesis on Proust and Faulkner, Princeton University, 1989. Its implications are profound, for once we begin to map the currents of erotic energy within *Absalom, Absalom!* we find an unbroken circuitry of male–male bondings.

[11] How revealing it is that in this final "crescendo of inventiveness" Quentin and Shreve should choose to motivate Bon's pathos, as Moreland notes, by systematically vilifying his mother.

the final chapter – have little to say.[12] Most of them suffer the fate of the distaff side: the subjective dimension of their history of breeding is beside the patriarchal point. The pathos of this novel, of course, lies in Faulkner's passionate rehearsal of that distaff history, especially in its scandalous moments. But the obvious corollary to such an approach is that the women come into focus mainly as potential or successful breeders.

Sometimes they do not attain even this much narrative importance. Consider the first appearance of Sophonsiba Beauchamp:

> But at last a hand began waving a handkerchief or something white through the broken place in an upstairs shutter. . . . Then they stood in the hall, until presently there was a jangling and swishing noise and they began to smell the perfume, and Miss Sophonsiba came down the stairs. Her hair was roached under a lace cap: she had on her Sunday dress and beads and a red ribbon around her throat and a little nigger girl carrying her fan and he stood quietly a little behind Uncle Buck, watching her lips until they opened and he could see the roan tooth and he remembered how one time his grandmother and his father were talking about Uncle Buddy and Uncle Buck and his grandmother said that Miss Sophonsiba had matured into a fine-looking woman once. Maybe she had. He didn't know. He wasn't but nine. (10)

Handkerchief, perfume, cap, ribbon, fan, roan tooth: these components establish Sophonsiba as a composite thing, a creature of surfaces and effects. Granted that the narrator is only a nine-year-old boy and that nothing in this first chapter is openly treated as problematic, Sophonsiba is nevertheless singled out for uniquely distortive narrative rendering. Her pattern of speech summarized on the next page, with its bumblebees and flowers and desert air and honey and queen bee, is "marvelous" as no other speech is in "Was." (Hubert and Buck and Buddy are permitted to speak an unremarkable English; they immediately understand each other.) Sophonsiba here emerges as a grotesque, and the question may arise: how can this woman be Ike McCaslin's mother? I think that to ask the question is to see that Faulkner's text bypasses rather than answers it. Sophonsiba has no narrative reality whatsoever as Ike's mother; this dimension of her being is simply omitted. Although he is amply supplied with four fathers who all enjoy a substantial narrative history – Buck, Buddy, Cass, Sam Fathers (and we could add Boon and Hubert to this list) – Ike has no mother. The interesting thing is that he doesn't miss one.

[12] Miss Worsham strikes me as the egregious false (because sentimental) note of "Go Down, Moses." "It's our grief" (381), she tells Gavin Stevens, but that haunting black chorus of woe has no white voice in it.

Less bizarre than Sophonsiba, but equally represented in the narrative as irreconcilably other, is Ike's unnamed wife. This woman appears as though out of nowhere. He is married to her within four lines of our first hearing of her (311), and in bed with her a page later. The narrative interest in her is as intense as it is limited. It focuses entirely on her archetypal sexual identity and her localized sexual gestures and utterance. "Lock the door. . . . Take off your clothes. . . . Promise": these terse phrases punctuate Ike's furious cerebration. She is rendered as the unthinking desire of the body, he as the tempted but scandalized witness to the spirit. They are worlds apart. At the end of their intercourse (and of the five pages of Go Down, Moses that attend to her), we read:

> he thought she was crying now at first, into the tossed and wadded pillow, the voice coming from somewhere between the pillow and the cachinnation: "And that's all. That's all from me. If this don't get you that son you talk about, it won't be mine": lying on her side, her back to the empty rented room, laughing and laughing. (315)

"Cachinnation" suggests so much: a woman who laughs violently (it could be mistaken for crying), a word one needs the dictionary for, a scene riddled with nonrecognition. Ike neither gets his son nor keeps his wife; neither event later receives emphasis. Like Lorraine in The Sound and the Fury, like Bobbie or Mrs. Hightower in Light in August, this woman can enter the narrative only as a nonrelational and disruptive fragment of the male protagonist's continuing history. All bodily desire and cunning, archetypally complete in herself, she has no story of her own. Obstacle, mirror, or target: she can be any of these, but she cannot be a subject.

The women who do matter in Go Down, Moses are black. Cleansed of sexual threat by the role of victim they are forced to play, these women – Eunice, Tomasina, Fonsiba, and especially Molly – are portrayed with dignity and pathos. But insofar as the sympathizer (Ike) and the victimizers are white, male, and McCaslin, the narrative interest in their stories is wrested away from the women. Despite the considerable black population of this novel, they are rarely seen in relation to each other. Carothers McCaslin intervenes between mother and daughter, causing the former's suicide; his great-grandson Zack intervenes between husband and wife, almost wrecking their marriage. The narrative logic of Go Down, Moses simply does not permit Eunice and her daughter to make common cause (if only in the form of commiseration) against their intruder, nor can it attend to Molly's dilemma as anything other than the tripartite male struggle (narrated at great length) between Lucas on the one hand, Zack on the other, and old Carothers somewhere in the middle.[13] Molly herself appears as virtually a foil, a figure reduced to the single quality of breeder, an indiscriminate breast for children black and white. She is denied the complications of either desire or outrage. (These responses are left to the males.) Not, of course, that she necessarily is innocent of desire, outrage, or any other motive of her own. Rather, like Lucas (through whom we read her), we cannot know:

> She went on, neither answering nor looking back, impervious, tranquil, somehow serene. . . . He breathed slow and quiet. *Women,* he thought. *Women. I wont never know. I dont want to. I ruther never to know than to find out later I have been fooled.* (59)

And so even Molly – insistently described throughout this novel as small and weightless, preternaturally aged, wizened, and resignedly maternal – even Molly turns out, through the narrative deployment of her sexual difference, to be inscrutably other: a sister of "sister." Like the other women examined in this chapter, she too appears as "wonderful" and "marvelous," with the attendant narrative posture, the combination of isolation and display, that these adjectives imply.

&

I should like to conclude speculatively. The patterns I have traced may complicate our admiration, but they do not detract from Faulkner's interest. Rather, we see his narrative sharing in the larger mystification of women common to so much Western literature. Faulkner's "marvelous" women are "marvelous" in the service of a narrative urge, present throughout his career, to probe the deepest recesses of his men. His ways of doing the one involved ways of doing the other. For his men to become themselves, his women had to take the shape they have. And in this creative move he shares in a larger Western project, aptly summarized by Simone de Beauvoir:

> [W]hat he [man] really asks of her is to be, outside of him, all that which he cannot grasp inside himself . . . because he must project himself into an object in order to reach himself. Woman is the supreme recompense for him since, under a shape foreign to him which he can possess in her flesh, she is his own apotheosis. Treasure, prey, sport and danger, nurse, guide, judge, mediatrix, mirror, woman is the Other in whom the subject transcends himself without being limited, who opposes him without denying him; she is the Other who lets herself be taken without ceasing to be the Other, and therein she is so necessary to man's happiness and to his triumph that it can be said that if she did not exist, men would have invented her. (186)

---

[13] Because the resonance of this strangely "overpopulated" scene implicates Faulkner's construal of race even more than his construal of gender, I return to it at greater length in the second half of Chapter 2 (my chapter on race).

De Beauvoir goes on to say that men *did* invent her and that many of her subsequent troubles come from this imposed and unwanted identity. This last is our story more than Faulkner's – that is, he reveals it whereas we are eager to tell it; indeed I shall be telling it throughout this study – but I want to close this exploration on another tack, by suggesting in what ways the biases I have been tracing do and do not "tell." They do "tell" because Faulkner approaches his women differently from his men. Only a New Critical insistence on universality, on the work of art as heroically complete in itself, could have blinded us to the differences made by gender.[14] Seen for the most part from outside, deprived both vertically in time and horizontally in space of their own subjective history, Faulkner's women move through their world as "wonderful" creatures, but considerably handicapped, from a narrative perspective, when compared with his men.

Yet these biases do not "tell" against Faulkner in the sense that they do not undo his claim to our attention. No writer, no text, can be free of biases, complete, for completeness is a notion incompatible with the gendered lineaments of human achievement itself. It is we Faulknerians, not Faulkner, who have wanted him complete, wanted him not only to say it all but to say it all right.[14a] What he wanted – and what he achieved – was not completeness but something closer to delivery, the delivery of his "impossible heart's desire." Faulkner became Faulkner by making his mark upon the stone, by having the courage to let that mark mark him reciprocally, and mark us projectively – both markings unforeseeable in their consequences. His entry into words is simultaneously an accessing, revising, or refusing of his culture's discursive resources: it is to the hilt complicit, gendered, and contestatory. His every literary move, both voluntary and involuntary, is enabled by other moves not made, as well as by the unpredictable moves we critical readers have made (and will continue to make). This ratio looks different now from the way it looked twenty-five years ago; in twenty-five years it will look different again. For the maculate process of seeing him anew within the conceptual frames of both his culture and our own – of relentlessly turning Faulkner

---

[14] Jane Gallop suggests the way in which, behind the discursive model for discussing "subjects" as universal and sexually neutral – a model that dominated New Criticism – there lurks a far from universal male paradigm: "The neutral 'subject' is actually a desexualized, sublimated guise for the masculine sexed being. Woman can be subject by fitting male standards which are not appropriate to, cannot measure any specificity of, femininity, and difference. Sexual indifference is not lack of sexuality but lack of any different sexuality, the old dream of symmetry, the other, woman, circumscribed into woman as man's complementary other, his appropriate opposite sex" (*Daughter*, 58).

[14a] I explore in Chapter 3 the Imaginary trajectory we commentators enact, in our yearning to fuse Faulkner's say with our own, to produce in our words the "real" meaning of his.

into "Faulkner" – constitutes the only immortality his works will ever know.

"IF I COULD SAY MOTHER": CONSTRUING THE UNSAYABLE ABOUT FAULKNERIAN MATERNITY

My title sounds insistently psychoanalytic, promising to un-cover the covered-up, to find the key that will unlock the mystery and reveal its hitherto concealed treasure. This game of penetrating/master-ing is itself distinctly phallic; there must be a better way to pursue the mother. I concede at the outset that I cannot say the Unsayable about Faulknerian maternity, that my argument bears most directly on the brilliantly disturbed novels between *Flags in the Dust* and *Light in August,* and that the text I shall examine at length – the source of the quotation in the title – is *The Sound and the Fury.* Faulkner's rendering of Mrs. Comp-son is, within the representational economy of that novel, uniquely punitive. I intend to identify the discursive model that underlies that rendering, then to reconceive the model, drawing on some contempo-rary feminist criticism, and finally return to Mrs. Compson. At the end I shall suggest ways in which Faulkner's texts of this troubled period are trying to say Mother and how they are succeeding.[15]

"If I could say Mother" recurs twice in Quentin's section of *The Sound and the Fury,* and in each case the phrase arises out of the memory of an April 1910 conversation between Herbert Head and Mrs. Compson:

> What a pity you had no brother or sister *No sister no sister had no sister.* Dont ask Quentin he and Mr Compson both feel a little insulted when I am strong enough to come down to the table I am going on nerve now I'll pay for it after it's all over and you have taken my little daughter away from me *My little sister had no. If I could say Mother. Mother*
> Unless I do what I am tempted to and take you instead I dont think Mr Compson could overtake the car.
> Ah Herbert Candace do you hear that *She wouldn't look at me soft stubborn jaw-angle not back-looking* You needn't be jealous though it's just an old woman he's flattering a grown married daughter I cant believe it.
> Nonsense you look like a girl you are lots younger than Candace color in your cheeks like a girl *A face reproachful tearful an odor of camphor and of tears a voice weeping steadily and softly beyond the twilit door the twilight-colored smell of honeysuckle.* (108)

In the second passage, near the end of Quentin's section, the smell of gasoline on his shirt reevokes this same scene of Herbert and the car, and

---

[15] I want to express here a general indebtedness to my colleague Abbe Blum, who made my path through contemporary feminist criticism more manageable.

it concludes with *"if I'd just had a mother so I could say Mother Mother"* (197).

Quentin's arresting phrase of abandonment is embedded, both times, in the context of Mrs. Compson's own fantasy return of adolescence. As she flirts with Herbert, drawing on the social model she used to know, that of the Southern belle, her son registers her maternal absence from his life. "Color in your cheeks like a girl *A face reproachful tearful an odor of camphor and of tears*": these are the only roles Mrs. Compson can play – premarital coquetry or postmaternal grief. Her abandonment of her children emerges here as saturated in the rituals and assumptions of her own virginal past. Between her childless adolescence and her child-complicated middle age no other viable script has become available to her. Between virginal flirtation and postmaternal complaint Mrs. Compson literally has nothing else to say.

As though to emphasize the alienation of her married state, the text rarely pairs her with her husband. Faulkner often has Benjy's first memories of Mrs. Compson join her instead with Uncle Maury. The novel signals recurrently that the man most on her mind, the man she uses as a shield between herself and her husband, is Uncle Maury. In this textual sense he vies with Mr. Compson for the position of husband. (One might argue that her textual husband is her son Jason, with whom she maintains a peculiarly intense relationship. In this regard they echo Gerald Bland and his mother, also an oddly incestuous pairing in which the titular husband has been conveniently removed.)[16] In either case Mr. Compson himself is arguably the third male in his wife's life. Appearing most saliently in Quentin's chapter, he registers textually more as his son's father than as his wife's husband.

Her brother Maury seems to serve as her way of remaining a Bascomb, of refusing to consummate her entry into Compsonhood. (My discovery at the Faulkner and Yoknapatawpha Conference in 1986 that Faulkner's family pronounces Maury as Murry, the name of Faulkner's father, may strengthen this fantasy conflation of the mother's brother with the mother's husband.)[17] Incestuous pairings thus suggest themselves at the parental level as well, and Mrs. Compson's preference for her brother leads with compelling logic to Quentin's preference for his sister. Refusing to be a wife, Caroline Bascomb refuses to be a mother, and Caddy must therefore – and fatally – play that role for her brothers.

The picture of Mrs. Compson that emerges is of a woman whose life ceased to be narratable after her entry into marriage and its sexual consequences. She has no stories to tell that can accommodate in a positive way

---

[16] André Bleikasten's *The Most Splendid Failure* briefly notes this point. See 225, n. 24, for commentary on the Blands.

[17] I am indebted to conversations with James Hinkle for this information.

even a grain of her postconsummation experience. Her entry into mature sexuality is swiftly followed by her exit. Having delivered her children, she takes to her bed – the childbed, not the marriage bed – acting like a child, exacting from her children the sustenance she should be offering them.[18]

She speaks obsessively of the rules she learned before marriage, and of her refusal to learn anything different since:

> "Yes," Mother says. "I suppose women who stay shut up like I do have no idea what goes on in this town."
> "Yes," I [Jason] says, "They don't."
> "My life has been so different from that." Mother says. "Thank God I dont know about such wickedness. I dont even want to know about it. I'm not like most people." (299)

I am still a virgin, her camphor and tears keep saying: I don't know anything about checks, about report cards, about business deals, about what girls do on the street or within their own bedrooms. Weeping and mourning, ritually heading for the cemetery throughout the novel, she registers her marital and maternal experience as a curse that makes a mockery of all her training: "when I was a girl I was unfortunate I was only a Bascomb I was taught that there is no halfway ground that a woman is either a lady or not" (118).

This rigid either–or posture indicates that it is Mrs. Compson, not her husband, who is possessed by the binarisms of the Symbolic order – but possessed by them as only someone locked into Imaginary identifications and repudiations can be. Despite John Irwin and other critics who fault Mr. Compson for not upholding paternal authority, his considerable appeal resides in his shrewd perception that a Symbolic order based upon traditional notions of morality and virginity is bankrupt, that it is an invented script.[19] He relates to this order as a produced structure, not an inalterable essence, whereas his wife would live it as the Real itself. She thus incarnates what Roland Barthes terms the cultural code, the already known: "If we collect all such knowledge, all such vulgarisms, we create a monster, and this monster is ideology," Barthes writes (S/Z 97). Mrs. Compson is such an ideological monster.

We touch here upon the source of her failure as a mother. Deformed by her social training – a training shaped by class and race to the require-

---

18 Clément and Cixous's portrait of the hysteric captures succinctly the economy of desire transformed into suffering that characterizes Mrs. Compson's behavior: "The hysteric . . . tries to signify eros through all the possible forms of anesthesia. . . . A witch in reverse, turned back within herself, she has put all her eroticizing into internal pain" (39).

19 Irwin develops this reading of Mr. Compson throughout his *Doubling and Incest;* see especially 67, 75, 110–13, and 120–2. Bleikasten reads the father also in terms of his failure "as lawgiver" (*Splendid* 113). See also Bleikasten's "Fathers in Faulkner."

ments of virginity – she abandons her own flesh and blood upon the loss of that virginity. She has outlived her image of herself. Simultaneously rushing forward to death and backward to childhood, she repeats herself and takes to black. The novel's attack upon her seems to be this: mothers are meant to nourish their young; their trucking with (male-authored) ideological scripts can only lead to overlectured and undernurtured offspring.[20]

This paradigm of ideological insistences perverting maternal function may shed light on that strange scene in which Jason wrestles with his mother over the key to Quentin's room. Noel Polk has pointed to the repression wrought into this image of the key-laden woman ("Dungeon" 61–93), but there is a sexual dimension to the assault as well. Faulkner takes a full page to show us Jason all over his mother, "pawing" at her skirt, while she resists the attack. Finally, "'Give me the key, you old fool!' Jason cried suddenly. From her pocket he tugged a huge bunch of rusted keys on an iron ring like a mediaeval jailer's" (325). Pawed at, pressed, her invaded pocket reveals its cache of hideous keys like a grotesque parody of the children who should instead have come forth from her womb. And indeed her womb is terrifying – a space imaged here as rusted, iron, a jailor's fortress, as was also earlier implied by Quentin's image of the dark place in which he was imprisoned: "The dungeon was Mother herself" (198).

No child escapes from this dungeon, and insofar as the dungeon is a womb, no child gets fully born. In place of nourishment she feeds her children repressive ideology, and they sicken on it. From Mrs. Compson's failure to mother we move through her daughter Caddy's failure to mother and finally, reductively, into *her* daughter Quentin's refusal to conceive. "Agnes Mabel Becky," the phrase spoken by the man in the red tie upon seeing that shiny container connected with Quentin, is the term used half a century ago in the South for a three-pack of condoms.[21] Mrs. Compson's inability to nourish here literalizes into her granddaughter's well-earned decision to seal off the reproductive functions of her womb.

Noel Polk helps us to generalize the model that Mrs. Compson fails abysmally to uphold. He writes of Faulkner's mothers of this period as "almost invariably, horrible people," failing to meet "even minimal standards of human decency, much less . . . the ideal of mother love as the epitome of selfless, unwavering care and concern" ("Dungeon" 66).

---

[20] This is one of the reasons that Lena Grove (not to mention Dewey Dell or Eula Varner) can be rendered with such affection: she does not meddle in the Symbolic order. Her unflappable comments about a family needing to be together "when a chap comes" (*Light in August* 18) are tonally the reverse of Mrs. Compson's outraged protestations of the flouted system.

[21] Paul Gaston, professor of history at the University of Virginia, supplied me with this enlightening bit of information.

"Selfless, unwavering care and concern": this is exactly what these mothers lack. It is also what they are posited by the culture as *supposed to possess,* and what they are excoriated for not possessing. Freud writes in his study of Leonardo: "A mother's love for the infant she suckles and cares for is something far more profound than her later affection for the growing child. It is in the nature of a completely satisfying love-relation" (*Standard* 11:117). Freud assumes, as does Faulkner, that, unlike fathers (unlike all other human beings), mothers enjoy "a completely satisfying love-relation." They *naturally* fulfill their identity in this bond with the infant. Mothers are defined as just those creatures whose subjective needs are supremely realized through the act of nurturing their own offspring.

Freed from ideology themselves, reservoirs of milk and loving kindness, mothers are meant to be sacred servants. *The Sound and the Fury* hammers this point home in the fourth chapter through the massive comparison, move for move, of Mrs. Compson with Dilsey, the latter a perfect instance of how mothers should care for offspring. And what is Dilsey's model if not the Virgin Mary herself, celebrated in the Reverend Shegog's sermon as Jesus' inexhaustibly loving "mammy [who] suffered de glory en de pangs," who "helt him at de nightfall, whilst de angels singin him to sleep," and who filled heaven with "de weepin en de lamentation" (342) at his death? This model of what a mother is supposed to do resonates throughout not just *The Sound and the Fury* but countless narratives in Western culture.

ॐ

Such a model assumes that the Word – the realm of spirit, of the Symbolic – is articulated through a male voice, announcing the Kingdom of Heaven. Mary serves as the bodily carrier of the spirit. Her function is to nurse her infant son and to bemoan his tragic death. She emerges thus – in her role as the suffering mother, the ubiquitous Pietà of Western art – as a register for the emotional loss suffered through Christ's crucifixion. She herself has no new word to utter, but her natural care for her child is the precondition for his divine utterance in which he reveals his kinship with his father.

If we secularize this text, we arrive at something like the following. The domain of the father is the domain of the Spirit, of all Symbolic activities that make up culture and that achieve articulation in the medium of language. This domain takes the inherently binary form of language, an endless series of constructed oppositions that constitute the (male) paradigm of meaning itself. The domain of the mother, on the other hand, is the domain of the unfissured, prelinguistic body. Her function is so to nourish the child that he (the model for the child is implicitly male) becomes somatically prepared for the vertigo and alienation that accompany entry into the Symbolic order of the father. In other words, the time of bonding exists as a prelinguistic, prelogical plenitude in which mother and child are each other, in which self and world, self and other, interpenetrate. If successful, this quasi-magical bonding bequeathes to the child somatic sufficiency – bodily grounding – that enables him to sustain his later and lifelong encounter with the world outside himself, and eventually to deliver his word within that world.

The gender distinctions essential to this paradigm are common to the discourses of both Christianity and psychoanalysis. The mother is simultaneously sacred and subservient, the enabler but not the speaker of the word. If we return to Faulkner with this script in mind, we can better place the anger toward the mother that suffuses the early novels. In those novels the mother fails at her sacred bodily task. Charged with preoedipal responsibilities, she not only neglects these but barges into the terrain of the law, often in its most outdated and repressive forms. The unnourished child therefore emerges into the world too soon. He has no somatic grounding that might hold the imprint of the culture's proliferating codes, consequently no basis for stabilizing the *"maelstrom of unbearable reality"* (AA 186). Thus we get Benjy, Quentin, Darl, Vardaman, and Joe Christmas: boy children unsure of the integrity of their own bodies, dizzyingly vulnerable to sensory overload, unable to maintain their identity within boundaries that might stabilize the relations between past and present, there and here, self and other, male and female, child and parent, brother and sister, white and black.

French and American feminists seem to agree that this male-scripted model of the nonspeaking mother is disabling rather than empowering. In "Stabat Mater" Julia Kristeva critically explores the myth of the Virgin Mary. Focusing on the iconography of breast, ears, and tears, Kristeva reads the Virgin as a figure of speechless succor. One of Kristeva's commentators, Mary Jacobus, writes:

> The function of the Virgin Mother in Western symbolic economy (according to Kristeva) is to provide an anchor for the nonverbal and for modes of signification closer to primary processes. In the face of the fascinated fear of the powerlessness of language which sustains all belief, the Mother is a necessary pendant to the Word in Christian theology – just as the fantasized preverbal mother is a means of attempting to heal the split in language, providing an image of individual signs, plenitude, and imaginary fulness. (169)

This subtext of the ideal mother as sanctuary, as preverbal plenitude, as pendant to the word and yet also a preserve against its possible emptiness, exerts a powerful punitive influence upon the representation of women in secular texts, including (as we have seen) Faulkner's texts. Kristeva, for her part, is in the difficult position of seeking to maintain the centrality of the pre-oedipal bonding without fetishizing it or making it immune to stress. Jacobus goes on to say that "for Kristeva, division is the condition of all signifying processes. No preoedipal language, no maternal discourse, can be free of this split." Kristeva enacts this split in her essay by inserting another discourse (this one fragmented, impulsive, lyrically focused on childbirth, breastfeeding, and body parts – what she calls the "semiotic") within the surrounding "Symbolic" portion of her text.[22]

The entry of the "semiotic" into the discourse of maternity would both restore the place of the maternal body within language itself and announce that the mother's desire is, like all desire, conflicted and tension-filled, rather than speechlessly satisfied through the suckling of her son. Thus Kristeva would revise the male-coded scripting of maternal desire – what she punningly calls "pèreversion." These feminist revisions (in their insistence that women's desire exceeds male scripts for maternity, that women's desire must find a way into language, that maternity must be demythologized and approached from the perspective of the mother herself) allow us to see how gender biases in that previous script polarize Faulkner's representational strategies.

❧

Let us now return to Mrs. Compson. What we see is a portrait of maternity crazily arrested in the "virginal" phase of the Virgin Mary model. Of the three divine components – succor, silence, and virginity – she has betrayed the two that Faulkner values and retained the one that he deconstructs. The ideal silent nourisher has degenerated into a non-nourishing nonstop talker. More, the language that pours out of her is wholly male-scripted; she speaks the defective Symbolic order at its most repressive.

Her white middle-class culture insists not merely that her desire be contained within mothering purposes. Rather, given the American South of the early twentieth century with its array of racial phobias and its constraining model of white womanhood, her desire is virtually taboo.[23]

---

[22] Kristeva describes the mother's extraordinary experience of one-in-two/two-in-one in terms that illuminate Faulkner's fear of and fascination with this figure: "For a mother . . . the arbitrariness that is the other (the child) goes without saying. For her the impossible is like this: it becomes one with the implacable. The other is inevitable, she seems to say, make a God of him if you like; he won't be any less natural if you do, for this other still comes from me, which is in any case not me but an endless flux of germinations. . . . This maternal quietude, more stubborn even than philosophical doubt . . . eats away at the omnipotence of the symbolic. . . . Such an attitude can be frightening if one stops to think that it may destroy everything that is specific and irreducible in the other, the child; this form of maternal love can become a straitjacket, stifling any deviant individuality. But it can also serve the speaking subject as a refuge when his symbolic carapace shatters to reveal that jagged crest where biology transpierces speech: I am thinking of moments of illness, of sexual–intellectual–physical passion, death" ("Mater" 117–18).

[23] Joel Kovel's *White Racism* attempts to chart psychoanalytically this intersection of latent racial phobias and overt gender models, as these operate within American black–white relations. Winthrop Jordan's authoritative *White over Black* attends as well to the fantasy

Enjoined to marry and procreate, Mrs. Compson is also enjoined to abhor her status as an incarnate creature replete with sexual organs. She may now appear to us more clearly what she is – a socially constructed figure – taught by her culture in such a way as to be unable to survive her own sexual initiation. The only story she has learned is a virginal one, and on this she dwells, within this she hides from the unbearable facts of her own parturition: a son whose idiocy indicts the very fertilization of egg by sperm; a daughter whose burgeoning sexuality promises, at best, the same disaster she has undergone; another son whose needs she did not (could not) assuage, and who punished her for it by committing suicide; and a third son whose fantasy name of Bascomb assures her that he is hers alone: no Compson seed in him, she is still a virgin.

Why has her adoption of the virginal script kept her from also participating in the nurturance script? Why does the tension (always latent) between these two "stories" become so inflamed in Faulkner's narratives? To answer this, we might look at Faulkner's representation of the female body in *The Sound and the Fury*. In so doing we discover that the other story for Mrs. Compson, the nurturance story, is simply intolerable in its fetishistic focus on the body and its linkage of fecundity with filth. The polarization of these two narratives reveals the suffocating binarism of the culture's texts of female maturation:

> Because women so delicate so mysterious Father said. Delicate equilibrium of periodical filth between two moons balanced. Moons he said full and yellow as harvest moons her hips thighs. Outside outside of them always but. Yellow. Feet soles with walking like. Then know that some man that all those mysterious and imperious concealed. With all that inside of them shapes an outward suavity waiting for a touch to. Liquid putrefaction like drowned things floating like pale rubber flabbily filled getting the odor of honeysuckle all mixed up. (*SF* 147)

If the virginal story presupposes a blank body (a body, as Luce Irigaray puts it, that is "pure exchange value . . . nothing but the possibility, the place, the sign of relations between men" [181, translation mine]), the body that Quentin fantasizes here is unbearably full, though no less constructed through a male lens. (How telling that Mr. rather than Mrs. Compson speaks to Quentin of menstruation.) This "delicate" body is more urgently imagined as huge, moonlike (moons that sway the blood tides, moons that are her hips and thighs), filled with liquid rot, spaces that you desire to enter and in which you drown. This is a disaster site. It is also a female womb. A place of periodical filth, this womb is obsessively scripted within an economy of decay: what could grow here?

structures subtending American racism, while James Snead's *Figures of Division* usefully places the issue of racial polarization within the larger problematic of Western philosophy's falsely polarizing yet inescapable binarisms.

The mother's threat seems most to inhere in her leaky and fluctuating wetness, a female wetness that menaces all projects of male enclosure and mastery.

Luce Irigaray has written suggestively of the male hostility to fluidity ("La mécanique des fluides," in *Ce Sexe qui n'en pas un*), and Jane Gallop discusses her argument as follows: "Fluidity has its own properties. It is not an inadequacy in relation to solidity. In phallic fantasy, the solid-closed-virginal body is opened with violence; and blood flows. The fluid here signifies defloration, wound as proof of penetration, breaking and entering, property damage. . . . [But] menstrual blood is not a wound in the closure of the body; the menstrual flow ignores the distinction virgin/deflowered" (*Daughter* 83). Most of Faulkner's males recoil in horror from this female economy of the blood. *Sanctuary* and *Light in August* are concerned with male-induced penetrations of the body. The blood their male protagonists focus on is the blood they can make flow, the blood whose flowing signals male mastery of the object. Or it is the symbolic "blood" of patriarchal lineage or racial difference, not the material blood that simultaneously – and so troublingly to the male mind – carries growth and decay.[24]

A "dry" virginal script that denies desire and repudiates intercourse, a "wet" adulterate script that concedes desire and equates the fertile womb with rot and drowning: there are no other alternatives in *The Sound and the Fury*'s lexicon for constructing maternity. "I was taught that there was no halfway ground that a woman is either a lady or not" (118). In Mrs. Compson's desiccated Symbolic world, ladies and sex organs are incompatible notions. This polarization means that, here and elsewhere, Faulkner's narrative treatment of white maternity takes a schizoid form.

On one side there is the "wet" drama – always illicit, always for not-ladies – of a sexed and rebellious younger woman heading toward unsanctioned labor (Caddy, Dewey Dell, Lena, to a certain extent Temple,

[24] Adequate consideration of this point would take more space than I can allow here. In Chapter 2, I return to the fixation with blood letting in *Light in August* and the investment in patriarchal lineage in *Go Down, Moses*. In Chapter 4, I examine at length the social mapping of male and female bodies in all four of the novels under scrutiny. More broadly, the male penchant to treat errant liquids as containable solids is a strategy of colonization that surfaces in the well-constructed plots – built upon oppositions encountered and satisfyingly overcome – of male narrative itself. Gallop writes, "This problem of dealing with difference without constituting an opposition may just be what feminism is all about" (*Daughter* 93). Roland Barthes sees the work of the critic as an attempt to keep difference from degenerating into opposition: "[D]ifference dispenses with or triumphs over conflict. Conflict is sexual, semantic; difference is plural, sensual and textual; meaning and sex are principles of construction, of constitution; difference is the very movement of dispersion, of friability, a shimmer, what matters is not the discovery, in a reading of the world and of the self, of certain oppositions but of encroachments, overflows, leads, skids, shifts, slips" (*Roland Barthes by Roland Barthes* 69). Teresa de Lauretis explores the gendered bias of (male) plots throughout *Alice Doesn't*.

Charlotte, and Eula). This drama, suffused with narrative empathy, focuses intimately upon the scandal of the penetrated and/or swelling body itself. Faulkner seems mesmerized by the image of the female body escaping the propriety of its male proprietor, usually the husband/father/brother who would confine its activity within the scripts of the Symbolic order. Because that order is (and needs to be shown as) without grounding, this drama is usually narrated with understanding. But the mothers-to-be in this drama are mute; they are mainly subsumed within their own bodies. When, later (as with Temple and Eula), Faulkner does endow them with speech, they have become defenders – often tragic defenders – of the Symbolic. It seems that they cannot simultaneously break the law and speak.

On the other side, there is the "dry" retrospective drama within which are imprisoned the proper wives, the repressed older women heading toward menopause or death. Mrs. Compson, Joanna Burden in her final phase, and of course Addie Bundren – a case unto herself – come to mind.[25] In general Faulkner cannot keep his narrative eye on the *same* woman moving through all the stages of the female life cycle. (Addie and Joanna cross into and out of sexual activity at the expense, so to speak, of their lives.) Maternity is thus a sort of narrative Waterloo: an incoherent zone his fiction can lead up to and away from but which none of his women can traverse and still remain themselves. Is it too much to say that once his pregnant women *deliver,* they cease to be figures of empathy or desire, for he has then entered the fantasy role of their infant needing succor? In any case, the representation of maternity ruptures on this incoherence.

With these constricting representational scripts in mind, I conclude by returning to Mrs. Compson's plight. As the quotation in my title indicates, we see her – Faulkner sees her – only through the freighted and damaged lenses of her offspring. (Indeed, psychoanalytic discourse itself, and a fortiori its commentary on the mother, has centered until recently upon the [male] child in need. What treatment the mother has received has tended to come very sharply angled.) This narrative deprivation of sympathy is decisive. Yet Mrs. Compson's gestures, when attended to against the grain of the text itself, have their pathos. Her refusal to accede to the name of Compson, for example, is heavily marked as vanity or regression, though we might also see it as a desperate attempt to preserve

---

25 Addie Bundren is the exception to my schema, the closest Faulkner ever comes to narrating an unco-opted female's move from virginity through intercourse and maternity and child nurturing into adulthood. This move in *As I Lay Dying,* however, is rendered as anything but continuous. Addie's remarkable awareness of body and presence of mind are premised upon the spatially and temporally unplaceable scene of her protracted dying.

a shred of her own identity from the marital exchange that alters her name from that of one male to that of another. (If she were a male being exchanged, if she were Joe Christmas or Charles Etienne de St. Valery Bon, we would be invited so to read her.) Behind her tyranny within the house – she who changes others' names as though in revenge for the unwanted alteration of her own – we can espy a woman with no other moves to make.

"It is our duty to shield her [your lady mother] from the crass material world as much as possible" (258), Uncle Maury writes Jason: shield her while we men invest her money in the real world of business affairs. Jason, for his part, plays the check-burning ritual upon her once a month. Men know better, they are permitted to discard when necessary the unreal rhetoric of honor (the no longer valid terms of the Symbolic). Mrs. Compson may also, at rare moments, know better – "If you want me to, I will smother my pride and accept them [the checks from Caddy]" (252) – but she remains imprisoned within her learned rhetoric, forced to believe she is repudiating her daughter's money. Born and brought up within defective male Symbolic scripts, she spends each day dying within those same scripts. "The dungeon was Mother herself," Quentin thinks; his mother is the jailor. Yes, she is the jailor, but she is also the jail and the inmate. Alienated from the powers of her own body, deprived by male scripts of any language of access to her bodily desires, she is the prisoner of her own womb. The dungeon is not mother but motherhood.[26]

&

I have sought to indicate the ways in which Faulkner's representational strategies cannot say mother. Let me finish by suggesting that the fiction of this troubled period is nevertheless engaged, paradoxically, in "trying to say" Mother. "I was trying to say," Benjy tells us, and Faulkner invents an extraordinary rhetoric to convey to us the tangled torment of Benjy's "say." What American writer has refused more forcefully the blandishments of the "already said"? Although Faulkner never spoke of it as the Symbolic order, although he never thought of language as decisively marked by gender, although he would certainly have cringed at neologisms like phallogocentrism, in a certain sense he knew. He knew that language is the Symbolic, that it comes to us alienated from our speechless feeling, and that if words are to do more than be a shape to

---

26 Mrs. Compson's body that is not her own illustrates with uncanny aptness Foucault's claim that the body, rather than being one's private sanctuary, "is the inscribed surface of events (traced by language and dissolved by ideas), the locus of a dissociated Self (adopting the illusion of a substantial unity), and a volume in perpetual disintegration ("Nietzsche" 148). I return in Chapter 4 to a sustained commentary on the social annexation of "private" resources.

fill a lack, they must be tortuously reinvented, recombined, such that the "self" they articulate may appear in its incarnate, decentered, and insecurely gendered pathos. And he would have agreed with poststructuralists that, even in his most ambitious undertakings, he failed to make the words (which "go straight up in a thin line," *AILD* 160) ever cling to the earth.

What he created in his most experimental early work seems to me analogous to Kristeva's "semiotic": a use of language that gets behind the crisp and repressed male structures of the Symbolic, and that is seeking (in its gaps and incoherences) to make its way back to the mother. Radically nonjudgmental, open to the confusions of past and present, self and other, Faulkner's experimental rhetoric enacts so often (within the character, within the reader) an experience of immediate, undemarcated identification. "The process of coming unalone is terrible" (*AILD* 56), thinks Dewey Dell. Faulkner in his early masterpieces frees language from its conventional forms of thinking and feeling in just such a way as to articulate this terrifying collapse of ego boundaries that is common to psychosis, to discovery, and to motherhood. The regressive urge of Faulkner's work of this period – its focus on assault, on overwhelming, on the unchosen – testifies to his desire to find words for the subject's inexpressible vulnerability, its boundary-riddled plight.[27]

Identification is itself primordially rooted in the infantile relation with the mother; perhaps this is why Freud was so wary of its capacity to erode ego boundaries.[28] One of his recent critics writes that for Freud, "Maturity (that is, *masculine* maturity) means being well-defended against one's past, which amounts to the same thing as having a strong capacity for resisting identification. . . . In effect, Freud's picture of maturity is of a man driven to outrun . . . identification with the body of his mother, the original unity of mother and infant" (Swan 9–10).

This description sounds as much like Thomas Sutpen as it sounds unlike William Faulkner. Penetrated through and through by the history of his region and his family, Faulkner outran none of it, and he invented a rhetoric unequaled in its capacity to express penetrability, the phenomenon of being wounded. The biography and the representations in the fiction give us reason to construe him as damaged by his own mother,

---

27 In the second half of Chapter 3 and throughout Chapter 4, I pursue the implications of this claim as they illuminate the trajectory of Faulkner's career. Put too summarily, I want to argue the following: as Faulkner freed himself from his fascination with the "semiotic," as his narratorial voice took on coherence and cultural alignment, his rhetoric became increasingly predictable and his work began to lose its capacity for outrage.

28 Bleikasten has written of the relevance of Freud's "Mourning and Melancholia" to Quentin's inability to sever his "narcissistic identification with the lost object" (*Splendid* 116). In both of these accounts such identification is seen as a regressive and self-damaging move.

expelled too soon, not nourished enough.[29] But if this is so, the hunger it generated was for "chanting measures beyond the need for words" (*SF* 340), and the activity it inspired was an attempt to use words to get past the Symbolic itself, "to retrieve the plenitude of the origins," as Bleikasten puts it, "by remembering the . . . body of the lost, forgotten, and unforgettable mother" ("Praise" 140).

"There is at least one spot in every dream at which it is unplumbable," Freud writes in *The Interpretation of Dreams,* "a navel, as it were, that is its point of contact with the unknown" (*Standard* 4:iii). Freud's project of male autonomy makes him insist upon mystery here, but it is possible to know what that navel connects us with. In his early dream novels, where the experiments with language are greatest and the psychic wounds least concealed, where the mother is punished representationally and yet sought after rhetorically, Faulkner made that unsettling connection.

---

[29] For biographical information/speculation, see Minter (1–23) and Martin.

2

Race

During the 1980s scholarly attention to Faulkner's representation of race underwent a sort of sea change. So long as New Critical criteria commanded the production of literary commentary, race (like gender) tended to remain an aesthetically minor dimension of writing – its production, its orientation, and its reception. The great writer, it was generally agreed, transcended such secondary conditions as racial makeup in his embodiment and pursuit of the timeless and the essentially *human*. The writer and his subject were both, implicitly, "man" (thus my masculine pronouns). Henry Louis Gates's recent claim that "No poet, ultimately, knows more than 'race'" ("Dis and Dat") would have sounded barbaric in its proposing race to be a primary category through which we discursively produce our sense of self and other.

But our two best studies of Faulkner's representation of race – Eric Sundquist's and James Snead's – implicitly share Gates's convictions, first, that race is a crucial constituent of human identity and, second, that racial distinctions are matters of cultural construction: a discourse, a code of behavior, a set of expectations. As Derrida claims of racism, "It institutes, declares, writes, inscribes, prescribes. A system of marks, it outlines space in order to assign forced residence or to close off borders. It does not discern, it discriminates" ("Racism" 331). In the following discussions I assume that the hegemonic discourse of race has less to do with biological fact than with (in Wesley Morris's words) "a system of classifications within genealogy, and, therefore . . . a mode of writing and rewriting history, of defining difference (and sameness) as descent, of transcending history in order to produce mythic narratives which justify, legitimize racist discrimination" (228).

Finally, race relations and distinctions shifted in Faulkner's own career (during the 1930s and early 1940s) from the status of topic to obsession. During this period, the issue of how to represent race tore incessantly at

Faulkner's sense of himself as godlike creator of a cosmos of his own.[1]
His sixteen-year immersion within this problematic (from *Light in August* through *Intruder in the Dust*) – his revision of his own earlier rhetorical modes and then revision of the revision – reveals an increasingly powerful grasp of racism as a *discursive* dynamic: a disease perpetuated through language practices. That immersion seems to have produced in him as well a painful recognition of the alterable yet ineradicable role of racist tropes within his own "unique" discourse.

MARGINALIA: FAULKNER'S BLACK LIVES

"Marginalia," my title figure, suggests in a number of ways the subordinate status of blacks in Faulkner's work. We can begin this exploration with Webster, who defines marginalia as "marginal notes," "extrinsic matters," and "nonessential items." Each definition works by way of a stabilizing opposition. We understand the marginal by opposing it to the central, the intrinsic, or the essential. In what follows I want both to contest and to uphold the claim that the role of black lives in Faulkner's canonical texts is marginal.

To contest it because, as Derrida has eloquently argued with respect to "the supplement," the center does not merely "permit" the margin to exist at its side; rather it is constituted by the very notion of marginality.[2] Take away the margin and you have lost the center; it is that outside the center which allows us to conceive of "center." Faulkner's blacks are in this sense the key to his whites (how could you know what white means without black to silhouette and make salient the construct of whiteness?).

---

[1] Much of Grimwood's study (and all of his chapter on *Go Down, Moses*) is devoted to exploring this unease.

[2] The relation of the object to its supplement echoes the relation of the center to its margin. In both cases an independent major term apparently commands a dependent minor one, yet on reflection we see that the dependence works both ways. In thinking through this unstable mutual dependence, Derrida's argument embraces the larger problematic of the signifier and its referent/concept. On the one hand, the signifier merely supplements the thing (object, concept, etc.) it points to (as margin supplements center). The primary thing remains "full," unaltered by its supplement. Yet, on the other hand, the fact that this thing must be supplemented (by being put into language, signified) in order to reach us at all means that the thing in its "original" state was not "full" but lacking. Its independent status is belied by its dependence upon a signifying system that can "deliver" it only within the intervening medium of the sign. "For the concept of the supplement . . . harbors within itself two significations whose cohabitation is as strange as it is necessary. The supplement adds itself, it is a surplus, a plenitude enriching another plenitude, the *fullest measure* of presence. . . . But the supplement supplements. It adds only to replace. It intervenes or insinuates itself *in-the-place-of*; if it fills, it is as if one fills a void" (*Of Grammatology* 44–5).

Black and white intimately coexist so as to make up the discursive racial economy of Faulkner's texts.

I want to contest the marginality of marginalia for another reason as well. Like doodling, marginalia may comprise less examined markings: more able to escape the mind's censorship, more likely to accommodate fugitive energies not welcome within the central enterprise. Marginalia may give expression to fears or desires that the legitimate center could not absorb and still remain legitimate. Faulkner's blacks are recurrently the medium through which he imagines, with both longing and repugnance, how it might feel to be not-white.

Yet, though they may serve us as a semiotic key for interpreting the center, those in the margins *are* marginal. No amount of deconstructive privileging transforms the representation of peripheral lives into central ones. The positioning of blacks upon Faulkner's canvas may reveal to the critic a discursive network of unarticulated interdependence, but it likewise reveals the fact that – largely deprived by the narrative of interior voice, of point of view, of a sense of their own past and future (their memories and desires) – blacks as represented by Faulkner are truncated figures. These lives often take on incandescent symbolic importance for the anguished whites viewing them (and this means the white reader and the white novelist outside the novels, as well as the white protagonists within them), but their importance is mainly symbolic. These figures have no access to their own incandescence; their importance is for others alone. The plots through which Faulkner comes upon his black figures, the narrative positioning he accords them, rarely escape, despite his keen sympathy, the pinched options of tragic exploitation or crucifixion, on the one hand, or comic trivialization, on the other.

A small caveat might be entered here, however, for the living uncooptedness of Faulkner's blacks is not likely to be expressed through some grand assertion (at the level of gesture or word) of independence. Rather, as Moreland acutely suggests, "blacks in Faulkner's writing may well act and speak for their people most articulately precisely when they adopt attitudes of strategic *non*articulateness and humorous obliqueness . . . neither imitating the language and structure of a white-dominated society nor ignoring those structures, but appropriating and 'signifying upon' those same structures" (162). We are just now recognizing the extent to which "signifying" served the black community as a verbal form of liberation, a creative revision of someone else's previous words or gestures, a revision unpremeditated by Webster's dictionary with whose authority I began this discussion.[3] In this sense, as I shall explore

---

[3] Gates provides a wide variety of examples in his brilliant overview of the uses of this concept (which he spells as "signifyin(g)") within black discourse (*Monkey* 44–124).

further, Lucas Beauchamp's shenanigans with the white salesman and his treasure finder constitute a tonic instance of "signifying."

Faulkner's Black Lives: I mean the phrase in both senses – the detached lives of the black characters Faulkner's art records, and also the un-detached, fantasized black life Faulkner imaginatively projects from within himself as he creates these figures. Faulkner's world registers simultaneously the discursive world he inherited, and his unique transactions with that inheritance – simultaneously how his ambient culture generally construed things, and how his remarkable head and heart (re)construe them. Subjective projection and subjective introjection – the pressing out of internalized models, the taking in of external models – are continuous in the acts of both writing and reading.[4] Faulkner's Black Lives, as he writes them into his art, become (flickeringly) our Black Lives, as we read them out of his art. Those of us who are not black undergo black-ness the only way in which we can – imaginatively, fantastically – as we momentarily merge our own malleable psyches with the fictive black ones represented within his work.

This subliminal yet powerful identification – we are in a certain mea-sure what we read while we read it – is why the truncation matters, why the marginality needs to be assessed. What kind of space is accorded to black subjectivity in these novels? From what tropes is such subjectivity produced, within what narrative structures is it embedded? We need to know what shaping models of blackness we are absorbing (or resisting), what enabling or disabling traits the text is inviting us to identify as black. And we need to keep in mind that "we" is a pronoun whose bearing alters as the race and gender of its occupant alter. Dilsey, say, may look different according to the race and gender of her reader, and also according to the period (and country or part of the country) in which she is being read.

These, then, are the issues I am concerned with: the covert interdepen-

Drawing upon myriad examples over a century-long period, Genovese argues more broadly for a mutually transformative (rather than active–passive) encounter between the hegemonic white culture and the enslaved black one.

4 The most suggestive account I know of this argument – that a crucial dimension of reading involves a fantasy fusion with the text – is that of Charles Bernheimer. In the introductory chapter (1–44) of his *Flaubert and Kafka,* drawing on object-relations psy-choanalytic theory, Bernheimer posits that our initial experience of total immersion in an object is with the mother's breast, and that all subsequent attempts at merger seek to replace this absent object. He further claims that our experience of being is itself grounded in these activities: that we sustain the sense of self-presence by an insistent self-immersion in beneficent objects. Not surprisingly, this move that sustains the sense of self in the act of reading is balanced by its opposite: a (deconstructive) move toward greater and greater self-fissure, in which alterity reigns – alterity within the text one reads (but can never possess) and within the self that is reading. Drawing on Freudian termi-nology, Bernheimer calls these two moves that constitute reading (but not just reading) Erotic and Thanatopic impulses.

dence between marginal black and central white, the menace that black "draws off" as well as the eccentric longings it may conceal, the various ways in which Faulkner construes black as he imagines its intermingling with white, and finally the composite images of blackness – the ratio of subjective and nonsubjective positioning – the reader is invited to experience in the act of absorbing Faulkner's Black Lives.

&

> I didn't know that I really had missed Roskus and Dilsey and them until that morning in Virginia. The train was stopped when I waked and I raised the shade and looked out. The car was blocking a road crossing, where two white fences came down a hill and then sprayed outward and downward like part of the skeleton of a horn, and there was a nigger on a mule in the middle of the stiff ruts, waiting for the train to move. How long he had been there I didn't know, but he sat straddle of the mule, his head wrapped in a piece of blanket, as if they had been built there with the fence and the road, or with the hill, carved out of the hill itself, like a sign put there saying You are home again. He didn't have a saddle and his feet dangled almost to the ground. The mule looked like a rabbit. I raised the window.
>
> "Hey, Uncle," I said, "Is this the way?"
> "Suh?" He looked at me, then he loosened the blanket and lifted it away from his ear.
> "Christmas gift!" I said.
> "Sho comin, boss. You done caught me, aint you?"
> "I'll let you off this time." I dragged my pants out of the little hammock and got a quarter out. "But look out next time. I'll be coming back through here two days after New Year, and look out then." I threw the quarter out the window. "Buy yourself some Santy Claus."
> "Yes, suh," he said. He got down and picked up the quarter and rubbed it on his leg. "Thanky, young marster. Thanky." Then the train began to move. I leaned out the window, into the cold air, looking back. He stood there beside the gaunt rabbit of a mule, the two of them shabby and motionless and unimpatient. (98–9)

So much of *The Sound and the Fury*'s rendering of blacks is in this passage. Quentin on a train, disoriented; the black emerging out of nowhere on the road, as if for Quentin's benefit, to give him orientation ("You are home again"); the mutually ratifying verbal/gestural interchange, in which Quentin and the black man enact an older, hierarchical racial economy (the "young marster" offering "Christmas gift" to a thankful darky); the train moving Quentin away with increasing velocity, while the rooted black man and his mule (as stable and timeless and natural as the hill itself) etch themselves into his mind: "the two of them shabby and motionless and unimpatient." "Unimpatient":

Faulkner's urge to emphasize is so great that he invents this word, making us move through the original "patient," then through "impatient" (the train, the modern white world Quentin will soon be hurtling toward again), and finally into "unimpatient": an achieved capacity for moving with time rather than against or through it: a capacity possessed in this novel only by blacks.[5]

This black man appears as pure symbol, offered to us as naturalized and unchanging, a monument to a certain temporal sanity and a hierarchical mode of social relations that Quentin and his culture used unthinkingly to enjoy. Other blacks in *The Sound and the Fury* may be more prominent, but they are usually deployed in the same manner: as symbols, set pieces, monumental performances. Thus Deacon comes on the stage for five impressive pages in Quentin's chapter, and then is heard no more. Thus the Reverend Shegog is swiftly marshaled into his place in the last chapter, heard in all his eloquence, and then just as swiftly abandoned. (And it is indeed "his place": the black church where the power of black voices can be safely articulated because traditionally confined.) These figures, whatever their thematic importance, are marginal to the narrative movement itself. Deprived of the space and time necessary for narrative development (even when they represent "unimpatience"), they perform their essential being in one climactic burst. They lack the narrative freedom of unpredictability. As such, they appear (like Old Man Job) less as integral figures within the Compson drama (not to mention their own drama) than as gnomic counterpositions – enlightening yet narratively unconnected – to the irreversible process of Compson decay.[6]

Dilsey and her family operate in another mode. They are generously developed over space and time (though it does remain Compson space and time – the text grants these "retainers" little space or time of their own), and fully integral to the Compson drama. Dilsey is so immersed in the white family's troubles that her capacity nevertheless to live a normal

---

[5] Thadious Davis shrewdly discusses (*Negro* 99–101) this passage in related ways; I came upon her work after I had drafted my own argument. I should note here what will be increasingly clear later in my argument: that the "naturalness" of the "nigger on a mule" registers in fact Faulkner's strategic reifying of a socially produced phenomenon – the subordinate status of blacks in the rural South. This discursive move monumentalizes the black figure, keeps him from desiring any of the social changes that might come from moving "against or through" time rather than "with" it.

[6] The narrative deployment of all figures in this text (not just black ones) is commanded by a center–margin criterion that transcends race: that of family versus outsider. Yet blacks tend to be marginalized in their own predictable way. "Sister," for example, who is also pressed into a brief narrative space and kept from development, radiates a disturbance scrupulously denied the ancillary black figures. Other ambulatory nonfamilial whites, such as Shreve, Gerald, Dalton, and Earl, seem to ramble in and out of scenes. They register more as part of the text's everyday narrative furniture than as charged symbolic counterparts to the doomed white Compsons.

life might, indeed, give us pause. Perhaps the keynote to her success, and to that of her entire family, can be heard in the following interchange with Luster:

> "Reckin so," Luster said. "Dese is funny folks. Glad I ain't none of em."
> "Aint none of who?" Dilsey said. "Lemme tell you somethin, nigger boy, you got jes es much Compson devilment in you es any of em. Is you right sho you never broke dat window?"
> "Whut I want to break hit fur?"
> "Whut you do any of yo devilment fur?" Dilsey said. "Watch him now, so he cant burn his hand again twell I git de table set." (319)

Every time I reread *The Sound and the Fury* I smile at this passage (or I used to until I developed this argument), and especially at that phrase "Compson devilment." I think I know now why I used to smile: the phrase is immensely reassuring. So that's all it is that Benjy, Quentin, Caddy, Jason, and Caddy's daughter are afflicted with: "Compson devilment"! "Compson devilment" adroitly transforms idiocy, anguish, and sadism into normal prankishness. The effect for the reader of this tranquilizing counterpoint – this calm black lens, this comic and normative mirror – is to domesticate, to make more quotidian, the tragic descent of the Compsons. The blacks serve as a powerfully pastoralizing background, a continuous reminder of what survival is like, in the midst of white degeneration. Dilsey, Roskus, Versh, Frony, T. P., and even Luster form a sort of chorus of normality. Like trained nurses they enter the sick room without contracting the disease.

What is the disease they do not catch? I submit that it is "the sound and the fury" itself. Faulkner represents and positions these black figures as fully self-contained, free of the passion and impatience that afflict the Compson offspring. Presented from without (this distinction is crucial), the black family is conceived in nostalgia, Faulkner's nostalgia. He seems to have climbed back into his own childhood to find them, and he presents them not subjectively, as figures drowning in those conflicting internal urges and sanctions of his own (and which he creatively bestowed upon the Compson siblings), but instead objectively, as figures of stability, seen from a gentle distance, reminders of warm and witty talk, of the saving routines of childhood recollected.[7] Benjy may keep trying to say, Quentin may think *"Wait just a minute . . . I'll get used to it in a minute"* (130), Caddy and her daughter Quentin may whirl themselves out of the family, Jason may run as fast as he can to catch the stock market and his fleeing niece; but Dilsey's black family stays put. Idealized and

---

[7] David Minter discusses (91–100) the personal exposure – deriving from the most painful childhood experiences – that Faulkner imaginatively risked in the creation of the Compson children.

tranquilized by white nostalgia and unconscious condescension, "unimpatient," they *know*.

Immovably "rooted in a traditional folk culture that defies time while accepting mortality" (Davis, "Black Characterization" 82), blacks serve the whites in *The Sound and the Fury* as a sort of benign cultural memory, frozen in dialect and obedience. Their reported conversations may take *them* nowhere, but they take us (as no Compson talk, freighted with portent, can take us) back to a white dream of pastoral innocence. Quentin's mind lingers on Uncle Louis Hatcher's memories of possum hunts and of riding out the old-time floods (Quentin will soon enough drown in his own flood). More poignantly he remembers Versh's story about a man mutilating himself:

> He went into the woods and did it with a razor, sitting in a ditch. A broken razor flinging them backward over his shoulder and the same motion complete the jerked skein of blood backward not looping. But that's not it. It's not not having them. It's never to have had them then I could say O That That's Chinese I dont know Chinese. (132)

To put it in extreme form, when Faulkner imagines black in this novel, the vanishing point he strains toward is Chinese. He seeks to enshrine a ceremonious life of retained "cultural practices and racial values" (Davis, "Black Characterization" 85), a life free, precisely, of sound and fury. Unsubjectified, their lives are represented as narratively free of the internal stresses of stream of consciousness, and thematically free of trauma or desire: a memoryless, sexless, and therefore simplifying antidote to Compson pain. Yet the strain involved in producing such pastoral images insinuates itself everywhere – in the archaic ritual with the "nigger on a mule," in the insistent troping of black insubordination as comic "devilment," in the pattern of narrative containment that prevents their unpredictability from leaking out and making trouble, in the unpacifiable image of an anguished black man with a razor, wreaking damage on his body. In the novels that follow, this latent strain erupts; Faulkner was rarely again to see black as a simplification of anything.[8]

> His turn came. He entered the shed. It was dark. At once he was overcome by a terrible haste. There was something in him trying to get out, like when he had used to think of toothpaste. But he could not

---

[8] Faulkner's representation of black as a nostalgic focus of simplified life rhythms, though long held to be compelling (for its white audience), is by no means innocent. The pacifyingly represented black-authored mutilation (Versh's story) recalls uneasily a disturbingly real Southern history of white-authored mutilations. *The Sound and the Fury*'s portrayal of black as pastoral is enabled by a series of mirror projections and distortions – of white reading black as the site of its own fears and desires – that I have sought to identify throughout this discussion. I am indebted to John Matthews for helpful discussion of the ways in which racial ideology reveals and conceals itself within this and other Faulkner texts.

move at once, standing there, smelling the woman, smelling the negro all at once; enclosed by the womanshenegro and the haste, driven, having to wait until she spoke: a guiding sound that was no particular word and completely unaware. Then it seemed to him that he could see her – something, prone, abject; her eyes perhaps. Leaning, he seemed to look down into a black well and at the bottom saw two glints like reflection of dead stars. He was moving, because his foot touched her. Then it touched her again because he kicked her. He kicked her hard, kicking into and through a choked wail of surprise and fear. She began to scream, he jerking her up, clutching her by the arm, hitting at her with wide, wild blows, striking at the voice perhaps, feeling her flesh anyway, enclosed by the womanshenegro and the haste.

Then she fled beneath his fist, and he too fled backward as the others fell upon him, swarming, grappling, fumbling, he striking back, his breath hissing with rage and despair. (172)

What could this be but *Light in August*? Its graphically detailed violence is unmatched elsewhere in Faulkner's work; there is a release in this prose that borders on ecstasy. Though she is the occasion for this violent release, the anonymous black girl counts for very little in herself. Preceded by the dietitian (the smell/sensation of toothpaste), to be followed by Bobbie the prostitute, this girl has no traits of her own. The traumatic emotional history she rouses into semiconsciousness is not hers but Joe's. She smells of her entire race and sex. Her eyes betray no personal identity, giving off instead the "reflection of dead stars." Sentient, she screams when kicked, flees from "beneath his fist." She is never seen again.

Faulkner represents her importance in what she triggers in the male, not in what she is herself. Joe's foot moves before he knows it is moving; his breath hisses. He becomes a figure of total – almost epileptic – bodily release. She occasions the collapse of Joe's precarious identity, a collapse expressed through ecstatic fighting, the giving and receiving of pain. As elsewhere in *Light in August,* the private act of intercourse between male and female leads to the public act of male-to-male brawling. Sexual intercourse emerges in this brief encounter (as elsewhere) as that which crosses the culture's codes of racial difference – a constructed difference on which the frayed fabric of white male civility urgently depends.[9] And in this book, with some significant exceptions, sexual intercourse is disturbingly connected with black.

The connection is lethal. Black becomes an almost magic fomentor of sexual fantasies and male violence. (I say "becomes" but isn't this fatal scenario already in place: a culture trained to see the black male as over-

---

[9] John Tucker reads the novel suggestively as a "structuralist" hive of unstable binary oppositions, of inadequate codes meant to clarify and contain an uncontrollable welter of conflicting human activities. Sexual intercourse seems to serve as a figure for all boundary transgressions in this text.

sexed and undercivilized, waiting to rape the undersexed and over-
civilized white woman?) Pronounce the word nigger and Joanna Burden's murder becomes a rape; the white men's behavior moves into
satisfying ritual (" 'Get me a nigger,' the sheriff said"). There is more
beating, more hands laid brutally upon bodies, in *Light in August* than in
any other of Faulkner's novels.[10] The beating seems to be both an outraged censuring of illicit sexual release and a displaced indulging in the
same release – an occasion for males to penetrate other males the only
way they can in this code-obsessed and homophobic culture: violently.
As always, black in itself counts for nothing; it is needed only as a trigger
for setting off uncontrollable white passions. As James Baldwin puts it in
"Stranger in the Village," "the Negro-in-America is a form of insanity
which overtakes white men" (88).

If in *The Sound and the Fury* black is proposed as a sanctuary in which
the chaos of sexual impulses can be kept at bay and the normality of racial
and gender distinctions be maintained, here we have the reverse. (Indeed,
that seems to be one of the meanings of the title – this book's fascination
with what is on the other side of the boundary-marking light.) Joe's
putative blackness lies within him like an inexhaustible toxin, stinging
him into ritual forays of sadistic and masochistic beating. It is himself as a
culturally constructed incoherence that he cannot bear, and his death is
surely as much a suicidal immolation at the castrating hands of Percy
Grimm as it is a heroic coming to terms with his warring components.

In all of Faulkner's novels characters generalize about blacks, but rarely
elsewhere is the generalizing so rabid, the channels of transference and
repudiation so befouled. The other side of the light is always the other
side, always ferociously projected from this side. Nathaniel Burden's "A
race doomed and cursed to be forever and ever a part of the white race's
doom and curse for its sins. Remember that" (278) and Gavin Stevens's
"Because the black blood drove him first to the negro cabin. And then
the white blood drove him out of there, as it was the black blood which
snatched up the pistol and the white blood which would not let him fire
it" (495) – both of these crazily polarized abstractions occupy central
space in *Light in August,* blinding characters to the flesh-and-blood reality
of actual blacks. Racism proceeds here not through biological difference
but through discursive insistence. In fact there are very few actual blacks
in this race-obsessed novel. The few who are there are barely granted a
name, let alone a story of their own.[11]

---

[10] In Chapter 4 I explore at length the social mapping of the body within all four of the
canonical novels under scrutiny. That mapping occasions the greatest violence in *Light
in August* because the violation of its licensed categories of difference – male and female,
white and black – occurs most brutally here, epitomized in the lifelong ordeal of Joe
Christmas.

[11] We do find in this novel three blacks whose brief appearance is at least graced with

What then does Faulkner imagine when he imagines black in *Light in August?* If we take Joe Christmas as the relevant case, Faulkner has no interest whatsoever in black as biologically determinate. As Byron says about Doc Hines's murder of Milly's putative black lover, "Maybe the circus folks told him. I dont know. He aint never said how he found out, like that never made any difference. And I reckon it didn't, after the next night" (413). The facts become irrelevant. More precisely, the "facts" are invented, discursively disseminated, randomly internalized, fatally acted upon. Faulkner focuses in this text upon the lifelong nightmare of a white man imagining himself (and imagined by others) to be black, while black itself has been constructed by this culture as what no white man can possibly tolerate within himself. The only thing visible here – glaring, highlighted as though in infrared – is the virulent power of a shared racist discourse.[12]

Black may have nothing to do with the color of a man's skin, and that is indeed the community's problem. The warning attribute of color can disappear, leaving only the invisible, culturally constructed essence of blackness. In the early twentieth-century South of untracked strangers and unknown genealogies, race distinctions take on a new anxiety, for *anyone* could turn out to be black. "Towns that had been relatively stable suddenly experienced a sizable influx of strangers whose origins were wholly unknown. Where once it had been highly unlikely for a resident to have 'black blood' without the town knowing of it, the system of community genealogy was now doomed" (Singal 182). Black may now appear transparently as a murderously projective state of the white mind when traditional markers of racial difference have lost their "native" authority.[13]

From the perspective of race representation *Light in August* emerges as Faulkner's pivotal novel, the one in which he first explored his white male culture's (and his own) most deeply seated black preoccupations not as biologically grounded but as culturally constructed. These constructions, he reveals with unsurpassed power, are inseparable from the assumptions through which white male subjectivity generates and affirms its own coherence. He found, in the overdetermined chaos that is Joe Christmas, that the domains of racial difference, gender distinction, and sexual desire

names: Jupe (whom Joe Christmas passes on the road at night, before killing Joanna), and Pomp and Cinthy, Hightower's grandfather's faithful retainers.

12 See the second part of Chapter 3 for further discussion of the racial coding that, once internalized, produces Joe Christmas's inextinguishable vertigo.

13 Davis argues as well that "Faulkner dramatizes his conception that a social, not a biological, definition of Negro underpins southern thought" (*Negro* 131), and that *Light in August* does not "present Joe Christmas as a black man" (176). My study departs from hers inasmuch as she continues to regret that Faulkner did not deal with the "real thing," *"the Negro as Negro"* (177, italics in the original). I read Faulkner's attention to discursive rather than "grounded" realities as the strength of his major texts on race.

fuse into a single magnetic field as covertly appealing as it is officially taboo: miscegenation.

ᥤ

> It was not the nigger anymore than it had been the nigger that his father had helped to whip that night. The nigger was just another balloon face slick and distended with that mellow loud and terrible laughing so that he did not dare to burst it, looking down at him from within the half-closed door that instant in which, before he knew it, something in him had escaped and – he unable to close the eyes of it – was looking out from within the balloon face just as the man who did not even have to wear the shoes he owned, whom the laughter which the balloon held barricaded and protected from such as he, looked out from whatever invisible place he (the man) happened to be at the moment, at the boy outside the barred door in his patched garments and splayed bare feet, looking through and beyond the boy, he himself seeing his own father and sisters and brothers as the owner, the rich man (not the nigger) must have been seeing them all the time – as cattle, creatures heavy and without grace, brutely evacuated into a world without hope or purpose for them, who would in turn spawn with brutish and vicious prolixity, populate, double treble and compound, fill space and earth with a race whose future would be a succession of cut-down and patched and made-over garments bought on exorbitant credit because they were white people, from stores where niggers were given the garments free, with for sole heritage that expression on a balloon face bursting with laughter which had looked out at some unremembered and nameless progenitor who had knocked at a door when he was a little boy and had been told by a nigger to go around to the back. (292–3)

This passage suggests something of *Absalom, Absalom!*'s capacious frame for reading black lives. Rejecting the attempted pastoral of *The Sound and the Fury*'s rendering of blacks, *Absalom* is premised upon the same racial violence that suffuses *Light in August*. Unlike that earlier book, however, *Absalom* pursues a narrative strategy that would both distance and (in a certain measure) understand the violence. Here, black is inserted into an extensive social, economic, and historical network. Even as he strikes out at those "balloon faces," Sutpen realizes that it is a mediated cultural system, not an essential biological fact, that is wounding him.

Crucially, though, the registering consciousness at this visionary moment is white, not black, and the sympathetic victim of its insight is white, not black. "It was not the nigger" punctuates this revelation. The arresting but invariant figure of the laughing balloon face applied to blacks remains to the side of Sutpen's gaze. Where he focuses (and we with him) is upon the poor whites' patched garments and splayed bare feet, upon their intolerable status as "cattle, creatures heavy and without grace," and upon their foreclosed future generation after generation. The passage is built upon the language of the subject-shaping gaze – of Sutpen seeing through the eyes of the "balloon face," then through the eyes of the plantation owner, seeing himself and his entire family as caught up in an impersonal yet annihilating network of concessions and sanctions. Faulkner positions Sutpen so as to see all of this, and the readerly sympathy that such subjectively shared insight generates (the ideological work that Faulkner's representational strategy carries out) is considerable. Produced to satisfy the needs of a plantation culture, this network privileges blacks over poor whites. It finds menial jobs for blacks, clothes and feeds them, uses them to maintain its own function and image. Within such an emergent paradigm (privileged by its placement in the text as an overwhelming epiphany), black suffering under the plantation system becomes marginal. The victim we are invited to internalize here is the lower-class white.

There are in *Absalom* two white classes with but one ideology between them. The ideology is planter-centered, and although the poor whites share its claim of superiority to blacks, their daily experience of economic impotence contradicts the tenets of the claim. This situation of heartbreak – crystallized for Sutpen at the moment of the closed door – might lead either to rebellion or to joining up. Rather than choose between these options, Faulkner has his narrative develop them both. He has Sutpen join up while he narrates at the same time the collapse (both tragic and justified) of the entire plantation system: its masters destroyed by their treatment of both the poor whites and the blacks. This clash of different class and racial groups is the overt reason for collapse. The latent reason may be more sinister: that the three groups threaten to dissolve into each other, to become (in the single overdetermined figure – white trash child/spawner of black son/dynastic planter – that is Sutpen) indistinguishable.

In any event the impact of this system's economic brutality upon blacks (and not just poor whites like Sutpen and Wash Jones) remains to be explored, and *Absalom, Absalom!* would be even richer if Faulkner *had* explored it. That is, we would have a novel that seriously probed into the systemic damage done not just to poor whites but to Southern blacks as well – their insertion into the dehumanizing network of white powers and sanctions that was American slavery. We would have an inquiry that went further, in its representation of black subjectivity, than the marginal examples of Pettibone's nigger and the smiling balloon faces can take us. All of these figures are only so many stand-ins for the real subject, the white planter, whom the poor whites cannot otherwise harm. But he alone (the planter) can *do* harm, and this text seems compelled to revolve around his gaze, to fashion a counterresponse, to work out a proxy revenge. In none of this is the black man's fate central; "it was not the nigger." The most we can say is that *Absalom, Absalom!* prepares the way for this systemic inquiry into race rather than class, but Faulkner does not carry it out (insofar as he can carry it out) until six years later, in *Go Down, Moses*. Here his principal interest when he imagines black is different – primarily psychological and sexual, and only secondarily economic and class-focused.[14] Perhaps the most direct way to analyze that interest is to personify it in the figure of Charles Bon.

If Charles Bon is another "balloon face" (a container filled by other people's inspiration, a figure approached through mediation), he is nonetheless the most compelling figure in *Absalom, Absalom!* – compelling in the sense that no one (not Rosa, Mr. Compson, Sutpen, Henry, Judith, Quentin, Shreve – and not, therefore, the reader either) can take their eyes off him, or rest with others' versions of him. Charles Bon is the most extravagantly reinvented character in the novel. What does it mean that black in *Absalom, Absalom!* is primarily imagined through him? Like Joe Christmas, Charles Bon is only putatively black; he looks white. But whereas Joe appears to the reader as a white man caught in a nightmare, Bon is genuinely – culturally – different from northern Mississippi whites. Indeed, he becomes, in his difference, the erotic center of *Absalom, Absalom!* All who see him (except, ironically, his father) or get caught up in the telling or the reading of his story run the risk of falling in love with him. In other words, Faulkner is here proposing a relationship with Charles Bon that is the reverse of others' (and our own) encounters with the abused and abusive Joe Christmas: a dozen or so white characters in the novel (and countless white readers outside the novel) drawn to one black man. What makes this possible and why might Faulkner be inviting it?

Bon's appeal is inseparable from his exoticism. *Absalom* depends for some of its most memorable effects upon exoticism, or another way to put this is to say that *Absalom* can try out through geographic and cultural displacement what it cannot work through on its home space. New Orleans is where it goes to understand sexual and racial ease; Haiti is where it goes to understand racial and economic war; Cambridge is where it goes to understand the stories of Jefferson. Charles Bon, more than any other figure in the book, is the product of Haiti, New Orleans, and Cambridge. Exoticism is another word for his nonprovincial allure. He has been put together out of physical and spiritual traits not available in northern Mississippi.

---

[14] To say that Faulkner's principal interest is psychological and sexual is not to say that economic and class-focused issues are necessarily marginal. It is to say that their impact upon the strategy of race representation in *Absalom, Absalom!* is latent rather than overt, and would require a different analysis from the one I offer here.

Thus constituted, thus appealing, thus distinguished from the native black and white specimens, Bon can house Faulkner's most audacious fantasy: that black is more beautiful than white, that the unconscious desire for miscegenation lurks deep within the white psyche. Bon represents in his lithe body and unfailing civility the novel's inadmissible desire for racial union, a desire that compels even so recalcitrant a Southerner as Rosa Coldfield so long as his blackness remains invisible and the desire for union be denied its true name.[15] But of course the reverse is equally true in *Absalom, Absalom!* Once identified as black, he loses his exotic French camouflage, his menace is revealed, and he becomes (despite the persistence of desire) the target of every native code. He becomes anathema. In so doing he reveals the price of the displacement at the heart of Faulkner's racial strategy here. To probe Mississippi enslavement through the prisms of aristocratic New Orleans, romantic (Conradian) Haiti, and intellectual Cambridge is powerfully to broaden the analysis but also to whiten (to lyricize) the lenses of access.

The contrast between exotic black and homegrown black is pronounced in *Absalom, Absalom!* On the one hand there are (in addition to Sutpen's savage blacks, speaking in incomprehensible tongues) the tragic octoroon, the mysterious Eulalia Bon, her epicene son Charles, and his emphatically foreign-named son Charles Etienne de St. Valery Bon – all of these figures of physical energy, grace, or pathos. But on the other hand, there is the "coal black and ape-like woman" (257) whom Charles Etienne marries to fling in Judith's face: a black woman described more abusively than any other in Faulkner's fiction ("that aghast and automaton-like state in which she had arrived . . . [and] which she seemed to exude gradually and by a process of terrific and incredulous excretion like . . . sweat . . . how he had found her, dragged her out of whatever two dimensional backwater . . . her mentality had been capable of coercing food and shelter from, and married her, held her very hand doubtless while she made the laborious cross on the register before she even knew his name . . . [a woman whom he] kenneled . . . [a] black gargoyle . . . resembling something in a zoo" [257–62]). The offspring of this union, owing apparently everything to the mother and nothing to the father, is Jim Bond.

What is one to make of this genealogy? What has Jim Bond in common with Charles Bon? What does it mean that this black descent, unlike the white one in *The Sound and the Fury* and unlike the white and black ones in *Go Down, Moses,* feels both abbreviated and built wholly of extremes?

---

[15] Eric Sundquist brilliantly argues that *Absalom, Absalom!*, in its way of connecting Rosa with the miscegenation theme, "brings us to the verge of a recognition we are unwilling to make . . . [showing us] the moment that never will be in the certain tragic fullness of what *might have been*" (115).

Faulkner produces black in this novel with a schizoid intensity, the foreign pole as seductive and lingered upon as the homegrown one is either neutral or repellant: in any case marginalized. Another way to put it is to say that in *Absalom, Absalom!* Faulkner can imaginatively desire the union of white and black only by exoticizing black.

Finally there are *Absalom*'s missing narratives. In a novel that richly invents other missing stories, two black ones are crucially absent here: those of Eulalia and of Clytie. One the abandoned wife and the other the illegitimate daughter of Thomas Sutpen, these characters supply the unnarrated black underweave to the Sutpen design. Eulalia engineers the collapse of that design. Her role, only marginally represented, actually matches (and eventually overmasters) Sutpen's point for point in plot import. But the subjective focus for her ordeal always lodges outside her – in Sutpen who betrayed her or in Bon through whom she wreaks her revenge.

As for Clytie, she both presides over the repercussions of the collapsing design and sees to it that, when the time is ready, the house burns down too. Beyond her plot function, though, Clytie emerges as the semiotic center of the novel, the foregrounded figure in whom Faulkner's tormented racial imagination fuses a white paternity and a black career, the figure who finally serves for Quentin as the key to the entire enigma. For Clytie incarnates the otherwise invisible racial transgression of Thomas Sutpen. She patiently awaits a reader or character capable of decoding her genesis, of realizing that if Sutpen could impregnate one black woman, he could impregnate others.[16] Here again Faulkner's positioning of subjectivity is critical. The awaiting object, silent but pregnant with signs to be decoded, is the black woman; the advancing subject, vocal and eventually producing the key that will decode, is the white man. Indeed, Clytie is pregnant only in this figurative sense. Faulkner ignores her erotic life (unlike his plunge into Rosa's), depriving her not only of mate or offspring but also of regret or desire. She remains, thus, a mute key to the mystery, her meaning eloquently residing in the pigment of her skin rather than the quality of her soul or the revelation of her words. For something of her subjective experience – what it must feel like to be a marginalized black in the South – we must leave *Absalom, Absalom!* and turn to *Go Down, Moses*.

❧

"Ah lets hit lay," he said, and cast, and moved as the white man moved, catching the white man's wrist before his hand reached the dice, the two

---

[16] Peter Brooks's case for construing Clytie as the semiological key to the otherwise indecipherable mystery of miscegenation at the core of the novel seems to me irrefutable. See his "Incredulous Narration."

of them squatting, facing each other above the dice and the money, his left hand grasping the white man's wrists, his face still fixed in the rigid and deadened smiling, his voice equable, almost deferential: "Ah kin pass even wid miss-outs. But dese hyar yuther boys –" until the white man's hand sprang open and the second pair of dice clattered onto the floor beside the first two and the white man wrenched free and sprang up and back and reached the hand backward toward the pocket where the pistol was.

The razor hung between his shoulder-blades from a loop of cotton string round his neck inside his shirt. The same motion of the hand which brought the razor forward over his shoulder flipped the blade open and freed it from the cord, the blade opening on until the back edge of it lay across the knuckles of his fist, his thumb pressing the handle into his closing fingers, so that in the second before the half-drawn pistol exploded he actually struck at the white man's throat not with the blade but with a sweeping blow of his fist, following through in the same motion so that not even the first jet of blood touched his hand or arm. (153–4)

If we compare this passage from "Pantaloon in Black" with the passage of Joe Christmas's violence against the black girl, we can see how the luxuriant detail works in each passage to different effects. In the earlier novel the accent is upon pain, upon the brutal and dehumanizing activity of one body pummeling another. Here the stress is upon Rider's exquisite physical grace. There is no pain in this passage, just Rider's flawlessly coordinated strength. (Birdsong, the man whose throat he is cutting, has no narrative reality; this is the first page on which he appears.) If we further compare this passage with the passage about Versh's story of a man mutilating himself – "A broken razor flinging them backward over his shoulder the same motion complete the jerked skein of blood backward not looping" (*SF* 132) – we can see how the same gesture has been put to quite a different use. There the move was toward peaceful depletion, here it is toward aggressive fulfillment. Indeed, the real hold this passage from *Go Down, Moses* exercises upon us comes from its hypnotic illicitness: a black man is, detail by beautiful detail, killing a white man. Placed narratively within his powerful mind and body, we as readers participate in the act.

I begin with this sequence from "Pantaloon in Black" in order to claim that *Go Down, Moses* focuses with unprecedented intensity upon black males, and that it is fascinated with a variety of illicit moves available to them. As I argued in the last chapter, the black women here have no such instigating power. Rousing desire in others but narratively deprived of it themselves, they rarely escape the tragic, but passive, role of being taken and abandoned by their white lovers. The other empowered black males in *Go Down, Moses* are Lucas Beauchamp, centrally, and Samuel Beauchamp, peripherally. But the most difficult figure to assess (and the one to whom critics are irresistibly drawn) remains Rider. "Pantaloon in Black" is unique in Go Down, Moses in its abiding focus on a black man's physical prowess. The story is keyed to Rider's body, the sentences moving in mimicry of his powerful motion: "He drank again, swallowing the chill liquid tamed of taste or heat either while the swallowing lasted, feeling it flow solid and cold with fire, past then enveloping the strong steady panting of his lungs until they too ran suddenly free as his moving body ran in the silver solid wall of air he breasted" (148). I do not mean to slight the importance of Rider's mental state – his ungovernable anguish over the death of Mannie – but this mental state is everywhere conveyed not by conceptual abstractions but by Faulkner's lyrical prose of the body in motion. Physical grace alone can of course be read as a stereotyping of black as body. To a certain extent we must read it so: a writer's choices at this level profoundly – because involuntarily – revealing. It seems to me, though, that Faulkner's investment in the representation of Rider's physical moves goes well beyond the static ease of cliché. Faulkner's verbal attention to Rider's body is so unfalteringly fine that through this bodily notation we are invited to construe the more-than-bodily lineaments of a being in torment. In any case, I would argue that it is attention, rather than attitude, that most conveys a writer's investments. By this criterion Faulkner has deeply invested himself in the portrait of Rider. Paralleling Ike McCaslin's pain-fully won prowess in the wilderness – but never announced as such – is Rider's mastery of his natural conditions.

Lucas Beauchamp has something of Rider's uncanny natural facility – "Then he whirled and leaped, not toward the sound but running parallel with it, leaping with incredible agility and speed among the trees and undergrowth" (40–1) – but this is not the virtue of Lucas that Faulkner stresses most. The narrative positioning of Lucas involves much more than physical movement. Rather, his behavior seems to represent Faulkner's meditation on what a cunning black man does when the things a white man might do are not available to him. Behind Lucas's big bank account lie some stark facts: the land he farms is not his own, the vocation he practices is not a choice, the territory he inhabits may not be es-caped.[17] If Ike McCaslin's story is one of precious options, Lucas Beau-

---

[17] Though Lucas's "plot territory" is always constrained (in Intruder it will shrink to the confines of a prison cell), his "discursive territory" is richly open to revision. Faulkner's most profoundly suggestive character revisions arguably take place within this figure, and in the second half of this chapter I pursue the implications of his three different scriptings between 1940 and 1948. With respect to his nonownership of the land, I base my claim upon the abundant evidence of "The Fire and the Hearth" itself. Of Lucas's coming of age Faulkner writes: "Within the year he married, not a country woman, a farm woman, but a town woman, and McCaslin Edmonds built a house for them and

champ's is one of given conditions adroitly accepted and exploited.[18]

Unlike Rider, Lucas is a game player. He runs an illegal still, he believes in buried treasure, he buys a special machine to find it with. These adolescent maneuvers (one imagines a slightly older Tom Sawyer doing such things) lack the soul-testing seriousness of Ike's drama, and that is their point. A black man living marginally, at the sufferance of the white landowner, with his own options long ago circumscribed, can either release his spirit in harmlessly illicit games or roll over and play by the rules. On the margin there is room only for childish play – Faulkner seems unable to imagine anything else for an established black to *do* – and the usual effect on the reader of these clever machinations in "The Fire and the Hearth" is to convict Lucas of frivolity.

Yet what I'm calling "childish play" suggests something more. The long-sanctioned commercial exploitation of blacks by whites gets nicely "signified upon" by Lucas's reversing the expected roles and playing the gadget owner rather than its renter. (In like manner George Wilkins's irrepressible wisecracks "signify upon" Lucas's humorless authority in the only way open to a constrained black – by repositioning the terms of the contest rather than inventing a new game altogether: a sign of wit unvanquished where there can be no question of a genuinely reshaping power.) Further, although Lucas is a man of custom, he nevertheless feels the siren call of progressive capitalism.[19] He alone in *Go Down, Moses* is

allotted Lucas a specific acreage to be farmed as he saw fit as long as he lived or remained on the place" (110). Throughout the foregrounded scenes of "The Fire and the Hearth" Cass's grandson Roth acts consistently as the long-suffering landowner chafing at Lucas's pranks, threatening to take matters in his own hands:

> "And remember [Edwards is speaking]. Aunt Molly gets the house, and half your crop this year and half of it every year as long as you stay on my place."
> "You mean every year I keep on farming my land."
> "I mean every damned year you stay on my place. Just what I said."
> "Cass Edmonds give me that land to be mine as long as I –"
> "You heard me," Edmonds said. (126)

Edmond's ownership of the land seems indisputable in these passages, yet in *Intruder in the Dust* Lucas pays taxes on the land, a sure indication that by 1948 Faulkner imagined him to be in possession. I am indebted to James Hinkle and James Carothers for a fuller sense of this issue. In the second half of this chapter I speculate on the reasons why Faulkner chose later to make Lucas a landowner.

18 Craig Werner, drawing on the work of Robert Stepto, proposes cogently that Faulkner's work in general constrains black narratives within the Euro-American genre of "the narrative of endurance," as opposed to Afro-American genres of "the narrative of ascent" and "the narrative of immersion." Lucas and Rider, like Faulkner's other blacks, remain condemned to "an essentially static pattern for black experience" – or they pay with their lives. Davis makes a kindred point in "Black Characterization."

19 Flem Snopes of course has this progressive urge with a vengeance. But Flem's schemes, though undoubtedly grander, are all egotistical and passionless – as well as accessible to us only through others' speculations (Faulkner refuses to open him to subjective voice).

interested in machines, in renting out equipment, in having his investment return a profit. His secret dream is to find that buried Civil War
treasure and to retire: a dream of release from the thralldom of the earth,
a dream of unacknowledged revenge against the landed white Southerners whose money would fall into his enterprising black hands. Faulkner's
portrait of this black man is thus poised between manifest admiration for
Lucas's fidelity to his ancestry, on the one hand, and latent respect for his
unco-opted capacity for a future, on the other. Though Lucas has only
games to play, he remains open (unlike the dignified Ike McCaslin) to the
fertile possibilities of scandal. He takes his chances as they come, intrepid
enough to risk a good deal of trouble, clever enough to get out of it once
it arrives.

The black women in Go Down, Moses lack the men's wit and ag-
gressiveness, but at least they possess (as compared with the earlier fiction) their own history. It is a history of sexual abuse; and Faulkner
passionately rehearses it through the figures of Eunice, Fonsiba, Molly,
and the "doe" in "Delta Autumn." Though rarely told in their own
voices, it nevertheless registers with great emotional impact, in the form
of the white male subject's appalling discovery of inherited racial guilt.
Black suffering and white guilt are now inextricably intertwined. Indeed,
by the end of Go Down, Moses Faulkner is straining to have the entire
community bear witness to the sorrow inscribed upon black lives.

The final story of an escaped, executed, and returned black man is
offered as aftermath, as dirge. Samuel Worsham Beauchamp is dead on
arrival, set up for capital punishment the moment we meet him. Faulkner
invests his subjective life with no narrative value, for the chapter's focus is
upon the traditional community that receives his corpse back into the
fold. The organizers of the reception, Miss Worsham and Gavin Stevens,
strike a curiously strident note, however. His piety is too officious, hers
too assured – the black grief is not really theirs – though Faulkner seems
to reveal this unintentionally:

> Now he could hear the third voice, which would be that of Hamp's wife
> – a true constant soprano which ran without words beneath the strophe
> and antistrophe of the brother and sister:
> "Sold him in Egypt and now he dead."

He shares nothing of either Lucas's somatic quickness or his ability to interest himself in
the "instruments" of progress. Peripheral figures in several of Faulkner's novels – Jason,
Max and Mame, Armstid, any number of lesser Snopeses, and others – are of course
prone to the lure of the fast or illicit buck, but these remain figures we are urged to read
against (at least during such vignettes), whereas we are ambiguously invited to read both
with and against Lucas's shenanigans. Lucas's being black may give him greater latitude
than Flem (or "lesser" whites) to escape Faulkner's disapproval of his pursuit of non-
traditional goals. In any event, his being black prevents him from succeeding enough to
disturb the status quo.

"Oh yes, Lord. Sold him in Egypt."

"Sold him in Egypt."

"And now he dead."

"Sold him to Pharaoh."

"And now he dead."

"I'm sorry," Stevens said, "I ask you to forgive me. I should have known, I shouldn't have come."

"It's all right," Miss Worsham said. "It's our grief." (381)

"It's our grief," she says – as though to distinguish her intimacy from Stevens's isolation – but Miss Worsham's voice is not heard in that overwhelming chorus of woe, a chorus uniquely black. The reference goes back to the pariahs, to Jews destroyed by Egyptians, to blacks deformed, uprooted, and executed by whites. These are the marginal people, and they suffer; they are done to. Faulkner can point to their grief, he can be anguished over it, he can quote its dialect voice, but neither he as narrator nor his white delegates can speak it inwardly, subjectively, freshly. Nor can he envisage that those blacks who suffer under it might, through their own activities, escape its burden.

When Faulkner imagines black in *Go Down, Moses,* he imagines a 150-year-long history of oppression (sexual, political, economic, emotional) of blacks by whites of the same family.[20] This is a history that the black women stoically endure and that the black men seek alternately to confront and (in illicit, appealing, and foredoomed ways) to escape. We have come a long way from *The Sound and the Fury.* The blacks and whites – men and women – of this novel emerge as thematically integral to each other's destiny. (How they emerge narratively is another question. Their outward stories come to us, rarely their inner voices.)

Bound to each other through seven generations that begin and end with miscegenation, the blacks see in the whites the conditions they cannot escape, the whites see in the blacks the guilt they cannot assuage.[21] Inescapable because the traditional South is the only setting Faulkner can imaginatively endorse, even for his blacks; and unassuageable because the act that Faulkner would have to legitimize (ceremonialize) for his whites to get clear of guilt, the act of miscegenation, remains within his frame of values a taboo act. The traditional South would, it

---

[20] The narrative *donnée* of a single family governs the entire analysis of racism in *Go Down, Moses.* In Chapter 4, I speculate on the critical limitation – the recurrent sense that this is a saga of unruly black offspring trying the patience of their white progenitors – imposed by this frame.

[21] This chapter, while attending to seven generations of racial abuse, has hardly touched upon the impersonal economic conditions that also guaranteed the continuation of racism from the Emancipation Proclamation of 1863 to the Voting Rights bill of 1965. The eternal "ledgers" in *Go Down, Moses* – arguably as effective in 1940 as in 1840 – carry metonymically this precise charge of an inescapable debt structure. For a compelling account of the recontainment of blacks after the Civil War, see Stephen Steinberg.

seems, collapse to its foundations if it were to assent to such a mixing of the races. And yet on the streets of every town and city of the South the effects of miscegenation are daily visible, wrought through illicit inter-course (when not rape) and inscribed in the pigment of the skin, that silent and eloquent testimony to a history heartbreakingly at odds with the simplistic strictures of the white Symbolic.

ॐ

Let me conclude by briefly comparing three marginal figures, each one the end of his line: Benjy Compson, Jim Bond, and Samuel Worsham Beauchamp. To set up the comparison is to see where it comes out. In Benjy, Faulkner took a marginal figure and made him central. Not that Benjy can escape his suffering or overcome his handicaps; his future is hopeless. But Faulkner made compelling art out of that hope-lessness. Spurred by its silent sound in his own mind, he created the most moving subjectivity in all of his work. Benjy is central because Faulkner makes him matter. He matters narratively (all Faulkner's art is in getting Benjy to matter narratively), and therefore he matters to us, his readers. We can hardly read *The Sound and the Fury* without registering his human wholeness.

Jim Bond and Samuel Worsham Beauchamp do not matter in the same way, nor to the same degree. Jim Bond is heard, not felt. Only Clytie is there to care for him, and it is a caring we do not see. He frightens white people; his single recorded interaction with them is to pick Rosa Cold-field off the floor at the end of *Absalom, Absalom!* He may have a putative soul, a unique interiority through which he registers his world, but Faulkner has not produced it textually, and so we as readers do not imaginatively credit it. His is not a black life we are invited to recreate from within.

As for Samuel Worsham Beauchamp, his mistake was to leave Jefferson for points north. This departure has simply undone his identity:

> The face was black, smooth, impenetrable; the eyes had seen too much. The negroid hair had been treated so that it covered the skull like a cap, in a single neat-ridged sweep, with the appearance of having been lac-quered. . . . He wore one of those sports costumes called ensembles in the men's shop advertisements, shirt and trousers matching and cut from the same fawn-colored flannel, and they had cost too much and were draped too much, with too many pleats . . . smoking cigarettes and answering in a voice which was anything under the sun but a southern voice or even a negro voice. (369)

Caddy and her daughter can depart from the Compson family and at least survive, if not triumph. Samuel Worsham Beauchamp is sentenced to death for leaving. In this portrait Faulkner proposes a total denaturing, as if the abandonment of his black and white family meant becoming unrecognizable – unrecognizable to Faulkner and therefore to us. All that remains of Samuel Worsham Beauchamp are his outward urban mistakes: his straightened hair, his overpriced and tacky clothes, his unplaceable voice. The portrait is suffused in disapproval; its subject has forfeited his soul by abandoning his native space.

Samuel Worsham Beauchamp's significance is produced by bypassing his own interiority. He matters because of the powerful communal response his returned corpse occasions back home, and this "homecoming" sends as well the following sinister message: Stay at home, grow up by accepting your overwhelming inheritance, by way of endurance. This is the significance, it seems to me, of a marginal character, one whom Faulkner cannot enter as he can enter Benjy Compson, one whom he turns into a symbol for the white spectators in and out of the story who regard him.

It is no discredit to Faulkner if we say that – despite some remarkable portraits of black courage, pathos, and cunning – the power of his racial imagination lies elsewhere. It lies in the extraordinary depiction of turmoil and hatred that the notion of black can unleash in the white male mind; it lies as well in the dramatized interdependency of black and white destinies; and it lies finally in the creative mix of feelings – longing, bafflement, and grief: always felt by whites – through which he explores (and therefore permits us to explore) this inflicted pain, this enforced segregation. But Samuel Worsham Beauchamp is on the margins and slips away from him. It will take another writer, Richard Wright, to see in this denatured corpse the seeds of escape, of Big Boy leaving home.

"HE COME AND SPOKE FOR ME": SCRIPTING LUCAS BEAUCHAMP'S THREE LIVES

The analysis proposed here differs from the one just conducted. There I sought to probe Faulkner's altering discursive practice – the assumptions at work, the subjective positions essayed, the tropes racially assigned, the fantasies released – as he textualized black lives in relation to white ones from *The Sound and the Fury* to *Go Down, Moses*. The scrutiny of each text was necessarily brief, the cast of characters large. Here I move inward, seeking to analyze the three "solutions" Faulkner negotiated during the decade in which he wrestled, three different times, with the representation of the same black man, Lucas Beauchamp. In attending to this single figure Faulkner reveals in small his entire repertory of discursive moves for articulating racial distinction: what he sees, what he comes to see through, what he cannot see beyond.

Who is Lucas Beauchamp? What does it mean to ask that question? I want to explore Lucas Beauchamp's subjectivity not as an unchanging essence but rather as a conflictual space. Conflictual, theoretically, because subjectivity itself is not an essence but a stance shaped by one's position within a signifying economy: as the economy alters, so does the subjectivity. Conflictual, practically, because Faulkner produces Luças Beauchamp within three different signifying economies: first, in a cluster of short stories that appeared in 1940 in *Collier's* and *The Atlantic Monthly;* then a second time in the sifted and revised versions of those stories that, two years later, make up *Go Down, Moses;* then a third time, six years later, in *Intruder in the Dust.*[22]

To pursue the subjectivity of Lucas Beauchamp is to analyze the language games Faulkner activated in producing this character. It is a question not of essence but of language: a discursive strategy, not a brute event. Yet this discursive strategy, while language, is never only language. It is rather the medium through which Faulkner predicts and solicits the response of middle-brow and high-brow audiences (the readers of the popular magazines, the more select novel readership) as he articulates racial difference in the mid-South in the 1940s. To say who Lucas Beauchamp is is to map the career of his creator within a ten-year history of trying in different ways to say black, and always failing.

Subjectivity: for at least two hundred years we have wanted to see in this word the arena of human freedom, that uncoerced interiority from which voluntary thoughts, feelings, and actions emanate. "A conscious and coherent originator of meanings and actions" (Smith xxviii), the human subject maintains a saving autonomy, a fragile sanctuary, an interiority within which – however turbulent the external conditions – the self remains recognizably itself. Subjectivity is thus the Imaginary answer to objectification, it is that deep unpredictable space of the essentially human within an otherwise charted world of Newtonian necessity. Within his own subjectivity, if nowhere else, the self remains an individual: literally, an undivided entity.

It is by now a well-known story how Marx, Darwin, and Freud, among others, have challenged this liberal notion of the autonomous subject by proposing a variety of networks – of class, of biology, of the unconscious – upon which subjecthood is constructed as a fissured entity but which subjecthood refuses to (or cannot) acknowledge.[23] To recog-

---

22 The standard account of the genesis of *Go Down, Moses* remains Early's. More recently, Jehlen, Matthews *(Play)*, Snead, and Grimwood have commented perceptively on the interplay of stories making up this novel.

23 The decentered self is a commonplace of recent theoretically informed criticism, and we are just now beginning to see a productive counterargument to such widely shared claims about the mystified subject. Paul Smith usefully probes this notion of a subjectivity wholly scripted by its entry into a Symbolic field. He argues that agency – empowerment rather than paralysis – can occur through recognition of one's own subjectivity as a site of conflicting positions within more than one signifying economy. I have already drawn intermittently (in the Introduction, in the second half of Chapter 1,

nize its constituent dependency upon such transpersonal structures is to see that the subject is not self-generative but rather produced, and (according to recent claims of French critical theory) it is produced in and by *language*. The subject, in other words, is subjected, thrown beneath, "something at the behest of forces greater than it" (Smith xxxiii). This embattled subject – one precisely not undivided, not master of his own house but beleaguered from within by "greater forces" – is of course the myriad focal figure of Faulkner's greatest novels. It is as though Faulkner explored himself most intimately and powerfully as a figure of tragic discord – a subjectivity irreparably fissured – and his memorable characters share this divisive (and ennobling) trait. Lucas Beauchamp, we shall see, attains such disturbing resonance in only one of his three avatars.

To say who Lucas Beauchamp is, I shall be looking at the language Faulkner provides for indicating how he looks, thinks, talks, and acts. What representational schema governs Faulkner's deployment of Lucas's body, what discursive practice accounts for his speech, what kinds of access do we have to his unspoken and unacted subjectivity? Michel Foucault alerts us to the ways in which the human body moves incessantly through channels of social inscription. The body, Foucault proposes, is "an inscribed surface of events (traced by language and dissolved by ideas), the locus of a dissociated Self (adopting the illusion of a substantial unity), and a volume in perpetual disintegration" ("Nietzsche" 148).

If the body is everywhere tracked by social coding, branded in the name of social norms, the voice is equally a register of a lifetime of social training. How we speak announces who we have and have not listened to, what "internally persuasive" accents of others we have made our own, what vocal communities we belong to as well as the ones we define ourselves against. As Mikhail Bakhtin writes, "the ideological becoming of a human being . . . is the process of selectively assimilating the words of others" (341). Utterance is inseparable from ideology, and the language we use to articulate our inner selves registers simultaneously our often involuntary affiliation within larger groups whose language has become our own. "He come and spoke for me," Lucas says to Zack at a climactic moment in "The Fire and the Hearth." He is referring to old Carothers McCaslin, but we may overhear a larger dynamic: that subjectivity is generated by the assimilation of the words of others, that Lucas becomes Lucas by speaking Carothers. More resonant yet, we may hear in these words Faulkner's own capacity to articulate Lucas – to speak for

in earlier notes, and in the first half of this chapter) upon some of these theoretical paradigms for the production of subjectivity. They become crucial instruments in conducting the analysis of the second half of this study, and I elaborate their assumptions further in the next chapter.

him – only in the ideologically laden accents of the white progenitor. For Faulkner's ways of speaking Lucas become his ways of speaking his own racial identity, and our responses to these speakings, submissive or resistant, emerge as so many minute activations of our own racial identity.

ða

The Lucas Beauchamp of "A Point of Law" (*Collier's,* June 1940) has not yet come into the patrimony of his own name. "Beauchamp" is as yet an inert patronymic; there is no Hubert Beauchamp/Uncle Buck/Tennie's Jim/Tomey's Terrel nucleus for his name to refer to. These figures will not be invented for at least another year, and Lucas is regularly shortened in conversation to "Luke." It could be any name; it is not yet talismanic, speaking of and summoning to the mind the absent old one. This story moves briskly and remains within the spatial and temporal confines of its plot: the comic troublemaking of "niggers" who run illegal stills on Roth Edmonds's land. There are no resonant memories here that escape the exigencies of plot.

Lucas is clearly a sharecropper in this early version, and Roth is unproblematically identified on the first page as his "landlord." When Lucas speaks, his dialect is thick. To his wife's (here, still unnamed) demand: "Whar you gwine dis time er night?" he responds, "Gwine down the road." He may be "gwine down the road" but we never see it. Rather, the text tends to limit Lucas's appearance to three main spaces: his own house, the veranda of Edmonds's house, and offices within the courthouse in Jefferson. All three of these spaces are constructed by whites; each constrains Lucas in such a way that we are watching him perform under pressure. The proportion of dialect utterance to narrated plot is high. And while Lucas is clever, he is also seen around. Even the deputies can chart his machinations: "So we set down and thought about just where would we hide a still if we was one of Mr Roth's niggers . . . and sure enough . . ." (217). "Niggers" are figures of fun here, and their behavior finally confirms rather than disturbs this epithet. Lucas Beauchamp emerges as wily in the way that "niggers" are wily. We read him in silhouette against George Wilkins but even more, perhaps, with George Wilkins: two black men negotiating domestic and nondomestic interests, one of them just foxier than the other.

Foxier in Faulkner's text, perhaps, but the *Collier's* readership would have been encouraged visually to remain within comfortable racial stereotypes while encountering this material. William Meade Prince's illustrations to "A Point of Law" (two huge drawings, each taking up a half-page of magazine space [20, 21]) stress not Lucas's agility but the play of bumbling black shenanigans. Prince's first illustration shows a tiptoeing Nat and a bottle-burdened George Wilkins trying to keep their illegal booze hidden from the authoritative gaze of white officers. The caption to the drawing – "About daylight, we see George and that gal legging it up the hill with a gallon jug in each hand" – neatly sabotages their aim, inasmuch as "we see" (we as white deputies, we as white readers – the positioning is identical) exactly what they are clumsily trying to keep from our gaze. The second illustration foregrounds the bottles and worm and jug of a homemade still, with Lucas and Molly stationed above this paraphernalia, their eyes and mouths wide open in astonishment. The caption reads: "'Git the ax!' Luke said. 'Bust it! We ain't got time to git it away.'" Once again the magazine version emphasizes the moment of comic ineptitude, in which the deputies, illustrator, writer, and reader join in a single, cliché-enforcing gaze: black as befuddlement, black as harmless antics, charted by a bemused and superior white intelligence.

"Gold Is Not Always" was written and published (*Atlantic Monthly*, November 1940) at about the same time as "A Point of Law." The same dynamics – prankish black men maneuvering within the confines of judgmental white men – activate this narrative. As Roth says, "As soon as you niggers are laid by trouble starts" (231), and the story delights in providing the trouble. Roth is still identified on the first page as Lucas's landlord, and Lucas's language remains heavily marked by dialect: "He done fotch the machine with him; I seed hit work" (227), Lucas says as the plot gets under way. Part of the comedy here resides in the racially pertinent move of Lucas's pretending to *own* Roth's mule. A certain measure of the ideological work of this tale consists in getting Roth's valuable mule back to Roth – restoring thus the racial norms of ownership – while it transfers the worthless treasure-finder from the foreign salesman to the clever black man. Lucas's admiration for this toy makes him childish. At the same time the salesman who trafficks in such useless fantasy objects receives his well-earned duping.

At stake here seem to be two options for the right management of the land itself: either a juvenile fantasy of discovering buried treasure that is figured in the machinations of a local black man outsmarting a foreign white one; or, in opposition to this scenario (with its comically "signifying" but potentially disturbing image of a white man enslaved by a black one), the proper relation to the land: hard work, no miracles. The trouble starts, as Roth says, once the "niggers" are "laid by" and the land does not properly occupy their energies. The implicit stereotype enacted by both these tales is that the blacks are idle and have plenty of time on their hands for such games. Indeed, Lucas is envisaged as better off than Edwards "since he owned nothing he had to pay taxes on and keep repaired and fenced and ditched and fertilized" (214). A hoary cliché speaks here, one that Faulkner at his most astute puts in the mouth of a

Jason Compson: namely, that the responsible handling of property and goods is a burden borne only by mature white men.

The Lucas Beauchamp of these stories is subordinated to a swiftly moving plot, and that plot cannot afford to dilate upon Lucas's subjectivity. Faulkner provides minimal interiorizing that might counteract the simplifications of Lucas's spoken dialect. His astuteness is never in question, in both senses: it is assured throughout the stories (the reader knows that Lucas's aplomb is not going to be disturbingly contested), and its lineaments hardly escape the containing stereotype of the wily black man. To put it more directly, the language that generates Lucas Beauchamp is not itself in question in these two stories. As a corollary, the stories are not likely to threaten their readers' commonplaces about racial identity. Complacent ideological alignments remain securely in place; the stories are, in their chosen and narrow way, extremely skillful.

As Faulkner's commentators have noticed, we encounter a sea change when we move from these stories into the revisionary world of *Go Down, Moses*.[24] Virtually the same passages take on a new aura of implication and value, as in the following pair of quotations:

> Edmonds stared at him [Lucas Beauchamp] as he leaned against the counter with only the slight shrinkage of the jaws to show that he was an old man, in his clean, faded overalls and shirt and the open vest looped across by a heavy gold watch chain, and the thirty-dollar handmade beaver hat which Edmonds' father had given him forty years ago about the face which was not sober and not grave but wore no expression whatsoever. ("Gold Is Not Always" 237)

> He [Edmonds] sat perfectly still, leaning forward a little, staring at the negro [Lucas Beauchamp] leaning against the counter, in whom only the slight shrinkage of the jaws revealed the old man, in threadbare mohair trousers such as Grover Cleveland or President Taft might have worn in the summertime, a white stiff-bosomed collarless shirt beneath a pique vest yellow with age and looped across by a heavy gold watch-chain, and the sixty-dollar handmade beaver hat which Edmonds' grandfather had given him fifty years ago above the face which was not sober and not grave but wore no expression at all. ("The Fire and the Hearth" 97)

The difference between these two passages tells us much about the genesis, procedure, and aims of *Go Down, Moses*. In revising the earlier

---

[24] Among recent critics Grimwood provides the most thorough and provocative new reading of the stories as entities conceived at different times and conflicting radically in their stance toward matters of family and race – the two central concerns of *Go Down, Moses*.

stories so as to make them cohere as parts of a larger narrative, Faulkner transforms his materials. Lucas Beauchamp's clothes take on a new register. What they register is the value-charged patina of time itself. Grover Cleveland and President Taft enter the "aura" of Lucas, his clothes become more luminously fine as they emerge from their long journey into the motley present moment, and the beaver hat undergoes a kindred rewriting. Its original value doubles, its age increases ten years, its source retreats another generation into the past.

"Lucas Beauchamp" is a new signified here. He has become a prism upon time itself, a departed time of heroes, of honorably crafted materials, of valuable bequests given in recognition of sustained service and worn talismanically. The first Lucas Beauchamp was a shrewd black man maneuvering on a largely contemporary stage, the second Lucas Beauchamp – time-immersed – is constructed as an extension into the 1940s of a set of nineteenth-century practices signifying honor, integrity, and determination. Time's mark on him has become his glory, not his scar. The representation of Lucas signals the degree to which *Go Down, Moses* has invested its energies in the survival – often critical but more deeply celebratory – of older modes of being and doing within a diminished present. The telos of *Go Down, Moses* is arche.

"The Fire and the Hearth" dilates upon Lucas's face – the face "which had heired and now reproduced with absolute shocking fidelity the old ancestor's entire generation and thought – the face which . . . was a composite of a whole generation of fierce and undefeated young Confederate soldiers" (118). As Myra Jehlen remarks, "It is a tortuous process by which a black man comes to look most like a Confederate soldier" (107). This throwback face, incredibly old yet perfectly intact, is antebellum in its undefeat. What, we may ask, is Faulkner doing here? Perhaps an answer emerges when we notice that Lucas's face is twice described as "Syriac," with this gloss added: "Not in a racial sense but as the heir to ten centuries of desert horsemen" (108). Systematically exoticized, Lucas's face is being rewritten: the rewriting proposes an identity to be understood "not in a racial sense." Lucas's heroic status is conditional upon his being figuratively removed from his own black heritage.

If a suspect logic governs this rewriting of Lucas's face, an odder one governs the writing of his blood:

> Yet it was not that Lucas made capital of his white or even his McCaslin blood, but the contrary. It was as if he were not only impervious to that blood, he was indifferent to it. . . . He resisted it simply by being the composite of the two races which made him, simply by possessing it. Instead of being at once the battle-ground and victim of the two strains, he was a vessel, durable, ancestryless, nonconductive, in which the

toxin and its anti stalemated one another, seetheless, unrumored in the
outside air. (104)

It seems to me that this passage proposes a desperate resolution. The
two races are said to stem from incompatible bloods – a toxin and its anti
– yet Lucas is imagined as overcoming this racist opposition by some sort
of sublime indifference. "Ancestryless," Faulkner calls him here – intran-
sitive, self-sealed – but "The Fire and the Hearth" tirelessly draws upon
(what else?) Lucas's ancestry in order to establish his stature. For reasons
that lie deep within the culture's racist ideology, Faulkner simply will not
imagine the two bloods as merging in time – Lucas must be seen as
nonconductive, raceless – yet this figure's clothes, gestures, and habits of
thought are soaked in the passage of time and have now become a source
of irreplaceable value. One might speculate that the text wants all of
Lucas's history, on condition that it be cleansed of its racial coloration. I
shall return later to the mystified scripting of Lucas Beauchamp in both
Go Down, Moses and Intruder in the Dust, but now I want to move from
the problematics of his face and blood to the elaboration of his body and
mind. Here Faulkner goes beyond cultural givens and generates perhaps
the most compelling black portrait in his entire oeuvre.[25]

This new Lucas of Go Down, Moses is a figure in intimate relation to the
land itself. "He knew exactly where he intended to go, even in the
darkness" (36), and when he hears the almost inaudible sound of Nat
following him, he whirls not toward her sound but parallel with it,
"leaping with incredible agility and speed among the trees and undergrowth" (40–1). Like Sam Fathers, like Rider, like the elaborately trained
Ike McCaslin, Lucas Beauchamp reveals a bodily agility beautifully at-
tuned to natural setting and obstacle. Rather than "performing" on a
white-constructed stage, as in the stories, he lives in Go Down, Moses as a
woodsman as well, incandescent in the body whatever shackles have been
placed upon his mind. Indeed, the land itself knows him here, striking
him a blow as the earth about him suddenly heaves, "a sort of final
admonitory pat from the spirit of darkness and solitude, the old earth,
perhaps the old ancestors themselves" (38).[26] Finally, this Lucas's intimacy with the land is beyond any white deputy's mapping. When they

---

[25] The only challenge to this claim is Dilsey in The Sound and the Fury. As I have argued,
however, the power of her portrait is suffused in racial "innocence," Faulkner's sense of
her as separately blooded from his white Compsons and spared the turmoil (psychic and
genealogical) that besets them.

[26] As the mythic tenor of this passage suggests, Go Down, Moses makes the land itself
numinous. The buried treasure of "Gold Is Not Always" is transplanted in revision so as
to emerge within the economy of ancient Indian rituals. The "old Injun's mound"
(where Lucas is now digging) marks a considerable departure from the originally unplaced shenanigans about a new-fangled treasure finder.

find his concealed still this time, it is because he has chosen to have them find it so as to keep them ignorant of the buried treasure.

The body is new here; more important, so is the mind. "A Point of Law" moves within a few lines to plot and dialogue; the first chapter of "The Fire and the Hearth" devotes nine pages to establishing Lucas Beauchamp's interiority: his views about George Wilkins, his complex plans for the two stills, his many-generational history with Cass and Zack, his sense of possession of his land ("it was his own field, though he neither owned it nor wanted to nor needed to" [35]), his dignified position as "the oldest living person on the Edmonds plantation" (36), his strenuous maneuvers with the land itself (trying to bury his still) leading to the earthslide, the glimpse of gold, and the pursuit of Nat, and finally his revision of his plans. Within these nine pages we enter a subjective drama more compelling than any plot it may release. The tensions are not centrally between white landlord and black sharecropper (Roth is never referred to as landlord in the revised version).[27] Rather, they open inwardly, subjectively, into the inexhaustible genealogical history of Lucas Beauchamp himself.

For he has now come into his name – not only a new signified, but a new signifier. No Luke here: this is the offspring of Lucius Quintus Carothers McCaslin, and the text knows him as Lucas with a near-religious scrupulousness. The "Lucas" part of his name reflects his voluntarily revised place within the line of white McCaslin descent (Lucas "signifies upon" Lucius), but the involuntary "entailment" on this genealogical inheritance surfaces in his matrilinear surname. He may be Lucas all he wants, yet he is not McCaslin but Beauchamp. The matrilinear surname conveys his slave/distaff descent, inasmuch as slave mothers and children were kept together for economic purposes, and the offspring of Tomey's Terrel and Tennie – at least those born before 1865 – would be given the name of Tennie's owner Hubert Beauchamp. Lucas's voice too has altered; he may speak dialect but not (like Rider) barely articulate dialect. "He done fotch the machine with him; I seed it work" has become "He brought it with him; I saw it, I tell you" (79). The changes that matter most, of course – the ones that all commentators on *Go Down, Moses* are drawn to – involve not Lucas's enlarged setting, altered voice, or agile body. They involve his tragic memories of the battle with Zack over Molly, when Zack's wife died at childbirth and Molly replaced her.

These scenes have been richly interpreted already; my aim is less to celebrate than to probe them. Probe, not attack: for I too am moved more by this remembered agon than by anything else in "The Fire and the

---

[27] Roth is no longer referred to as landlord because in *Go Down, Moses* he has been, as it were, disinherited. He is now seen as five generations removed from the original landowner, and on the distaff side as well. The text repeatedly suggests that the land passes to Roth because Ike could not rise to its responsibility.

Hearth" (unless it be the mirroring agon of Roth's tragic alienation from Henry, his black alter ego). Why are we so moved? The answer lies embedded within the white male psyches of the writer, of this reader, and (paradoxically) of Lucas himself as he rehearses these memories. The scenes are of enacted and failed male bonding. Females drop out of the drama once their purpose as catalysts for the encounter has been served. We never even learn the name of Zack's dead wife. Her narrative purpose is simply to produce an heir (naturally male) and then to disappear so that her widower Zack can meet his rightful mate on the other side of that matrimonial bed: Lucas. As with Roth and Henry later (also a question of beds not taken, intimacies forsworn upon entry into the culture's racist ideology), the bonding that matters is between men. Roth registers the loss of Henry with an intensity of grief starkly absent from his tight-lipped evasion of the "doe" in "Delta Autumn."

It is a male scene; it is also a white one. On the evidence of Lucas's memories in "The Fire and the Hearth" we could take him to have only one progenitor, white and male and two generations removed. The re-membered struggle is doubly articulated as an affair of males: Lucas and Zack, Lucas and old Carothers. It unfolds as a chivalric ritual of honor-bound moves, advantages offered but not accepted, the enemy cherished even as he is pursued. It is indeed a love scene – the most concretely represented and intensely narrated in the entire novel – and it dramatizes not desire (in which the boundaries of subjective identity risk being overwhelmed) but respect coupled with aggression (a coupling that exalts selfhood even as, in its intimacy, the one man draws murderously near to the other). We white male critics have been lauding this scene for decades now. Is it because it sublimates eros into principle, turns the stickiness of a self-altering exchange into the ritual of a self-affirming one, and finally locates in the male–male encounter and the struggle with the white male grandfather the sources of Lucas's indestructible dignity?

"He come and spoke for me" (58) indeed. Lucas thinks of this acces-sion to the progenitor's voice as the final understanding earned from this identity-enshrining encounter. He has been, as the French theorist Al-thusser would say, "interpellated." A bid for his identity has been made, and he has accepted it. This is the moment in which he fully assumes the ideological frame of his own subjectivity. As Althusser puts it:

> I shall then suggest that ideology "acts" . . . in such a way that it "recruits" subjects among . . . individuals . . . by that very precise op-eration which I have called *interpellation* or hailing, and which can be imagined along the lines of the most commonplace everyday po-lice . . . hailing: "Hey, you there!" Assuming that the theoretical scene I have imagined takes place in the street, the hailed individual will turn round. By this mere 180 degree physical conversion, he becomes a *subject*. Why? Because he has recognized that the hail was "really" ad-

dressed to him, and that "it was *really* him who was hailed" and not someone else. (174)

Who is Lucas Beauchamp? He is who he sees in his internal mirror, who he allows to speak for him; he becomes himself by saying himself within the signifying economy of McCaslin. Rednecks and white trash may think him a nigger, but "The Fire and the Hearth"'s dearest move is to refuse that outward appellation, to move inwardly and replace it with: McCaslin. Not just any McCaslin, but the old man himself: through him Lucas accedes to an empowering subjective identity consolidated by the passage of time. That is, he attains a genealogical memory.

To possess a memory is not only the essential human privilege celebrated by *Go Down, Moses;* it has also been, at least since the Enlightenment, the sign of humanity itself. Henry Louis Gates argues persuasively that during the eighteenth century memory was certified by the presence of writing, and that a people who could not write (in European languages of course) had no memory – and therefore were not quite human. "Without writing, no *repeatable* sign of the workings of reason, of mind, could exist. Without memory or mind, no history could exist. Without history, no humanity . . . could exist" (Gates, "Race" 11). We know with what tenacity many slaveholders resisted the notion of slaves becoming literate, and we know as well the attempts to deny that nineteenth-century slave narratives were really written by the black subjects in question. For reading, writing, and remembering powerfully promote the interiority of subjecthood itself. I refer to this passage of cultural/racist history in order to suggest what is at stake in Lucas Beauchamp's attainment of a genealogical memory. He becomes a full participant in humanity, a blood brother to Faulkner's brood of resonant, memory-laden, white protagonists.

Lucas can join them, however, only as a white man. Virginia Woolf's haunting phrase – "For we think back through our mothers if we are women" – tells us how pinched and conditioned Lucas Beauchamp's liberated humanity is. He can think back neither through his mother nor through his blackness. He speaks himself, or he allows himself to be spoken, within a white signifying economy. His moments of supreme authority are thus deprived of their racial component. If you will, he is permitted to become human only universally, not regionally, and his incapacity to think about his black mother surely plays its role in his callous treatment of his black wife.

Finally, the Lucas Beauchamp who attains white stature in "The Fire and the Hearth" also accepts the standard discourse of white responsibilities, the discourse of the Bible. This Lucas Beauchamp speaks scripturally of his "allotted span" (75) of life; he tells Zack that "even the Book dont ask a man to forgive them he is fixing to harm" (58); and he waxes eloquently, in the privileged last paragraph of "The Fire and the Hearth," upon the Book's injunctions and his obedience: "Man has got three score and ten years on this earth, the Book says. He can want a heap in that time and a heap of what he can want is due to come to him, if he just starts in soon enough. I done waited too late to start. . . . I am near to the end of my three score and ten, and I reckon to find that money aint for me" (131).

Note the inscription here within an interpellative signifying economy. The Book has "come and spoke for him"; he reads his interiority in the light of its commands. Accepting its script, he voluntarily chastens his wants. It is not only that he ceases to search, but – more sinister – that he inserts himself within a finished and regulatory discursive structure: "that money aint for me." The containment is complete. He has, we are meant satisfyingly to feel, finally grown up.[28] That he does so by relinquishing his wants, by understanding maturity as white, male, and scripturally ordained, by recognizing and affirming his place within such a system – that he does so carries out the ideological work of "The Fire and the Hearth." Lucas can be left alone now; he will behave himself.

This sardonic note is not the right one, though, for completing my discussion of *Go Down, Moses*. Faulkner was never again to imagine black lives so richly intertwined with white ones. If in the magazine stories we find Lucas in the present company of, mainly, George Wilkins and Roth Edmonds, in the novel he lives in the present and absent company of a rich array of reflecting lives. To name a few, we read him against Rider and Samuel Worsham Beauchamp, two blacks whose uncontrollable passion or "defective" training keeps them from Lucas's open-eyed prudence. We read him, as well, with Sam Fathers and Ike: a trio of woodsmen, of aged men of integrity, at odds with the culture they must live in. At his most compelling, Lucas rises into the sinister but sustaining force of his McCaslin ancestry. Ultimately he will rise beyond family altogether, and we will read him against Old Ben, solitary, childless, mythic, unapproachable. This will be Lucas's final avatar in *Intruder in the Dust*.

&

> [Lucas] . . . always in the worn brushed obviously once-expensive black broadcloth suit of the portrait-photograph on the gold easel and the raked fine hat and the boiled white shirt of his own grandfather's

---

28 Molly's emergence in the third chapter of "The Fire and the Hearth" drives home this moral lesson. Touching Roth's heart as the only mother he ever knew, speaking to him (and us) with biblical authority ("Because God say, 'What's rendered to My earth, it belong to Me unto I resurrect it. And let him or her touch it, and beware' " [102]), Molly is placed by Faulkner so as to articulate decisively – as mother, wife, and religious seer – the text's rebuke of Lucas's rebellious moves.

time and the tieless collar and the heavy watch-chain .and the gold
toothpick like the one his own grandfather had carried in his upper vest
pocket. (24)

These lines are taken from a sentence five times this length in the early
pages of *Intruder in the Dust*. The perspective is Chick Mallison's, and
Lucas as seen in his eyes has receded in a number of ways from the mobile
figure of *Go Down, Moses*. "Portrait-photograph": the portrait we encounter here is locked into its mandatory legitimizing details: broadcloth
suit, raked fine hat, boiled white shirt, tieless collar, heavy watch-chain,
and gold toothpick. These details scrupulously accompany Lucas's every
appearance in this latest text. Faulkner cannot seem to find him except
through such fetishized objects. So powerful is this imprisonment within
clothes, watch chain, and toothpick that we seem to read not so much of
Lucas as of the enbalming accoutrements that announce him. And they
do "speak" him. They insert him within a sartorial nineteenth-century
tradition of white respectability that Chick tirelessly identifies with his
own grandfather.

Lucas Beauchamp has here become a congealed icon. How he looks is
textually more important than how he may feel. He emerges less as an
imagined subjectivity than as an object – reliably unchanging even if
impenetrable – of the male gaze that frets and fusses about him for page
upon page. A throwback to the past, he is imagined only once as feeling
something unpredictable to Chick – grief for the death of his wife Molly
– but the text uses this material with an unswervingly single purpose: to
open up the mind of Chick Mallison, not to explore the moves of Lucas
Beauchamp or to enter the subjectivity of the dead Molly. Moves are, in
fact, just what Lucas does not have in *Intruder in the Dust*. To put it most
broadly, the ways in which Faulkner's discourse frames Lucas Beauchamp
undercut the ways in which Faulkner's plot seeks to free him from a
frame-up. Let me elaborate.

Lucas is framed in his immaculate clothes and visible habits; they are all
he has. His wife and children have been taken from him; friends he never
had anyway; and now he is not only isolated but almost mute. He barely
speaks in this novel (the one time he must convey information to the
sheriff takes place, as it were, offstage, summarized by Gavin rather than
narratively lived into). Vertically he has lost old Carothers to talk to as
well as George Wilkins or Nat to scheme with; horizontally he has no
peers. The text everywhere insists on his being like Chick's grandfather
but like no black man. A taxpayer now, he proudly accepts this dis-
tinguishing difference. He tells Chick that he insisted on Molly's taking
her headrag off before the portrait photograph could be taken because "I
didn't want no field nigger picture in the house" (15). "Field niggers" is
his implicit term for most other blacks: no wonder they don't make
common cause with Lucas's plight.

He is also, in a figurative sense, castrated; only they sort of took both legs too. Lucas hardly possesses legs in *Intruder in the Dust*. We see him mainly as in a portrait photograph, from the shoulders up. He has none of that unpredictable physical mobility, that bodily quickness that flares up in "The Fire and the Hearth." The motion denied him is transferred to Chick Mallison. Chick moves incessantly throughout this novel, circling Lucas, trying to come to terms with him, traveling miles upon miles to refute the evidence against him. More, Chick is moving in the figurative sense as well. His feelings are continuously tracked by this narrative; he can still *be* moved; he is meant to move us. The Bakhtinian drama of authoritative dicta being challenged and replaced by others that are more internally persuasive lives in Chick alone.[29] Lucas does not speak, seems hardly to feel, has no subjective discoveries to make. He is already finalized.

This congealed Lucas responds predictably (if with impeccable dignity) to racial threats. Insulted in a white store by a white man as "You gaddamn biggity stiff-necked stinking burrheaded Edmonds sonofabitch," Lucas answers: "I aint a Edmonds. I dont belong to these new folks. I belongs to the old lot. I'm a McCaslin" (19). The enraged white retorts, "Keep on walking around here with that look on your face and what you'll be is crowbait." Unruffled, Lucas replies: "Yes, I heard that idea before. And I notices that the folks that brings it up aint even Edmondses." Well, this is sublime, way beyond what the Lucas Beauchamp of *Go Down, Moses* could afford; and we might ask: how can this Lucas afford it? The answer is that now there are inobtrusive whites stationed everywhere to shepherd him. Even as the white racist snatches up a plow singletree in order to smash Lucas's skull, the son of the store owner intervenes, grabs the racist, is aided by another white man. "Get out of here, Lucas!" the son hisses. "But still Lucas didn't move, quite calm, not even scornful, not even contemptuous." When finally he deigns to depart, he goes "without haste . . . raising his right hand to his mouth so that as he went out the door they could see the steady thrust of his chewing" (20).

The deeper fantasy-logic of *Intruder in the Dust*'s narrative emerges in such an episode. Pose is allocated to the black man; motion is reserved for the white man. Lucas's splendid demeanor is inseparable from his immobility. He can look free but not act freely. He is imagined here as saying things that no black responsible for his own safety in Jefferson in the 1940s could say because he need not be – cannot be – responsible for his

---

[29] Bakhtin develops a major distinction (341–9) between "authoritative discourse" and "internally persuasive discourse." Our journey as subjects from the former to the latter – from dicta that have been pressed upon us to those that we can internalize and make our own – is, precisely, our ideological maturation. Lucas undergoes no such linguistic trajectory.

own safety. Rather, he is an icon that the text proudly sports, while its central white figures almost seem to compete with each other to keep him unharmed. Consider this later moment in the text, when Chick, the sheriff, and his black convict-helpers unexpectedly encounter Nub Gowrie at the site of his murdered son's grave. The old man raises his pistol:

> But long before this he [Chick] had seen the sheriff already moving, moving with really incredible speed not toward the old man but around the end of the grave, already in motion even before the two Negroes turned to run, so that when they whirled they seemed to run full tilt into the sheriff as into a cliff, even seeming to bounce back a little before the sheriff grasped them one in each hand as if they were children and then in the next instant seemed to be holding them both in one hand like two rag dolls, turning his body so that he was between them and the little wiry old man with the pistol, saying in that mild lethargic voice . . . (160)

The passage is perhaps more revealing than it knows. Again, motion, protective power, and voice are reserved for the white man. He has anticipated the two blacks' moves, and like a cliff his superior substantiality grounds their aimless terror. Figured as "children" and as weightless "rag dolls" in this passage – offered up to us as testimony to the sheriff's adroitness and resolution – the blacks are safe enough. But they remain safe only within a discursive economy that identifies them as fetishized objects, as predictable children, ultimately as "Sambo." Their moves, in every sense of the word, are scripted in the reifying and limited terms of a white discourse.

Who are the other blacks in this text? Old Ephraim delights in domestic wisdom (when you want something done, get the women and children to help you do it); Aleck Sander, Chick's sidekick, is nearly voiceless, accompanying Chick into each dangerous foray, his own construing of this strange adventure largely kept out of the text's narrative. Instead, Aleck Sander is endowed with preternaturally keen senses; he can hear and smell better than whites. The contours of his mind, which might liberate him from this cliché of the hypersensed Negro, go almost uncharted. In their place we get vast generalizations about black workers in the fields – naturalized there, since time immemorial properly at work there[30] – and we get Gavin Stevens's discourse of "Sambo."

The appellation "Sambo" has been attacked by liberal critics almost since the book's publication, and there is no need to rehearse their commentary.[31] I note only that Stevens's desperate attempt to corral the black

[30] Jehlen comments aptly on the naturalized blacks working the fields, figures objectified and "invested with meaning only through the agency of a white observer" (132).

[31] Representative commentary can be found in Edmund Wilson (460–9), Cleanth Brooks

man within the epithet "Sambo" weirdly repeats the culture's traditional attempt to read him as "nigger," and that this move belies the plot momentum of the text that would spring Lucas free. The *discours* recontains what the *récit* would enfranchise, just as the frantic claim of communal homogeneity is undermined by the classed barriers recurrently operative in these pages: the uncrossable barrier between a few (moderately) liberal whites in the foreground and an anonymous mob of racists that surround them as background, as well as the barrier between the unflappable sartorial Lucas Beauchamp and the nameless black workers ("field niggers") toiling in the fields.

Finally, why is *Intruder in the Dust* such a safe book on matters of racial identity? Partly because of its Tom Sawyerish aura of security — we know right away that these kids are not going to get hurt, that Lucas is not going to be lynched — but also because Lucas is only superficially connected with the murder itself. He happened to be strolling in the wrong place and to see something he should not have seen. Faulkner goes on, implausibly, to have Crawford Gowrie seek to placate Lucas, as well as to have Lucas easily tricked by Crawford's wiles. (This Lucas is so ritualized, his fetish objects so well known, that Crawford has no trouble stroking his vanity and getting him to fire his 41 Colt at a stump from fifteen feet distance, thus enabling the 41 Colt to become the suspected murder weapon.) Perhaps the book's racial discourse is safe, finally, because we know too surely that Lucas *couldn't* have done the murder. Perversely, I would like to envisage a Lucas at least capable of murder, one whose embroilment within the racism of the South was reciprocal, unpredictable, threatening. Faulkner will not imagine this possibility in *Intruder in the Dust*. To glimpse what such a Lucas might have been, we must go elsewhere, go backward in Faulkner's career, and conceive a shadowy tripartite figure composed of Joe Christmas, Rider, and Samuel Worsham Beauchamp. Such a figure is monstrously unlike Lucas Beauchamp, but what is this to say but that Faulkner's most disturbing portrayals of racial turmoil have no place in his novel most explicitly dedicated to thinking through racial turmoil?

ò⋅

Although my focus has not been on Faulkner's differential uses of the short story and the novel, the scripting of Lucas Beauchamp seems implicitly to tell us something about the writer's treatment of race and the givens of his form. For Faulkner's genius is juxtapositional. He rises into power as he broods upon and revisits his materials, submits them to new

(*Yoknapatawpha* 420–1), Lee Jenkins (272–4), and Walter Taylor (145–65). More recently, Noel Polk ("Man in the Middle" 130–51) and Wesley and Barbara Morris (222–38) have sought to resuscitate *Intruder in the Dust*'s reputation, arguing for it as a morally compelling and coherent piece of work.

perspectives, finds in them hidden resources. Outrage, his thematic hallmark, occurs only in the encounter with the unexpected. In his best
work, form and content alike destabilize expectation; they do so through
unpredictable juxtapositions. *The Sound and the Fury, As I Lay Dying,
Light in August, Absalom, Absalom!, The Hamlet,* and *Go Down, Moses*
play off facet against facet, dance from one subjective point of view to
another, set into motion reading upon reading of the same (but never the
same) materials. "Maybe happen is never once," Faulkner wrote in *Absalom, Absalom!* In turning over his materials he rescripts them, sees them
as rescriptable – objects with no inherent meaning but rather capable of
taking on new meanings when inserted within new signifying economies. It is not a question of choosing between the short-story writer or
the novelist: Faulkner becomes a supreme novelist because he is a short-
story writer as well. It is the revisiting that makes him Argus-eyed, for
the repositioning of objects leads to the rethinking of subjects, to the
discovery (among others) that racial identity may be a matter more of
discursive practice than of biological destiny.

Intruder in the Dust, I would speculate, is a novel that has sacrificed the
play of juxtapositional (and definitional) possibilities to the insistence of a
singular demonstration.[32] We know too clearly how we are meant to take
both Lucas Beauchamp and the plot in which he is enmeshed; they come
at us with pedagogic urgency. This novel's shrillness, like that of *A Fable,*
resides in its knowing too much and its being locked into a single discourse of knowledge. Lucas Beauchamp emerges within such a discourse
as mythic, impenetrable, and immovable object; Chick Mallison as a
vulnerable and moving subject. Lucas's journey thus comes to an end.[33]

---

[32] "First, in order to take care of George Wilkins once and for all . . ." (33): this baffled
urge to conclude that spawns the opening sentence of "The Fire and the Hearth" is
comically sabotaged through Lucas's unavailing plots and tragically undermined in Ike's
unwanted autumnal discoveries. Grimwood and Morris both attend to *Go Down,
Moses*'s reverberations, its resistance to the male desire for willful closure. By the time of
Intruder in the Dust, however, Faulkner seems unironically to take care of Lucas Beauchamp "once and for all" and thus to complete his singular demonstration.

[33] Lucas was fated to appear one more time: a year later (1949), in another medium,
Clarence Brown's film of *Intruder in the Dust.* This last representation does him considerable credit. The film edits out the most dubious elements of the novel – Gavin's ser-
monizing about Sambo and the South, the narrator's exacerbated sensorium and consciousness – and renders a drama that is sober, surprisingly faithful to Faulkner's text,
and moving. The emergent lines of action are simple, but this is one of Faulkner's novels
in which the doings *are* simple. The film is quiet enough for us to hear the crickets, and
we *see* what the text itself scants: Lucas walking through the square, Lucas as a figure
belonging to the community of Jefferson. Camera angles emphasize Lucas's dignity,
showing him almost godlike as he looks down at Stevens and laconically demands his
"receipt." In place of the feverish intensity that suffuses the narrative consciousness of
the novel, we find a more "democratic" visual entry into all the principal figures in the
story. Gavin (here called John) is so strenuously edited that Lucas's speeches – mini-
mized in the verbal onslaught of the novel – take on finally their appropriate weight. It is
a fitting last appearance.

A wily "nigger" in the magazine stories, sprung as free as he would ever be in *Go Down, Moses* (his freedom here calibrated in a lithe body and a mind whose surface is black but whose depth is McCaslin), he settles down in this last novel as an antique, a source of his white creator's nostalgic delight.

His final words are a request – "My receipt," he asks Gavin. He has liquidated his debt and wants to depart from his white benefactors, to return to his impregnable, unknowable state. The concept of the debt bristles beyond its immediate usage here, for indebtedness – the ledger-recorded purchase of black men and women as chattel, the payment for their abuse in the form of money but not love – resonates darkly throughout *Go Down, Moses*. But *Intruder in the Dust* prefers to imagine the debt the other way, to have Lucas laboriously count out his quarters, dimes, nickels, and pennies, get his receipt, and disappear into the unnarratable. Such a refusal to continue scripting racial culpability – a refusal wrought into this fantasy image of debts cleared off, of ledgers audited and approved by both black and white – signals eloquently the weariness of the text, its insistence upon fetishizing a single black man in whose (mystified) aristocratic demeanor the racial turmoil of the 1940s is meant to reach a sort of figurative resolution. The racial debt is of course still not liquidated – only it is we, not they, who owe it – but William Faulkner, for his part, had exhausted in this book his twenty-year attempt to imagine it and, in the revisionary freshness of his racial discourse, to do his part in paying it off.

3

Subjectivity

We now turn inward, in order to probe the construction of the white male subject at the core of Faulkner's canonical fiction. Compared with the women and blacks whose representation, either nonsubjective or at best glancingly subjective, I have been analyzing during the earlier chapters, these males are relatively empowered within the novels themselves and centrally positioned in Faulkner's plotting. They would seem to share (with their author) a patriarchal subjective gaze that commands, for its part, the marginalized representation and behavior of both women and blacks. Yet no reader of Faulkner recognizes his tragic protagonists in the above description of white male hegemony and empowerment. Something has gone awry in the inheritance itself and in their relation to it. Indeed, we continue to read Faulkner because of the turmoil such supposedly privileged figures undergo, as they seek to regulate, revise, or revoke their involuntary (and often incoherent) allegiance to their culture's norms of white male subjectivity.

The first part of the chapter explores the production of (male) subjective identity in general, as a frame for approaching the ordeal of Faulknerian subjectivity in particular. Drawing on Althusser and Lacan, I seek to read the Faulknerian subject as New Critical assumptions do not permit us to read it: as a site of Imaginary and Symbolic crossings, a field brimming over with contradictory injunctions. My argument extends past New Critical bounds in another way as well, attempting to characterize the Imaginary and Symbolic dimensions not just of Faulkner's texts, but also of the conferences and commentaries we lavish upon him.

In the second part of the chapter I narrow the focus to two resonant figures, Joe Christmas and Ike McCaslin, in order both to probe the genesis of their subjectivities and to begin analyzing the diachronic dimension of Faulkner's career. *Light in August* gives us the becoming of male subjectivity most powerfully in a central character bound up within – yet disempowered by – his culture's subject-producing codes: a character who can physically but not conceptually "pass" within their confines. The upshot is Faulkner's most disturbing novel about the violation of race and gender norms, the crossed wiring of subjective scripts. By contrast, the writer who conceives of *Go Down, Moses* through the inaugurating story of "Delta Autumn" (penultimate in placement but the first story to focus for Faulkner [in 1940] the prospective arrangement of his novel as a whole) is a writer whose explorations of subjectivity and whose relations to both his culture and his reader have entered their own calmer, autumnal phase. This is a writer whose commerce with the Other (internal and external) has achieved orientation, with identity-sustaining boundaries now more or less in place. He has become "Faulkner" and he writes, henceforth, less of "semiotic" invasion than of strenuously achieved Symbolic alignment, of a sutured subjectivity.

"THINKING I WAS I WAS NOT WHO WAS NOT WAS NOT WHO": THE VERTIGO OF FAULKNERIAN IDENTITY

The title is dizzying. During this inquiry I shall be off-balance in my shift from the scrutiny of Faulkner's work to considerations of ideology, psychoanalysis, interpretive norms, and the institutional dynamics of "attending to" Faulkner. These are all issues of identity, I hope to show, and thinking about them can occasion vertigo. I turn now to Quentin's passage in *The Sound and the Fury* from which I take my title quotation:

> When it bloomed in the spring and it rained the smell was everywhere you didn't notice it so much at other times but when it rained the smell began to come into the house at twilight . . . it always smelled strongest then until I would lie in bed thinking when will it stop when will it stop. The draft in the door smelled of water, a damp steady breath. Sometimes I could put myself to sleep saying that over and over until the honeysuckle got all mixed up in it the whole thing came to symbolise night and unrest I seemed to be lying neither asleep nor awake looking down a long corridor of grey halflight where all stable things had become shadowy paradoxical all I had done shadows all I had felt suffered taking visible form antic and perverse mocking without relevance inherent themselves with the denial of the significance they should have affirmed thinking I was I was not who was not was not who. (194–5)

Spurred by the overpowering smell of honeysuckle, Quentin's thoughts go on to undermine relationships he has based his sanity on, by dissolving the difference between sleep and waking, night and day; by prying apart the connection between things done, felt, suffered, on the one hand, and their significance on the other. The smell of honeysuckle, invading him and triggering his unbearable sense of his own and of Caddy's sexuality, breaks down these stable relationships; and Quentin's attempt to talk himself into tranquility – "saying that over and over" – ends by doing the reverse. Nothing remains self-identical; all drifts away from its habitual moorings, becoming "shadowy paradoxical" as Quentin's language – the script by which he knows himself – chokes on its quest for coherence, dissolving into the babble of "I was I was not who was not was not who."[1] An alien body, a wandering mind, a dizzying sense of unowned doings, feelings, and sufferings: these come together in this passage as something we call Quentin. He belongs to them, but in what sense do they belong to him?

Faulkner's most powerful strategy for representing this disunity that is Quentin is the stream of consciousness technique itself. Here is Quentin early in the chapter:

> Because if it were just to hell; if that were all of it. Finished. If things just finished themselves. Nobody else there but her and me. If we could just have done something so dreadful that they would have fled hell except us. *I have committed incest I said Father it was I it was not Dalton Ames.* And when he put Dalton Ames. Dalton Ames. Dalton Ames. When he put the pistol in my hand I didn't. That's why I didn't. He would be there and she would and I would. Dalton Ames. Dalton Ames. Dalton Ames. If we could have just done something so dreadful and Father said . . . (90)

If things just finished themselves: Faulknerian stream of consciousness perfectly enacts the way in which things do not finish themselves. Within this rhetoric Quentin cannot finish his thought or firm up his identity, cannot keep Dalton Ames and Father and Caddy and honeysuckle from penetrating his being, cannot keep at bay the maelstrom of sayings by his mother, Herbert, Mrs. Bland, and others. When his desire to be with Caddy alone is denied, his only other desire is to put an end to all this uninvited company that fills his body and mind. Since he cannot finish himself, he will "finish" himself.

Let us generalize the model of identity implicit in Faulkner's stream of consciousness representation of Quentin's subjectivity. Unlike characters in the nineteenth-century classic novel (who are typically passed on to us by the narrator as coherent entities, summarized organisms existing over

---

[1] The best full-length study of Faulknerian psychic structures menaced by pressures they cannot control is Gail L. Mortimer's phenomenological *Faulkner's Rhetoric of Loss.* André Bleikasten's *The Most Splendid Failure* recurs frequently to this concern. See especially the chapters on Quentin, 90–143. For a reading of this vertigo in terms of the play of difference and deferral inherent in the system of language itself, see John Matthews's *The Play of Faulkner's Language* 63–114.

time), Quentin appears as a moment-by-moment involuntary recorder of others' voices, a sentient receptacle wounded by the shards of their utterances: the site on which the cacophony of the larger culture registers. Quentin is a memory box, a porous container of others' throwaway discourse. Unable to consolidate what he has absorbed, unable to shape his own thoughts into the coherence of a temporal project, he is a figure in motley. By representing him as thus maculate through and through, Faulkner reveals the pathos of his fantasy of preserving Caddy's immaculate virginity.

I have spoken only of Quentin, but even in the modified form of a non-stream-of-consciousness technique this paradigm of identity pertains to other characters of the novel as well. Not just Benjy and Jason, but Caddy, Mr. and Mrs. Compson: these figures are in different ways penetrated and controlled by alien formulas. Faulkner seems drawn to them in the measure that – fissured themselves, encoded within unworkable scripts – they seek ineffectually to impose unity upon, to preserve identity within, their own lives and the lives around them. They seek such unity and identity mainly through speech, and indeed *The Sound and the Fury* is full of sound, of puny humans contradictorily asserting their own authority. It is the *loud* world, we remember, that Quentin would rescue Caddy from.[2]

What is at stake in this desire to preserve identity, this urgent need to stabilize relations between the self and the world? Why is it so difficult (and for many readers painful) to read Quentin's section? What does it mean that we as readers insist on taking all novels – even Faulkner's and Joyce's novels, even Genet's and Beckett's – as "stories" about individual "characters" engaged in "plot"? The answer (to the last two questions) is that fiction has traditionally served as a privileged site for celebrating the suturing of individual identity, and many readers do indeed resist this Modernist text's refusal to affirm coherent selfhood through the vehicle of plot. Fiction is one of the arenas in which the culture tells its licensed fables of selfhood, of the successful negotiation between a self's energies, on the one hand, and a society's forms, on the other. This is what Jameson might call the master narrative of modern Western culture, and Faulkner's masterpieces come into sharpest focus as texts in which the negotiations of this master narrative are both urgent and impossible, in which the need for protected boundaries is as intense as the awareness that these boundaries cannot be protected. Virginity, incest, and miscegenation; Sutpen's Hundred, the McCaslin inheritance, and the wilderness – each of these phrases names a crucial Faulknerian space (psychic or

2 The ways in which normative social maps bind Faulknerian voice and body are explored in the second half of this chapter and more fully analyzed throughout Chapter 4.

material) in which boundaries have been erected and overrun. What is it that makes these enclosed arenas precious and (in Faulkner's great work) beyond preserving?[3]

ੴ

I suggest that identity is a privileged term within a Western vocabulary of individualism. In its primary meaning, that something is always itself, and its secondary implication, that that selfhood is different from all others, the concept of identity makes some large promises.[4] It promises sameness over time, an unchanging essence at our core. Our self-sameness is intrinsic (to be found within) rather than relational (to be found by way of our membership within a larger group). The term suggests, further, that we are unique creatures, essentially different from each other. To privilege individual identity in this way is to fantasize a protected sacred place, the place of ourselves, which would be immune to the vicissitudes of time, space, and culture. It is to allay our anxiety that we may not have an unchanging core and therefore may take on our meanings from our affiliations and conditions. It is to fix, enclose, and affirm our unique difference from others, to say: "That's who I am." By thus reifying our sense of ourselves, by charting it as a separable essence and putting boundaries around it, we repress that intolerable sense of *being-helplessly-caught-up-in-the-Other* that Faulkner represents in the plight of Quentin Compson.

This paradigm of identity as an essentialized sacred space commands not just how we want to think of ourselves but how for many years we have chosen to think of art objects as well. The critical position that best enshrines it is New Criticism.[5] Most readers of this book who (like its author) are over forty and under sixty were probably trained as New Critics. We learned that depth and unique difference are the hallmark of the work of art. Language is assumed, within this critical model, to be supremely manageable. Each work is to be studied in its precious difference from others, each character in a novel to be probed in his rounded wholeness, each master writer to be praised for the inclusiveness of his

---

[3] For a discussion of the idea of "sanctuary," see my "Precarious Sanctuaries."

[4] The self so identified is explicitly universal but implicitly (in its insistence on oppositional clarity, on being distinct from the Other) male. See Judith Kegan Gardiner for an excellent overview of the (usually concealed) gender problematic in psychoanalytic models of identity from Freud through Erikson and Chodorow. The decentered subject is, of course, a common theme of poststructuralist, psychoanalytic, and Marxist criticism.

[5] Despite their contemporary role as *bêtes noires,* the preeminent spokesmen of New Criticism – Allen Tate, John Crowe Ransom, Cleanth Brooks, and William Wimsatt, to name four – have decisively shaped the institutional study of literature in this country since the 1930s. Their major texts are too well known to need identification here. For critical assessments of their enterprise, see Lentricchia, Eagleton (*Literary Theory*), Cain, and Bove. For a reading of Faulkner's practice and reputation as affected by New Critical norms, see Schwartz and Moreland.

unique vision. (All along the tacit assumption was that life, in its murk and messiness, its ideological confusions, could not provide such fine-grained distinctions: but art could.)

"Close reading" was invented and became institutionalized as a class-room technique for exploring the essence, the identity, of the aesthetic object. Through close readings the uniqueness of the writer's vision was identified, and once the individual case had been scrupulously delineated, it was seen to partake (paradoxically) of the universal as well. That is, the unique vision is simultaneously, in its representative wholeness, a univer-sal or *human* vision. (My use of "his" in the previous paragraph assumed – as we were taught to assume – a universal, not a gendered, referent.) To speak of universal or human is to be in touch with essence, with that which is lodged so deeply within the individual that it escapes the acci-dents of condition or local affiliation and reflects instead something com-mon to the species. In the name of encompassing all groups, human actually disavows the power of any group to affect the essence of the unique individual.

As spectators in the presence of the human or the universal, essences freed by art for our disinterested appreciation, we are meant to praise. (How often a New Critical classroom assignment on a poem or a novel could be distilled to the following message: praise this object! say how finely, disinterestedly, inclusively it understands life in its inimitable weave of form and content!) The work, exquisitely beyond bias, stands self-complete before us, a microcosm of that ideal identity we would seek to posit within ourself: a sacred space. Like us, it may be embedded within other, potentially contaminating networks, but these networks are secondary and not the focus of commentary. The work's aesthetic tri-umph, like our own fantasized identity, resides in its freestanding whole-ness.

I have worded this in such a way that the connection emerges between how we view the identity of the work of art, how we view the writer's identity, and how we view our own. This distinction between the unique and universal, on the one hand, and the group-shaped and system-shar-ing, on the other, not only affects Faulkner's texts: it affects conferences on those texts. During 1985 and 1986 the Faulkner and Yoknapatawpha Conference chose to discuss those texts within the "group-shaped" frames of women and race, and one of the most urgent (though un-spoken) questions was: how can we still think of Faulkner as unique and universal when it becomes more and more obvious that he is also white and male?

For me, the most revealing moment at the 1986 Conference on Faulkner and Race occurred when a speaker eloquently reflected on latent complexities of motive in two of Faulkner's characters: the white deputy in "Pantaloon in Black" and the black man Jesus in "That Evening Sun." The speaker concluded that these characters, in their pain and bewilderment, should be thought of as neither white nor black, but instead as *human*. There was an immediate and audible sigh of satisfaction within a great portion of the audience, for this conclusion spoke to our continuous anxiety about racial difference - spoke to it by transcending all group differences and arriving at species universality, at the human. Yet what black reader of Faulkner will find it more illuminating to see that white deputy as human rather than white (white as crucial limitation and blindness), and what black or woman reader will want to see Jesus (who has beaten Nancy before and may now be about to slit her throat) as human rather than black and male (black as the site of racial abuse, male as the site where a code of manhood coils and clamors)? Gender and race pervade these scenes. The white deputy and Jesus act deeply out of their group identity, and to see them as essentially human is to obscure into secondariness the massive role played by these affiliations.

I should say, in closing this anecdote, that a woman came up after the talk to quarrel with the speaker's interpretation of Jesus, and I (who had also come up) raised a question with him about "human" but defended his (non)gender reading. In the interim between then and now I have pondered this event – it was in fact the germ of this argument – and I now see that the talk and the later disagreements were all of them instances of the legitimate shaping power of race and gender. As a white male, the speaker saw something in Jesus that a black reader might not focus upon (he being concerned with a racial context that the white reader might find ancillary); likewise the woman with a quarrel *had* a quarrel. She was interested in reading Jesus within a gender context that was for her primary, not secondary, though for the white male speaker the gender context might seem secondary to an existentialist one. Further, a reader with ideological interests might have come up to the podium and quarreled with us all, his focus arising from a matrix of class and economic issues that we had scanted. (These various reader orientations – white and black, male and female, existentialist and ideological – are here posited as cultural roles, not natural givens. Anyone *might* play any of them, though certain determinate conditions predispose readers toward some and away from others. And which ones get accented does matter: I am not arguing for some complacent pluralism. In practice – my practice in this study as well – we regularly scant one frame in order effectively to activate another.)

The obvious point is that each text, like each reading of the text, achieves its power through its omissions. Seeing some things is predicated upon blindness to others, and it is of the first importance to ascertain what is seen, what is scanted. The text, like the reader, is caught up in a variety of networks; it is inextricably part of its time and its place. Its identity is adulterate and reconceivable, a function of its angle of vision upon the world, the reader's angle of vision upon it, and the ideological economies operative within each of those optics. Roland Barthes makes this point shrewdly in his essay on that "universal" bestseller entitled *The Family of Man (Mythologies* 100–2). Barthes notes that this photographic celebration of our universally shared destiny – that all over the world we are alike in being born, in growing up, in working and playing, in growing old and dying – manages systematically to repress a countertruth: that we are born into different conditions, we grow up with different possibilities, we have different work and play options (depending on what part of the world we inhabit and our economic conditions), we die at different ages and of different diseases (depending on the culture we live in).[6] This countertruth is attentive to the differential of history, whereas *The Family of Man* focuses upon the immutability of nature. Both points of view are truthful, but only one concedes that it *is* a point of view. *The Family of Man* passes itself off as unedited pictures of nature, of the obvious: as how things are.

The text that claims to be universal tends to posit, then, an unchanging human truth, an essential identity uncontaminated by the accidents of time, place, and affiliation. Free of bias, it asks to be taken as a privileged portrait of how things are.[7] Such a text was the object of study of New Criticism, and there is a longing in many of us that still seeks to read Faulkner in this way. I want now to posit another model of identity, this one drawing on Althusser and Lacan, and then briefly to consider both *Absalom, Absalom!* and the transferential activity of reading Faulkner (or attending conferences upon him) from the perspective of this new model.

ૠ

Althusser is interested in the paradox at the heart of the term *subject*.[8] The subject is simultaneously the free human being and the human being subjected to an exterior system of beliefs and practices.

---

6 Barthes writes: "Any classic humanism postulates that in scratching the history of men a little, the relativity of their institutions or the superficial diversity of their skins (but why not ask the parents of Emmet Till, the young Negro assassinated by the Whites what they think of *The Family of Man?*), one very quickly reaches the solid rock of a universal human nature" (*Mythologies* 101).

7 Survey courses of English literature find it difficult to avoid the same idealist perspective. The "pageantry" of masterpieces from *Beowulf* to Virginia Woolf emerges as a sequence of works that resemble nothing so much as each other in their fine-grained and unbiased universality. The differential history that occasions the production and reception of all these works is usually marginalized in such courses, if not repressed.

8 The central Althusser text for my purposes is "Ideology and Ideological State Apparatuses." The major attempt to produce an Althusserian model of literary theory is Macherey's *Pour une Théorie de la production littéraire.* The work of Terry Eagleton and of Fredric Jameson is considerably indebted to both Althusser and Macherey. See especially Eagleton's *Ideology,* 136–54, and Jameson's *The Political Unconscious,* 9–102. Other useful commentary on Althusser includes Tony Bennett's *Formalism and Marxism,* James Kavanaugh's "Marxism's Althusser," and William Dowling's *Jameson, Althusser, Marx.*

Ideology is the missing term that enables this paradox, for ideological practice and the free human subject mutually constitute each other. "The category of the subject," writes Althusser, "is the constitutive category of all ideology . . . insofar as all ideology has the function (which defines it) of 'constituting' concrete individuals as subjects" (171). We obtain our sense of unpredictable inwardness through our spontaneous assent to the social scripts – the ideological economies – that surround us. We assent to arrangements so self-evident as to be invisible, and all smoothly functioning ideology is invisible in this sense. It is what goes without saying, it is our daily participation in a "natural" schema of how things are, our way of wearing our name, our clothes, our unconscious convictions about the rightness of our procedures.

But we do not generate names, clothes, and convictions out of ourselves. They may be the material of our identity, but they come to us from outside, already established and awaiting our spontaneous participation. We join in by activating the models thus proposed. If we are teachers we pursue some compelling image of teaching and we assent to the material conditions and goals of this profession. With whatever modifications or demur, we answer the call: by reading certain texts, teaching certain classes, proposing certain projects, ascribing to certain boundaries of norm and taboo, accepting certain salaries, framing our lives within certain calendars of work and nonwork. (Our strikes and reforms, group-organized and spurred by an equal if not higher commitment to the original call, follow the same dynamic.) In each case we stabilize identity by subjecting ourselves to a fixed cluster of expectations. We achieve focus and depth by internalizing and reaccenting external models. Althusser calls such a model ideology, a script whose acceptance ushers us into a particular version of social reality, a version that we enact insofar as we remain faithful to the gestures, practices, and beliefs sanctioned by the script. The key to this model is noncoercion: "the individual is *interpellated as a (free) subject in order that he shall (freely) accept his subjection,* i.e. in order that he shall make the gestures and actions of his subjection 'all by himself.'" (I might note here a certain brittleness in this Marxist model. It cannot account for our condition of "overscriptedness" – a recurrent Faulknerian dilemma – nor for the ways in which individual thought and behavior are less predictable than the concept of "scripting" suggests: less predictable but not random. For a model of subjective identity that escapes some of the rigidity of "scripting" without returning to the premise of individual free choice, I shall turn in the second half of this chapter to Pierre Bourdieu's notion of the "habitus.")

Identity on this model is decentered in the sense that its center is imported from outside ourselves. These social scripts focus and empower us. They do not, however, quite command our unconscious life and all its

wayward stresses. Is it too much to say that Faulknerian tragedy is generated by the civil war between these internalized social scripts and a something within the self that remains defiantly unamenable to social scripts? I
turn now to Lacan for a discussion of this more primordial resource.

According to Lacan we come into our identity only through a series of
alienations, and the earliest ones are decisive.[9] The infant, speechless
(*infans* means speechless), absorbs from its first days bits and pieces of
language into itself, and it absorbs as well the gaze of others. What it
knows in addition is the sensation of disconnected body parts; it has as yet
no totalizing image of itself. This momentous step occurs during what
Lacan calls the mirror stage: that phase (Lacan sees it beginning roughly
at the sixth month and continuing for another year) when the infant
begins to "recognize" itself as reflected either through the eyes of its
mother or in an actual mirror. The resultant external image is perceived
as a totality – a completed self – and it contrasts richly, in its wholeness
and mobility, with the infant's own interior sense of physical uncoordina-
tion and turbulent body parts. In other words, the infant recognizes itself
only in an alien image of wholeness. Lacan writes that "the total form of
the body by which the subject anticipates in a mirage the maturation of
his power is given to him only . . . in an exteriority" ("Mirror" 2). Or, as
he puts it more simply, "the first synthesis of the *ego* is essentially alter
ego; it is alienated" (Séminaire 3, cited by Ragland-Sullivan, 275).

This first moment of coherent self-knowing is thus a "mirage," and it
prefigures the process of unconscious identificatory merging with exteri-
or figures that will, for the rest of our lives, affect our identity as subjects.
Lacan calls this irrationally projective dimension of identity *Imaginary,* a
term I have found indispensable in this study. As Ragland-Sullivan
writes, "The ego is developed in a primordial discordance between natural being and identification with the forms of the outer world. In other
words, *alien* images – i.e., not innate – first constitute the ego as an *object*
of its own identificatory mergers" (2). The self is thus "constituted
through anticipating what it will become" (Gallop, *Reading* 81), built
upon fictions.

The second major stage of identity formation begins at about eighteen
months: the time at which the child begins simultaneously to acquire
language skills and to recognize the invisible presence of the father as a
barrier to its desire for merger with the mother. Reconceiving Freud's

[9] The most useful collection of Lacan's major essays in translation remains *Ecrits: A Selection.* The essay most relevant to this portion of my argument is "The Mirror Stage as
Formative of the Function of the I," 1–7. Lacan's work is notoriously difficult, and I have
benefited greatly from commentaries by Anika Lemaire, Fredric Jameson ("Imaginary
and Symbolic in Lacan"), Luce Irigaray, Jane Gallop (both texts), and Ellie Ragland-
Sullivan.

Oedipal drama, Lacan sees the child's entry into language as itself a substitute satisfaction for the lost object – the mother – that the infant shall never again possess. Language appears in this argument as an alien network made up of empty differences, of signs that mean only in relation to each other. It is a system outside the speechless somatic self. Henceforth caught up in this system (which Lacan calls the Symbolic – the paternal field of Culture's rules and regulations, of linguistic transactions, of the Law), the child must seek in the register of language a wholeness that language cannot provide. Language keeps sending us to other language. Thus we spend our lives trying to say what we want, chasing in the channel of language for an object that never existed in that medium in the first place.

These two stages of self-formation posit an inevitable self-fissuring. The human subject is a being precariously poised between Imaginary mergers and Symbolic distinctions. S/he does not master either arena. Identity is therefore decentered and from the beginning adulterate. There is no native self. As Lacan writes, "I think where I am not, therefore I am where I do not think" ("Agency" 166). Or, "clarifying" Lacan, we might say: "Thinking I was I was not who was not was not who." In each formulation we remain the last ones to know what we are up to – consciousness is not a window upon identity – though Faulkner's wording has an urgency and a sense of the cost of such vertigo absent from Lacan's witty phrasing. The social world – its language, its gestures, its images – penetrates us from the moment of our conception on. We have never been virginal. Drawing on Althusser and Lacan as formulators of a human subjectivity irrationally permeated by social networks, a subjectivity that lives its identity both through participating in ideology and through Imaginary mergers with surrounding others, I turn now to *Absalom, Absalom!*

ð

Faulkner knew nothing of either Althusser or Lacan, yet *Absalom, Absalom!* uncannily responds to their enterprises. The ways in which individuals are born and educated into alien systems of thinking, feeling, and doing – into ideology – and at the same time find themselves caught up in an Imaginary fusion with others in whom they see themselves mirrored: these concerns lie near the heart of the book. As John Irwin has shown, individual identity in this novel is a matter not of enclosed essences but of specular relationships.

The process of vicarious identification is rampant. Rosa and her identification with Judith and Charles's courtship, Henry and his shifting triangular identifications with Judith and with Bon (mergers in which the clarity of sexual difference itself seems to dissolve), Sutpen's identification with the planter in the big house, Wash Jones's identification with Sutpen,

Quentin and Shreve's identifications with Henry and Charles: in each of
these crossings an involuntary psychic merger takes place, often across
"the devious intricate channels of decorous ordering" (*AA* 173), the
boundaries set up by Culture that tell us whom we are like and whom
unlike, whom we can or cannot touch, where, and when. These crossings, my examples make clear, are saturated in Symbolic arrangements –
how else explain Sutpen's passionately class-shaped identification with
the planter or Wash's with Sutpen? – but the energy that fuels them rises
from a more primitive reservoir of identificatory (Imaginary) need. The
novel's primary image for this desire for illicit merger is touch itself, just
as the novel's primary image for the cultural regulation of touch is the
closed door.

Individual identity here remains poignantly incomplete. Even Charles
Bon, in Quentin and Shreve's final version of him, finds himself moving
past the cool stability of "breathing, pleasure, darkness" (374) and into
the helpless state of yearning. Needing his father's recognition and not
getting it he thinks, "*My God, I am young, young, and I didn't even know it;
they didn't even tell me, that I was young*" (401). *Absalom, Absalom!* insists on
the same kind of fluidity in its very form. Revising each finished version
of its characters' identity with another version, the novel melts down
whatever it has consolidated, infusing youthful instability and passion
into material gone rigid or dead. "Get on, now. . . . But go on. . . . Go
on" (325–6) – these generative phrases run like a leitmotif throughout the
narrative, fanning the glow of its stalemated materials into the bonfire of
an overpass to love, heating up painful but finished events into unbearably unfinished ones. Charles Bon enters this novel dead, is brought back
to life, is shot, is resurrected, is shot again, is resurrected again, is shot
again. Each time he dies it hurts a bit more, hurts Quentin and Shreve
who have lent him something of themselves, hurts the reader who has
lent Quentin and Shreve (and therefore Charles) something of the reader's self. The narrative keeps revisiting its most intransigent materials,
rejuvenating and replaying them as a living might-be, then as a medi-
tative might-have-been, then as a tragic was.

In this creative (yet foreclosed) move to revise its own inheritance, this
tormented overview of its own wasted terrain, *Absalom* goes past an
Althusserian vision of ideology as hegemonic consent. It does so through
the resurrectory energy of desire itself, the energy that psychoanalysis
respects as transference and that moves through the incompleteness of
individual identity – that of the doers, the tellers, the readers – and seeks
(hopelessly yet irresistibly) to merge with the other.[10] Rather than accept

[10] The best texts I know on the role of desire in the production of literary texts are those of
Roland Barthes (*The Pleasure of the Text*), Peter Brooks ("Freud's Masterplot"), and
Charles Bernheimer (1–44).

the limitations of a narrative in which everything has already happened (the conventional historical novel) or accept the illusory freedom of a narrative in which everything is yet to happen (the conventional novel of today), Faulkner combines these two frames into a narrative of tragic desire. Events come to us in the double perspective of having already happened, and yet – such is the desire of the teller – they are rekindled, still happening, being reimagined, reframed, compelling yet hopeless. This is the narrative of desire entrapped (can't matter) and desire released (must matter): *"they mought have kilt us but they aint whupped us yit"* (234).

Such involuntary mergers recall in certain ways the Lacanian field of the Imaginary, the restless movement of "the immortal brief recent intransient blood" (369) that never escapes from nor comes to terms with the normative boundaries put forth by the Symbolic order. Those boundaries, though, are beyond dismantling, and not because authorities dispense enough police to protect them. They are beyond dismantling because internalized, bred into the fabric of the subject's unconscious feeling and thinking. Henry Sutpen polices himself. His West Virginia father may touch blacks with impunity but, born and bred in the South, Henry cannot. He screams and vomits when his father does it, he murders at the intolerable prospect of his sister doing it. Ideology is inseparable from subjectivity itself, and Faulkner tirelessly shows us – in Quentin Compson, in Joe Christmas, in Charles Etienne de St.-Valery Bon – the implosion of the subject that follows upon the clash within of incompatible ideological scripts.

All great novels involve the clash of ideological scripts, but most do not represent that clash as beyond individual resolution. Indeed, as I suggested earlier, one of fiction's cardinal functions has been to produce subjective identity as a space for working through conflicts both Imaginary and Symbolic. One might even claim that the culture's most widely disseminated texts, its best-sellers, always affirm a dominant ideology (in the sense that we as readers are invited to assent comfortably to their assessments) even as they indicate stress within the available social arrangements. (What better way to promote the adequacy of ideology to desire than through the dramatizing of stress – internal and external – encountered, experienced, and finally brought to term?) We can test this claim by briefly considering the ways in which two masterpieces written in 1936, *Absalom, Absalom!* and *Gone with the Wind,* play out this issue of ideological clash and containment in terms of subjective identity.[11]

Narrative voice is fiction's most potent instrument for containment – for conveying the sense of an individual speaker subjectively abreast of

[11] Eric Sundquist touches briefly on this comparison. Peter Brooks brilliantly explores the logic of *Absalom*'s intertwined failure of narrative and genealogical authority in his "Incredulous Narration."

the conflicts that arise – and *Gone with the Wind* comes to us in a continuously satisfying narrative voice, an all-knowing voice equal to its task. *Absalom, Absalom!* comes to us, by contrast, in a variety of voices; and the fact that they all tend to sound alike does not help us out. Each of these voices either knowingly or unknowingly calls into question its own authority. This is a case in which more is less.

If we turn to the handling of time and theme, we discover a comparable stability in the best-seller, instability in the experimental novel. All of *Gone with the Wind* is written as though the past history it is unfolding took place recently. The novel never acknowledges its own seventy-five-year vantage point on the events it records – the pastness of the past. It does not acknowledge it, but it everywhere exploits it in the unified vision afforded by retrospect. Mitchell renders the defeat of the South as tragic, deserved, and – secondary. She does this by focusing the reader less upon the issues of the war itself than upon two larger-than-life figures (Rhett and Scarlett) who stand neither simply for nor against the lost cause. The trauma of the war – the ways in which it called into question (still calls into question) our nation's deepest social contract – is contained within Scarlett and Rhett's "immortal" love story, ending on the note of the unvanquished human will, the staying power of subjective resolve, of individual identity. (A comparison of the place of Tara and of Sutpen's Hundred within the economy of each novel's ending makes the same point.)

Absalom, Absalom!, by contrast, lives uneasily on both sides of Mitchell's satisfying time frame. In *Absalom* the pastness of the past – its unrecoverability – is foregrounded. Yet this disappeared past has refused, precisely, to pass: it is still present, still unfinished, still beyond managing. The years 1808, 1833, 1859, 1909–1910: the narrative moves bewilderingly back and forth among these time-frames, suggesting that the racial issues over which the war was fought retain their power to haunt and confuse. Who is black in *Absalom*? How much black blood does it take to be black? In place of *Gone with the Wind*'s easy separation between black and white, *Absalom* finds black and white to be inextricable components of each other's identity.

Gone with the Wind "masters" the trauma of the Civil War, then, by containing it within a love story of two strong individuals, narrated by a capable narrative voice that preserves key distinctions between white and black, self and system, past and present, energy and weakness: distinctions upon which twentieth-century American culture's most confident images of itself are founded. In *Absalom* all these distinctions have become problematic. No narrator can deliver this material because none has mastered it. None can speak from a later cultural vantage point of superior hindsight and sort it all out; no voice is in control. And this means literally that Southern culture since 1865 (as Faulkner can speak that culture) has been unable to provide the individual narrators with a perspective – a resolving ideological frame – that will contain that cataclysmic war and make it go down. It sticks in the craw, and in so doing it shatters the conventional fictional contract between a desiring self (the character's, the reader's) and the roles proffered by society to accommodate and socialize that desire. *Absalom* is an experimental novel, precisely, in its refusal of these blandishments, these conventions of retrospective mastery. Its frustrations are passed on to us as our own. We do not feel wise reading it, we do not feel sure of ourselves – of who we are – while reading it.[12]

In fact, Faulkner's novel (as opposed to Mitchell's) seems designed to frustrate our answer to the simple question that inaugurates all queries about identity: who is _____? Who is Thomas Sutpen (or Charles Bon)? It is not that the question cannot be answered but that the novel keeps on answering it in different ways. (There is no corresponding vertigo suffusing the identity of Scarlett O'Hara or Rhett Butler.) Who Sutpen is

---

[12] Not enough critical attention is generally paid to the sense of readerly empowerment or incapacity wrought by a given text's "narrative contract." (Warwick Wadlington's recent *Reading Faulknerian Tragedy* goes a long way toward meeting this need.) Insofar as a narrative invokes (in its forms even more than its themes) the comforts of the already-known, it consolidates the ideological bonding between reader and culture. It makes one feel rich in common wisdom. Virginia Woolf's commentary in *A Room of One's Own* on this aspect of reading is unsurpassable:

> But the effect [of an unconventional text that the narrator is reading] was somehow baffling; one could not see a wave heaping itself, a crisis coming round the next corner. Therefore I could not plume myself either upon the depths of my feelings and my profound knowledge of the human heart. For whenever I was about to feel the usual things in the usual places, about love, about death, the annoying creature twitched me away, as if the important thing were just a little further on. And thus she [the author of the unconventional text] made it impossible for me to roll out my sonorous phrases about "elemental feelings," the "common stuff of humanity," "depths of the human heart," and all those other phrases which support us in our belief that, however clever we may be on top, we are very serious, very profound and very humane underneath. She made me feel, on the contrary, that instead of being serious and profound and humane, one might be – and the thought was far less seductive – merely lazy minded and conventional into the bargain. (95)

It would be unfair to leave this sustained bashing of the "lazy minded and conventional" novel by the experimental one without conceding that, within the "literary establishment," their relative status has long been reversed. For at least thirty years *Absalom* has been the darling of Faulkner criticism, and its brilliant demonstration of Modernist premises – self-reflective narrative, pervasive irony, shifting points of view, foreclosed present scene – reveals that one generation's maverick experimentation becomes the next generation's canonical procedures. In the next chapter I seek to identify some of this text's traditional moves. For a provocative reading of *Absalom* as severely limited by its adherence to the canonical tenets of Modernism, see Moreland.

depends on when and where you look at him, and who is doing the looking. He looks one way to a woman, another to a man, another to a disowned son, another to a disillusioned classicist, another to that classicist's quietly desperate son, another to a bemused Canadian. These competing views of Sutpen's identity do not embarrass the novel; they enable it. Character in *Absalom* lives openly in someone else's *talk;* there is no illusion here of unmediated identity, of identity as enclosed essence.[13] A different narrator, a different issue (miscegenation, say, rather than incest) produces a different identity.

What indeed is *Absalom, Absalom!* "itself"? Is it the material 378 pages within the Modern Library covers that most of us used to know (or the 471 pages of "corrected" text that we are now obliged to know)? John Irwin has shown its astonishing intertextually shared life with *The Sound and the Fury.* Less spectacularly, Noel Polk's "corrected" edition of *The Sound and the Fury* indicates the difficulty of containing any text within its material bounds. Consider the history of *The Sound and the Fury*'s Appendix.[14] To do so, we should first go forward to *Absalom, Absalom!*, for in concluding that novel in the mid-1930s Faulkner composed a chronology, a genealogy, and a map. Charmed, perhaps, by the illusion of containment that such instruments seem to convey, Faulkner went on to write, some ten years later, an Appendix to *The Sound and the Fury* (liking it so much that he negotiated its appearance as the opening material in the next edition of the novel, though perversely insisted on calling it an Appendix). I say "seem to convey" because even these moves toward containment in *Absalom* reveal in their conflicting claims – 1909 or 1910? smallpox or yellow fever? – the unmastered dialogic restlessness of the text.

Likewise, *The Sound and the Fury*'s Appendix has hardly stabilized readings of the text. How could it do so when it has been moving around so much itself? For sixteen years the text with the Appendix at the beginning held sway; then, at the time of Faulkner's death, a new edition appeared with the Appendix placed more discreetly at the end of the novel proper. Some twenty-two years later, in 1984 and under the supervision of Noel Polk, the most recent edition of *The Sound and the Fury* appeared, this time minus the Appendix. Which is *The Sound and the*

13 John Matthews (*Play* 115–61) richly opens up this dimension of characterization in his chapter on *Absalom, Absalom!* For a study of the ways in which the novel's entire representational project is dependent upon voice, see also Stephen Ross (*Fiction* 185–233).

14 Noel Polk discusses these issues at length in his *Editorial Handbook for* The Sound and the Fury. In a telephone discussion of 3 July 1987, Polk spoke to me of some of Faulkner's reasons in the mid-1940s for wanting to give a privileged position to the Appendix, yet without "pandering" to those who would refuse to struggle with the body of the text itself. For a tonic discussion of the Appendix's refusal to pacify Faulkner's unruly Yoknapatawpha texts, see Lester.

Fury? If I have told the story properly, the question will sound naive. The amount of critical exegesis dependent upon the originally absent, temporarily present though shifting, and now discarded Appendix is weighty indeed, and it is not limited to undergraduates who do not know better. There are several *Sound and Fury*s afloat (not that they are all of equal value), and whichever we prefer changes in yet other ways when we try to calculate its interaction with *Absalom, Absalom!*

ᐰ

Character and text not only exhibit changing identities; literary history is founded upon such changes. The discontinuous reputation of Milton and of Donne, the current reconceiving of *Jane Eyre* and of *Uncle Tom's Cabin*, the (temporary?) slippage of Lawrence from the twentieth-century canon: these are not capricious changes. They testify to the fact that we do not so much receive masterpieces, intact, as produce them, adulterate.[15] The identity of texts is not essential but contextual; their value is inescapably conditioned by current canons of assessment. No writer comes to us "as he is," Faulkner included. How can we see him except through the interpretive eyes of Sartre and Malraux, or Olga Vickery, or Cleanth Brooks, or John Irwin, or John Matthews – which is to say through the concomitant lenses of Sartre and Malraux's existentialism, Vickery's New Criticism, Brooks's sympathy with Southern culture, Irwin's Nietzsche and Freud, Matthews's Derrida? I have in this sentence immersed Faulkner within a fog of names, yet this is, whether we are conscious of it or not, the only access we have to him. "Faulkner" is misleading shorthand for a complex and many-voiced enterprise that operates under the cover of his name.

Individual identity is likewise misleading shorthand for a complex and many-voiced enterprise that operates under the cover of that phrase. So long as we are physically separate from each other, demonstrably lodged in separate bodies, we shall probably never concede the degree to which

[15] To Marx's question, "Where does the eternal charm of Greek art come from?" Etienne Balibar and Pierre Macherey respond as follows:

> There is no good answer to this question, quite simply because there is no eternal charm in Greek art: for the *Iliad*, a fragment of universal literature, used in this instance as a vehicle for memory, is not the *Iliad*, produced by the material life of the Greeks, which was not a "book" nor even a "myth" in our sense of the word, which we would like to apply retrospectively. Homer's *Iliad*, the "work" of an "author" exists only for us, and in relation to new material conditions into which it has been reinscribed and reinvested with a new significance. . . . To go further: it is as if we ourselves had written it (or at least composed it anew). Works of art are processes and not objects, for they are never produced once and for all, but are continually susceptible to "reproduction"; in fact, they only find an identity and a content in this continual process of transformation. There is no eternal art, there are no fixed and immutable works. (Quoted in Bennett, *Formalism and Marxism* 68)

we depend upon the other and upon system in order to constitute the self. So long as we look solid, we shall deny the terrifying extent of our liquidity. Yet it is, so to speak, the liquid in us – what Faulkner sometimes thinks of as the blood – that engages incessantly in acts of transference, of identificatory merger. Because our identity is perpetually unfinished, because we are never coincident with ourselves, we read books, teach students, write essays, and attend conferences.

I have been using the pronoun "we" with abandon, but the "we" in this enterprise is no common entity. At any conference we attend, our orientations unfailingly accompany us, differentiating us from some and joining us to others. It is customary at such gatherings for the participants to wear a small badge conspicuously displayed, and this badge notes that we are here in our bodies but not only here. We are also there, lodged in our affiliatory institutions (and if the badge says Berkeley it suggests something different from Buffalo, something different again from Swarthmore or the University of Mississippi). We speak out of our training within these institutions, and are heard in terms of them (rightly or wrongly), as we speak out of and are heard in terms of our race and gender (rightly or wrongly).

Yet we Faulknerians do come together under a common umbrella that is appropriately named "Faulkner." It is the site less of our individual than of our transpersonal professional identity. Many of us are rewarded, either figuratively or literally, for publishing essays, coming to conferences, and attending to our place in the Symbolic field of reputations. I close by suggesting, however, that such conferences – like our solitary (yet never solitary) acts of reading him and writing about him – are the site as well, and more profoundly, of our common acts of Imaginary transference, the locus of our hopeless desire to merge our incompleteness with Faulkner's beckoning authority, to make his voice encounter our own and issue, finally, in our own accents. Dead, he lives. Continually reinvented, he speaks from us and to us. "Freed . . . of time and flesh" (*Sartoris* 19), like old Colonel Sartoris or Colonel Sutpen, he broods over us all in the form of our impassioned and incompatible inventions of him.

BECOMING JOE CHRISTMAS AND IKE McCASLIN

"The most crucial need of literary theory today is for the development of conceptual instruments capable of doing justice to a post-individualistic experience of the subject in contemporary life itself as well as in the texts" ("Imaginary and Symbolic" 382). So wrote Fredric Jameson some years ago, and Faulkner's narratives of the decentered subject calls out for such a theoretical account. In the brief comparison that follows, I shall probe the genesis of Faulknerian male subjectivity within a variety of contemporary frames – with as much attention to the frames as to the two protagonists being inserted within them. Several "post-individualistic" instruments for this analysis are available, and I draw on the following in order to highlight the social constructedness of Joe Christmas and Ike McCaslin: Althusser's formation of the subject within socially propagated ideological scripts, Lacan's placement of the subject within an unstable interplay of Imaginary and Symbolic registers, Bakhtin's conception of the subject as the site of ongoing dialogic encounters, Jameson's reading of the subject as textualized participant within the culture's "political unconscious," Foucault's work on the subject as modeled by disciplinary and discursive practices, Bourdieu's understanding of the subject as responsive to the culture's maps for being human (its "habitus"). All these recent systems for thinking about subjectivity share a conviction of the subject as produced, networked, decentered: the other of the mythically unified and autonomous subject of liberal capitalism.[16]

Jameson seems to want to do away altogether with the troublesome category of the subject[17] – here Althusser, Lacan, and Foucault buttress his sense of the subject as irremediably mystified – but I pursue my analysis with a different conviction. Postindividualistic, yes, but it remains the *subject* that we are concerned with. To abandon the term, to opt for a vision of the self as a wholly determined entity, is to give up agency

---

[16] I shall try to keep this note manageable. The major texts on the decentered subject draw upon Marx for articulating ideological contradictions, upon Freud for articulating unconscious fissuring, and upon Saussure for articulating linguistic affiliation within more than one signifying economy. Lacan's *Ecrits* suggestively combines the last two orientations by formulating a model of the unconscious based upon the primacy of the Saussurean signifier – showing the subject's inescapably mystified dependence upon cultural coding – and his work is crucial to Althusser's and Jameson's (later) writings about the subject. Gallop, Ragland-Sullivan, Moi, and Rose – drawing upon Kristeva and Irigaray – usefully open Lacan's project to feminist commentary and criticism. Carroll and especially Smith seek to approach the category of the subject without falling into either holistic or necessarily decentered mystifications. I realize that my practice in this discussion runs the risk of "fitting" Faulkner's novels too neatly within currently approved paradigms of subjectivity. Given my sustained attention to the nuances of Faulkner's own texts elsewhere in this study, it is a risk I am willing to run, if only because it makes explicit that we always read through theory-shaped lenses. I hope it is clear, nevertheless, that I do not see Faulkner simply replicating any of these theoretical paradigms. Rather, they serve to open his texts to some of the questions that matter most to contemporary readers.

[17] Jameson justifies his move from Freud to Frye as a refusal of the merely *personal* or *familial*: "[T]he need to transcend individualistic categories and modes of interpretation is in many ways the fundamental issue for any doctrine of the political unconscious, of interpretation in terms of the collective or the associative" (*Political* 68). He does concede, though, that a Lacanian analysis, with its recourse to the social by way of the Other, may well escape this limitation.

and empowerment. As Jacqueline Rose puts it, "No politics without identity, but no identity which takes itself at its word" (157). Paul Smith has strenuously argued against the wholesale devaluation of the subject in contemporary psychoanalytic, ideological, and deconstructive enterprises. He urges that we see subjectivity as a differential construction, yet a precious one. Speaking of the contradictory subjectivities enjoined upon self-aware women today, he writes: "What binds subject-positions is precisely their difference. That is, the contradictions between them are a product of the negativity which enjoins the 'subject' to construct, recognize, and exploit difference. It is negativity which also and simultaneously produces the human agent" (150).

Smith's "negativity" is the energy that comes from subjective consciousness's refusal to align itself wholly within any one of the conflicting social roles proffered to it. This capacity for unpredictable response to one's insertion within contradictory roles is, he argues, the empowerment of agency itself. The bearing of such meditations upon the fiction of William Faulkner is massive. I shall argue that Faulkner's iconoclastic early work understands subjective negativity as disabling rather than enabling, while his later work endorses subjective agency at the price, precisely, of negativity. The subject his work ends by articulating is sutured, self-knowing; it has found its fit.[18] But the subject who opens up the spectacle of incoherence is the subject who pierces the reader's own illusion of unity. In what follows these two subjects will take on their Faulknerian names of Ike McCaslin and Joe Christmas.[19]

How much the names themselves tell us. McCaslin, the inheritor of a concrete nineteenth-century lineage (a stabilizing identity tag however much it may also overbear): Ike McCaslin enters the world "old" – his paths have been familially laid down for him since before birth – and

[18] In a (1956) interview with Jean Stein, Faulkner described the moral trajectory of his protagonists (and implicitly of his own career) in terms that reinscribe the autonomous centered subject. He spoke of a "trinity of conscience: knowing nothing, knowing but not caring, knowing and caring" (75). These remarks, which privilege the increase of knowing as Faulkner's career advances, have been much cited by admirers of the later work. In this way we move from the confused Benjy and Quentin of the late 1920s to the informed Ike and Chick of the 1940s and 1950s: protagonists who have gone much further in figuring out themselves and their world, and who do something about it. Faulkner seems not to have recognized (at least not in 1956) that his most compelling protagonists are those who enjoy no such enabling fit between their subjective energies, on the one hand, and the licensed practices of the culture in which they find themselves, on the other.

[19] Snead's deconstructive/ideological argument is especially illuminating here. He shrewdly explores the play of hierarchical binarisms in the genesis of subjectivity in Light in August, and he touches as well on the fantasy of virgin space – a territory prior to naming – in Go Down, Moses. He is not interested, as I am, in the diachronic implications for Faulkner's career of such a rewriting of the subject.

his drama unfolds as the taking up or refusing of his two proffered patrimonies. Christmas, the orphan, the abstract religious symbolism of his name savagely, parodically applied: Christmas enters the world illegitimate – his nonpath has been laid down for him by the confused circuitries of his culture's Symbolic order.[20] His drama unfolds as the impossibility of acting in accord with what Bourdieu calls the "habitus": a "cultivated disposition, inscribed in the body schema and in the schemes of thought" (15), which – half-subjective, half-objective – bonds the subject's expectations to the culture's offerings.[21] In Christmas this "disposition" has become nightmarishly incoherent, a mix of white and black "habituses" imploding within the subject who houses them.

Ike McCaslin is not only born old; he is born often. Conceived elderly in 1940 as the central autumnal figure in "Delta Autumn," he is rejuvenated seven months later when Faulkner writes "The Bear" and then reshaped and inserted retrospectively into the newly revised "The Old People," replacing Quentin Compson.[22] His youth thus follows his age, and this is to say that Faulkner explores his formative years only after establishing his mature place in the already stabilized world of the Symbolic. Indeed, Ike's formative years are but retrospectively imposed rehearsals of his lifelong mature identity as hunter. We never see him younger than the ten-year-old boy (in "The Bear") entering the woods, protected and guided by his tutorial relationship with Sam Fathers.

Joe Christmas is born only once, and disastrously. His entire life resembles his conception: something between a rape and an unwanted intrusion, an intolerable boundary-crossing. His spawning incarnates the illicit entry of (black?) male into (white) female, and his subsequent violent career will repeat (in several keys and on several stages) the illicit entry of male into female, female into male. The dietitian, the nameless

---

[20] Bleikasten explores this nightmarish dimension of Christmas's plight in "Fathers in Faulkner," in "The Closed Society and Its Subjects," and (at greatest length) in his chapter on *Light in August* in *The Ink of Melancholy*, 275–351.

[21] Bourdieu glosses "the habitus" as "the immanent law . . . laid down in each agent by his earliest upbringing, which is the precondition not only for the coordination of practices but also for practices of co-ordination" (81). The advantage of speaking of subject behavior in terms of "habitus" instead of "scripts" is that the unpredictability of behavior in time is permitted to surface in the analysis. "To substitute *strategy* for the *rule* is to reintroduce time, with its rhythm, its orientation, its irreversibility" (91). Indeed, "[b]ecause the habitus is an endless capacity to engender products – thoughts, perceptions, expressions, actions – whose limits are set by . . . historically and socially situated conditions . . . the conditioned and conditional freedom it secures is as remote from a creation of unpredictable novelty as it is from a simple mechanical reproduction of the initial conditionings" (95). Therefore, Bourdieu argues against any rigid application of linguistic paradigms to human behavior: "As soon as one moves from the structure of language to the function it fulfills, that is, to the uses agents actually make of it, one sees that mere knowledge of the *code* gives only very imperfect mastery of the linguistic interactions really taking place" (25).

[22] Grimwood offers the fullest reading of this genetic history.

black girl, Bobbie the prostitute, Joanna Burden: these women condition his shaky emergence into and out of selfhood. He is as suffused in (and suffocated by) the "aura" of black and female as inescapable matrix as Ike is freed of those racial and gendered frames.

The missing mother and the threatening lover loom over all of Joe Christmas's career. In Joe's lifelong violence Faulkner spells out the damage a male child can suffer from and inflict upon the female.[23] The lack of pre-Oedipal nourishment scars irreparably this text's central male subject. *Light in August* focuses again and again on the earliest years of identity formation: Joe in the orphanage, Joe at the McEacherns. As Lacan has argued, subject status is intrinsically fragile, open to – shaped by – the unpredictable desire of the Other.[24] Joe Christmas, from his infantile naming to his death thirty-three years later, is of all of Faulkner's characters the one most at the mercy of the unpredictable desire of the Other, while all the while desperate to protect his "virginity," to keep his precarious boundaries intact. His career is monstrously Other-directed. He learns who he is from others – from being called "nigger" first by other children in the orphanage (they having been tutored probably by Doc Hines), then by the dietitian and Bobbie in the wake of their own exposure and fury, and finally by the citizens of Jefferson when the murderer of a white woman is to be named. Each time the epithet is hurled at him when someone's (or some group's) integral identity is under pressure and found lacking. As for "nigger," Joe learns what that means by the disgust all the whites he knows *must* feel toward the black. Of such a culturally imposed abhorrence Bourdieu writes: "Because the dispositions . . . inculcated by objective conditions . . . engender aspirations and practices . . . compatible with those objective [conditions], the most improbable practices are excluded . . . as *unthinkable*" (77). One such unthinkable practice in the American South of the 1930s is that a white man interiorize as his own the subjectivity of a black man. Joe has been led to absorb into himself the most poisonous codes of his racist culture: a white man somehow contaminated with black blood, he "knows" himself as what it is unthinkable for him to accommodate.

Joe's emergence into adulthood aptly illustrates Foucault's disciplinary paradigm for subject formation. His interiority has been formed by the

---

23 Bleikasten comments acutely and at length on Joe Christmas's maternal privation/fixation in *The Ink of Melancholy*.
24 Lacan scorns the "moral tartufferies of our time" that are "forever spouting something about the 'total personality'" of the subject. In its place he characterizes this scene of desire's dependence on the Other thus: "Who, then, is this other to whom I am more attached than to myself, since, at the heart of my assent to my own identity it is still he who agitates me? . . . If I have said that the unconscious is the discourse of the Other (with a capital O), it is in order to indicate the beyond in which the recognition of desire is bound up with the desire for recognition" ("Agency" 172).

punitive disciplinary technologies of society – the operative rules of the orphanage, of McEachern's religious catechism, of Bobbie's professional prostitution – and his finished soul is the crowning touch of this fabrication. "The history of this 'micro-physics' of the punitive power would then be a genealogy . . . of the modern 'soul,'" Foucault writes: "A 'soul' inhabits him and brings him to existence, which is itself a factor in the mastery that power exercises over the body. The soul is the effect and instrument of a political anatomy; the soul is the prison of the body" (*Discipline* 29–30).[25] On this argument the soul comes last, like a brain carefully designed and inserted at the final moment into a robot in order to supervise all the activities his body has been already programmed to undertake. In Joe Christmas, though, this programming deconstructs, loses its efficacy; yet it cannot be revised. Who Joe Christmas is – how he reads his own interiority – is the consequence of what has been done to him: literally, the moves that have been made upon his body, the marks (physical or fictive) his body is read (by himself and others) as containing. The minuscule element that remains his own is wholly negative: his attempt to refuse these proffered (or already internalized) versions of himself.

This fashioning of Joe Christmas's subjectivity resonates as well within a psychoanalytic economy of meanings, inasmuch as that framework can articulate the becoming of selfhood, its primordial beginnings in the nonself. Lacan speaks of the *me* that precedes the *I* in the formation of identity. The *me* is a composite of the introjected gaze and words of others, that ineradicable portion of identity that is laid down prior to entry into the Symbolic. Phonic and visual residues are introjected from the time of infancy, and these fuse into unconscious networks of signification. Fueled by Imaginary identifications, consumed with boundary transgressions, locked into polarized antagonisms, the *me* radiates that sense of self that is involuntary, inaccessible to conscious change, helplessly responsive to the desire of others. On this chaotic scene of identity the linguistic *I* is a latecomer, an adroit manipulator of surface language games the logic of whose moves is all the while being cathected at a lower level, unawares.[26] Joe Christmas is as arrested in the Imaginary phase – a *me* that never coordinates his introjected scripts into the coherence an activated *I* – as Ike McCaslin is conceived from start to finish as a citizen of the Symbolic: an already matured *I* sanctioned by its grounding in the

---

[25] Foucault emphasizes that "this is the historical reality of this soul, which, unlike the soul represented by Christian theology, is not born in sin and subject to punishment, but is born rather out of methods of punishment, supervision and constraint"(*Discipline* 29).

[26] I have been aided in this discussion of the *me's* relation to the *I* by Jameson's discussion of "Imaginary and Symbolic in Lacan" (esp. 349–71) and by Ragland-Sullivan's lengthy analysis of pre-Symbolic subject formation within the Lacanian schema.

hierarchized values of the big woods. He is as securely named and placed as Joe is lacking in both.

Faulkner comes at Ike through repeated scenes of training. "The Old People" locates him between Sam Fathers and Cass. "The Bear" situates him between Sam and Cass again, but also inserts him in scenes with Boon and Hubert – and indeed with Lion and Old Ben – in which his tutelage proceeds apace. Even from his wife (in some of the novel's strangest scenes) he manages to learn. He learns from everyone; he seems infinitely educable. By the time of "Delta Autumn" he has become sententious in his amassed education, and the power of that story resides in its capacity to shock Ike out of his settled knowing. But Ike cannot be shocked for long; Faulkner is too deeply invested in Ike's orientation to leave him seriously unfocused. (It is not primarily a question of ironic or unironic stances toward Ike. The issue is, rather, the extent and quality of attention he receives. Faulkner's attention to Ike, like his later attention to Gavin, commits this text to the articulation of his positions in a way that makes the question of irony pertinent but secondary.)[27]

Joe is by contrast virtually incapable of education. (The impact of Faulkner's early texts often resides in their resistance to pedagogic motives, their embrace of what Malraux called the irreparable.) Each of Joe's formative scenes unfolds more as trauma than as education: from the dietitian and Bobbie he "learns" how women frustrate your expectations, from McEachern and Hines he "learns" how fathers train your mind by abusing your body. He is, magnetlike, exposed to everything – there is no aggressive energy in the novel that will not at some point find its way into him – and none of his encounters is remotely empowering. All the *me*'s he has internalized coil and recoil inside him – he vomits early, spills blood and semen later, releases his own blood at the end – but these relational exchanges never establish a microcommunity, never facilitate an *I*.

When, for example, Joanna proposes that he publicly validate his black identity within the Symbolic field by going to law school, *he* does not respond: his mouth does. "'To school,' his mouth said." She repeats the offer. "'To school,' his mouth said. 'A nigger school. Me.'" Patiently, intently, she reiterates this invitation to enter into the public domain. "'But a nigger college, a nigger lawyer,' his voice said, quiet, not even argumentative; just promptive" (303–4). No argument, no dialogic test-

---

27 For at least twenty-five years, New Critically inspired commentary – privileging the concept of irony – has debated Faulkner's stance toward Ike McCaslin. I propose instead that the character of the writer's *attention* conveys imaginative orientation in ways that go deeper than tone: Jason Compson, for example, is presented with unremitting irony, but his portrait, unlike his mother's, reveals a tremendous subjective investment on the part of the writer. For earlier discussion of this point, see my remarks on Rider in Chapter 2.

ing of the proposition, no conscious confrontation in which his fragmented subjectivity might refocus through the encounter and become an *I*.[28] Instead, his voice and mouth speak in his place, automatically refusing the proposed orientation. Only the energy of negation is his, and if he can be said to choose his destiny, it is in the sense of stubbornly refusing every partial and positive option available to him. In Joe Christmas the necessary line between subjective learning and objective training verges upon disappearance, for he is incapable of reaccenting (digesting) anything he has absorbed. Foreign to himself, he is foreign to others, and *Light in August* appropriately loses him to the mangling gaze and hands of others some 185 pages before the novel's conclusion. At the end he does not so much disappear as enter a state of permanent disruption. He is the blood that won't go down, that chooses not to go down: as sinister a sign of this text's disturbance as Ike (whose medium is words, not blood) is *Go Down, Moses*'s icon of peace.

Ike's peace is most nourished by his accumulated stock of memories. *Go Down, Moses* dilates in the flashback memories of Ike McCaslin – lovely vignettes of Ash and Boon and earlier hunts juxtaposed against later ones. These memories locate his identity as a sutured entity centered in space and amalgamated over time – not a discrete stance arrested in the violence of a single action – and they play their part in his far-reaching pronouncements. "Sam Fathers set me free," Ike tells Cass. It is the most radiant claim in the novel. Whether it is true or not counts less than Ike's capacity to think and say it. He has seen himself in Althusser's ideological mirror. Interpellated, he has answered the call. Dialogically defending himself against Cass's probing, he has strengthened his grasp upon this centering call. In doing so he enters his true patrimony, one of a space he does not own (the wilderness) and of a discourse that has become his own. Ike talks; he talks his envisaged and accepted place within the scheme of things, his role within the Symbolic. Protector of blacks, cherisher of wild things, articulator of God's plan for the post-Civil War South, he embodies the most authoritative stay against confusion – of the cultural coming to terms with the natural and the divine – in all of Faulkner's work.

Joe Christmas has no memories. (Traumatic memories have him, but that's a different matter, one of blind repetitions rather than the pedagogic narrative of recollection and working through.) Each of his vignettes etches him in our mind; his accumulated life is less than the sum of its

---

[28] "The ideological becoming of a human being," Bakhtin writes, "is the process of selectively assimilating the words of others" (341). Joe Christmas's assimilation of others' words is the reverse of purposively "selective": he absorbs (without reshaping) the most baleful utterances of his culture as these have been pressed upon him. He is, devastatingly, linguistically inert.

parts. More, he can barely talk; he is a hundred times more interesting than anything he manages to say about himself. And this muteness is telling. "The speaking person in the novel is always, to one degree or another, an *ideologue*," writes Bakhtin, "and his words are always *ideologemes*" (333). The speaking person presses toward self-possession, toward a critical grasp of the structure of values – the implicit ideology – lurking in his discourse. But Joe Christmas is spoken, he does not speak, and by not speaking he can in no way revise the culture's assumptions wrought into the language by which he confused knows himself. Rather, all that is unworkable in that discourse and those assumptions surfaces in his disaster. His final bodily annihilation maps the failure of the whole scene of unconscious training:

> If all societies . . . that seek to produce a new man through a process of "deculturation" and "reculturation" set such store on the seemingly most insignificant details of *dress, bearing,* physical and verbal *manners,* the reason is that, treating the body as memory, they entrust to it in abbreviated and practical, i.e., mnemonic, form the fundamental principles of the arbitrary content of the culture. The principles em-bodied in this way are placed beyond the grasp of consciousness, and hence cannot be touched by voluntary, deliberate transformation, cannot even be made explicit; nothing seems more ineffable, more incommunicable, more inimitable, and, therefore, more precious, than the values given body, *made* body by the transubstantiation achieved by the hidden persuasion of an implicit pedagogy, capable of instilling a whole cosmology, an ethic, a metaphysic, a political philosophy, through injunctions as insignificant as "stand up straight" or "don't hold your knife in your left hand." (Bourdieu 94)

Joe's imprisonment within his culture's religious and racial insistences – "She ought not to started praying over me" (117), "I think I got some nigger blood in me" (216) – reveals glaringly the suffocation of these scripts. His moves during the last 185 pages, tracked as they are by a variety of countrymen speaking out of their own orientations (not his), say nothing about "genuine" racial traits and everything about the discursive practices through which racial identity is produced and recognized.[29] He finally returns, parades about in Mottstown, calmly awaiting his arrest and execution as a "nigger." Like a kind of Irigarayan mimicry, in which the text "makes 'visible,' by an effect of playful repetition, what was supposed to remain invisible" (Irigaray, *This Sex* 76), *Light in August* plays out the virulence of racial constructs in such a way as to emphasize their arbitrariness. "Every established order," Bourdieu writes, "tends to

---

[29] Davis notes the constructedness of Joe Christmas's portrait. Snead and Duvall go further and analyze the social dynamic at work in such a scapegoating discursive practice. See also my discussion of *Light in August* in the next chapter.

produce . . . the naturalization of its own arbitrariness" (164). This claim seems to me as true for *Go Down, Moses* as it is stood on its head by *Light in August*. Ike represents the successfully trained body and mind, integrated into the "habitus" of a fading culture at once idealized and found wanting. Joe incarnates the nightmare flip side of such accommodation.

ஐ

This brief comparison of novelistic practice intimates a sea change in Faulkner's strategies for representing subjectivity between 1932 and 1942. (Joe and Ike, of course, are not the only subjectivities Faulkner enters in those two novels, but it seems fair to claim that each embodies the most representative accents of his respective text. This is especially true of *Go Down, Moses*, where the musing narrative voice of "The Old People" and "Delta Autumn," not to mention heightened passages in "The Fire and the Hearth" and "The Bear," sounds remarkably like Ike.) The writer's relation to his culture's discursive practices shifts massively, and this shift entails a different relation with the reader. A Modernist aesthetics of shock cedes to a conservative aesthetics of mourning and nostalgia. The early text pursues a subjectivity shattered into uncohering parts; it does this by staging within its reader something like an implosion. We exit from *Light in August* shaken, the "cosmology, ethic, metaphysic" we had internalized now revealing something of its untenable artifice.[30] The role of the unthinking *me* in the gestures made by the deliberate *I* has been revealed; the intolerable play of the other in the fashioning of the subject has "abrupted" upon the scene. The later text, by contrast, stages a subjectivity enabled by memory, grounded by the wilderness, sutured into utterance. We exit from *Go Down, Moses* reconstituted, refreshed by our enheartening complicity with the text, resecured as communal figures within a Symbolic domain all the more moving for its imminent disappearance.

Lacan might help us to see what Faulkner's measured perspective (his hopelessness in the face of the Delta's advancing autumn) perhaps glimpses as well: that this security is itself but the classic move of the Imaginary register. To envisage identity as whole and self-knowing is to reenact the lifelong fantasy of autonomy inculcated in the mirror stage.[31] The earlier text's painful exposure of fractured subjectivity testifies to a

---

[30] Bernheimer seeks to articulate a general poetics of reading as a continuous oscillation between moments of unthinking identification with the text and moments of deconstructive recoil from it. Wadlington, more specifically, has proposed a model for the dynamics of reading Faulkner. He claims, persuasively in my view, that the shaping or refusing of subjectivity in terms of proffered cultural roles is the central activity – shared by writer, characters, and reader – in the drama of acknowledgment or repudiation that fuels Faulkner's texts.

[31] Cf. Lacan: "The mirror stage is a drama whose internal thrust is precipitated from insufficiency to anticipation – and which manufactures for the subject . . . the succes-

harder-earned sense of identity as castration – selfhood as irremediably fissured and involuntarily inserted within alien economies.[32] This recognition that we are aleatory creatures contingently defined and self-defining according to the conflicting structures we live within constitutes the sobering hallmark of Symbolic awareness. But William Faulkner seems to have found that he could continue to become William Faulkner – to "grow up" finally – only by eluding this castration at the heart of selfhood, by moving backward in time for his dreams and by orphaning once more his speechless and abandoned orphans: Ike McCaslin was calling, and behind him lay Gavin Stevens.

sion of phantasies that extends from a fragmented body-image to a form of its totality . . . and, lastly, to the assumption of the armour of an alienating identity, which will mark with its rigid structure the subject's entire mental development" ("Mirror" 4).

[32] Julia Kristeva envisages escape from gender scapegoating in visionary terms that draw upon something like this voluntary and internalized castration: "I see arising . . . an attitude of retreat from sexism (male as well as female). . . . This process could be summarized as an *interiorization of the founding separation of the socio-symbolic contract,* as an introduction of its cutting edge into the very interiority of every identity. . . . This in such a way that the habitual . . . attempt to fabricate a scapegoat victim . . . may be replaced by the analysis of the potentialities of *victim/executioner* which characterize each identity, each subject, each sex" ("Women" 210). The bearing of these terms upon *Light in August* seems to me remarkable.

4

Culture: A Cosmos No One Owns

"A cosmos of my own," Faulkner claimed; "sole owner and proprietor," he penned across the map of his fictional kingdom. I have written this book as a sympathetic challenge to the premises upon which that claim is grounded. Gender and race enter Faulkner's texts not as natural facts he independently records but as cultural constructs already embedded within discourses he must accept or revise – his "saying" gender and race articulates his cultural alignment, not his sovereignty – and I have examined his necessary complicity with, and resistance to, some of these discursive options.[1] Subjective identity itself emerges, as the last chapter sought to show, as a wayward interiorizing and reaccenting of external models of being. In this final chapter I want to pursue further the social shaping of subjectivity in two related ways: by attending to some of the social norms that constrain Faulknerian body and voice, and by probing the discursive economies within and against which Faulkner, as a writer responding to these social norms, produces body and voice in the canonical texts.

A full-scale inquiry into Faulkner's materials along these lines would be a book in itself. That such an inquiry, in its privileging voice and body, would seem to enshrine human subjectivity is in my view not a reason against it. For the subject – decentered, not whole – remains an indispensable focus for assessing the interplay between "individuals" and the social roles they endorse, revise, or refuse: an interplay operative at the

---

[1] Gary Stonum argues that Faulkner's insistence on control over his materials is doubled by an awareness of the materials' control over him. Of the map of ownership that accompanies *Absalom, Absalom!* Stonum writes: "But the confidence displayed on the map should not obscure the fact that *Absalom, Absalom!* presents a kind of art in which the writer's proprietorship over his material is less likely to be secured than strived for or at best tenuously maintained" (146). Certainly Sutpen's disastrous trajectory bespeaks some such awareness. Moreover, as Martin Kreiswirth has recently argued, the summarizing map is itself unreliable, its dates suggestively unaligned, its predications a touch out of phase (yellow fever? smallpox?).

level of author, character, and reader. Here I read only two components of subjectivity, voice and body, as items already inserted within larger social practices, items always "totally imprinted by history" (Foucault, "Nietzsche" 148). Voice and body are of course in a certain sense conjoined (especially at the level of fictional character), and this study, while it pursues each separately, will recurrently suggest their copresence. Yet my argument requires their separation as well, for I see body as a continuously (and in the early texts tragically) tracked entity, whereas Faulknerian narrative voice enjoys (and enjoins upon its reader) a remarkable range of moves: none free, but none nearly so harnessed as the beleaguered body.

To develop my argument about voice and body as items no one owns, I shall draw again upon Foucault and Bakhtin. "I would like to show with precise examples," Foucault writes, "that in analysing discourses themselves, one sees the loosening of the embrace . . . of words and things, and the emergence of a group of rules proper to discursive practices. These rules define not the dumb existence of a reality, nor the canonical use of a vocabulary, but the ordering of objects" (*Archaeology* 48–9). Rather than accommodate already established human subjects and objects, positioning within these discursive practices constitutes the players *as* subjects and objects. The writer who activates such a practice comes upon his materials already "subjectified" and "objectified" according to its terms.

Foucault's concept of bio-power is even more germane for my inquiry here. Increasingly, he argues, Western society has shaped subjective identity through disciplinary practices that chart and manipulate the body. Accordingly, the soul itself is not, as in Christian theology, "born in sin and subject to punishment, but is born rather out of methods of punishment, supervision, and constraint" (*Discipline* 29). The sustained social modeling of the body (as I claimed earlier with respect to Joe Christmas) eventually produces the desired conception of the soul. Beginning with the birth of the prison and then considering the emergence of medical technology and the social science disciplines, Foucault moves from literal incarceration to the subtler, quasi-institutional procedures for anatomizing and controlling an individual: surveillance, judgment, examination, and confession. In these activities the body is subjected to an increasingly rigorous programming, as it moves within a set of normative social practices.[2]

---

[2] Foucault's major text that focuses upon the formation and deployment of discursive practices is *The Archaeology of Knowledge*. Bio-power is a later concern in his work, surfacing most powerfully in the texts of the late 1970s, *Discipline and Punish* and *The History of Sexuality*, vol. 1. Useful commentary on both these themes of Foucault's work can be found in Dreyfus and Rabinow (44–78, 126–83).

The bearing of these ideas upon Faulkner's texts is, as we have already seen, manifold. On the one hand, his fiction is almost constitutively drawn to scenes of crisis, scenes in which an individual subject undergoes traumatic assault, and a Foucauldian schema allows us to thematize the role of the socially channeled body within these crises.[3] On the other hand, Foucault's idea of discursive practices opens the way to interrogating the relationship between a writer's specific narrative practice – complicit, contestatory – and a culture's reservoir of narrative options. The following questions become pertinent: In what ways do social norms regulate the career of the Faulknerian body? What discursive practice does Faulkner draw on – in producing the body – so as to give it point and purpose, and to position it in relation to the reader? To what extent does Faulknerian narrative either highlight the social coding of the body or contest discursive norms for its representation? How do Faulkner's ways of representing the body alter during his career?

"The ideological becoming of a human being . . . is the process of selectively assimilating the words of others," Mikhail Bakhtin writes (341).[4] Utterance is on this view always saturated in ideology. The formation of selfhood, as I argued in the second half of Chapter 2 and throughout Chapter 3, is a social phenomenon consisting in the adaptation and modification of others' language, others whose language has been likewise adapted and modified from that of yet others. The key to selfhood – the selective language we use to articulate our "inner selves" – is simultaneously the trap of subjecthood: our often involuntary affilia-

---

[3] One of Foucault's unsettling insights, however, is that power (as it becomes more fine-tuned) operates characteristically in situations the reverse of crisis. He speaks of "the capillary functioning of power" (*Discipline* 198), an invisible, normalizing activity such that the subject polices him/herself within the appropriate disciplinary structures. Further, he insists that "we must cease once and for all to describe the effects of power in negative terms. . . . In fact, power produces; it produces reality; it produces domains of objects and rituals of truth" (*Discipline* 194). I have sought recurrently to identify this "positive" dimension of power as the "inevitable" structures within which Faulknerian voice and body take on recognizable identity by coming into harness. Elsewhere in this chapter (and especially in the Conclusion) I assign to the most artistically enabling form of this power economy its proper name – Modernism, with its tenets of deracinated consciousness and experimental form, tenets tremendously suggestive for the young Faulkner during his apprentice years in the 1920s. Throughout the study I have also focused, of course, on more traditional negative instances of power as that which coerces the subject.

[4] Ideology is one of the most abused words in current critical commentary, and I hope I do not here extend that abuse. By ideology I do not mean false consciousness, but rather a set of beliefs and practices that propose coherent subjectivity by securing the individual's alignment within a repertory of roles generated by larger power structures. My understanding of the term derives from Althusser, and my sense of its bearing upon literary production is informed by three critics who have themselves been influenced by Althusser: Macherey, Eagleton, and Jameson. A succinct overview of the role of ideology in narrative can be found in Belsey.

tion within the larger groups whose language we have adapted as our own. As Bakhtin writes, "Language is not a neutral medium that passes freely and easily into the private property of the speaker's intentions; it is populated – overpopulated – with the intentions of others. Expropriating it, forcing it to submit to one's own intentions and accents, is a difficult and complicated process" (294).

This perspective sheds light on what is ideologically at stake in the fractured verbal performances of many of Faulkner's characters as well as in his own evolving relationship with the literary tropes he inherited. It allows us to glimpse the competing discursive practices, the contextual weave of affiliations and repudiations, within which those performances take place. A central aim of this chapter will be to propose the shifting ideological orientation (of the writer, of his characters) that is wrought into an altering rhetorical practice – an altering way of producing his characters' and narrators' voices – as Faulkner moves from the Modernist *The Sound and the Fury* to the more traditional *Go Down, Moses*.[5]

These then are my concerns: Faulkner's way of employing or contesting his culture's normative tropes for the rendering of subjects and objects, the ideological schemas that implicitly constrain the represented body within his texts, his deployment of the utterance as that charged field in which individual selfhood emerges as a negotiation of society's verbal/gestural resources. Finally, the inquiry that subtends all the others is the following: in what ways are we as readers invited to respond to Faulkner's complex and changing practice? For it is here, in the strategic soliciting of our response, that the text's ideological work itself does or does not take place. I suggested in the second half of Chapter 3, and here I argue explicitly, that this ideological work (this inviting of certain kinds of response) changes radically between 1929 and 1942. *Go Down, Moses* seeks to activate within us a vastly different repertory of social roles than those we are invited to play when engaging *The Sound and the Fury*. To put the aims of this final chapter in one sentence, what kind of culturally

---

[5] I use "voice" to include both the specificity of characters' and narrators' spoken (and unspoken) utterances and the more elusive dimension of narrative behavior that we think of (with whatever deconstructive modifications) as authorial voice. A poetics of absence does not undo the illusion of "hearing" a text as a composition of voices, but it certainly complicates (by textualizing) our understanding of that illusion. The fullest explorations of voice in Faulkner occur in Wadlington and Ross (*Fiction*). Wadlington elaborates the dynamic of role playing enacted by author, character, and reader in the process of engaging the vocal (or written yet apprehended as vocal) performance of others. Ross proposes an analytically useful set of vocal categories – phenomenal, mimetic, psychic, and oratorical – for conceptualizing and mapping the primary role of voice in literary experience. I have benefited considerably from both these studies. For a strong deconstructive reading of Faulknerian voice, see Matthews (*Play*). For further suggestive commentary on voice in Faulkner, see Lilly and Zender.

inflected cosmos does Faulkner (re)produce through his shaping of voice and body, and what subject roles do we as readers perform as we engage that cosmos?[6]

ക

In *The Sound and the Fury* that cosmos is off-balance. Entering the fiction through Benjy, we stumble through his verbal/somatic field. Immersed in him, we register his alienation not only from his culture's norms of thinking and behaving, but also – more basically – from the elements and events of his own body.

> *I got undressed and I looked at myself, and I began to cry. Hush, Luster said.*
> *Looking for them aint going to do no good. They're gone.* (84)

What is Benjy seeing in that place of scar and absence? What can he know of his own sexuality? When the girls tease him and he breaks free of the fence, his only language for his longing is "I was trying to say" (60). Likewise, when his hand goes into the fire or the barn runs away or the box "hit me on the back of the head" (46) or his throat keeps making a sound, he does not know that the fire is burning him, that his drunkenness is causing him to fall, that the liquid exploding from his mouth is vomit. Benjy is the text's radical image of somatic dispossession: his body is a cosmos whose internal workings and external transactions he fails to make his own. Yet, from birth to death that body remains socially mapped, inscribed ("every mans brow even Benjys" [203]) in the somatic norms of his culture.[7]

---

[6] For a good collection of basic texts on the dynamics and theoretical implications of the reader's response to texts, see Tompkins. Charles Bernheimer suggestively argues for reading as a perpetual oscillation between the poles of transferential investment and deconstructive alterity. Reader-response concerns have recently broadened and deepened, going well beyond their formalist phenomenology (what we do step-by-step as we read) in the early Fish and Iser. See Booth and Miller (*Ethics*) for the ethical dimension wrought into the reading experience itself. For a brilliant revaluation of Faulknerian tragedy as premised upon reading as a quasi-physical acknowledgment (not interpretation) of the text's offered roles, see Wadlington. I should note again what will be explored in more depth later: that the ideological trajectory of Faulkner's texts that I trace from 1929 to 1942 is simultaneously a mapping of his entry into and exit from the larger project of literary Modernism. See Moreland for a critical reading of the thematic and rhetorical stances enjoined upon Faulkner by this temporary allegiance to Modernism. My own view (surely explicit in my argument by now, but to be elaborated further in this chapter and in the Conclusion) is that Faulkner's deepest hold upon us – his most powerful impact upon our own subjectivity as readers – is inseparable from his Modernist alignment.

[7] Gwin has pertinently noted that, if Benjy lacks a Symbolic self-image, he yet retains a minimal identity, thanks to the cohering vision of himself reflected back from the mirror of Caddy's attentiveness and the insistence of her voice: "Benjy has lost Caddy but he remains within her maternal discourse, for her voice has imprinted both itself and *himself* upon the receptacle of his memory" (43). The Lacanian dimension of identity as construed through the mirror of the Other is striking in early Faulkner.

The Sound and the Fury, especially its first chapter, is riddled with these somatic norms, in the form of incessant threats of physical punishment. "Your momma going to whip you for getting your dress wet" (19), "Mr. Jason say if you break that tree he whip you" (44) – these phrases and their echoes punctuate the text. The seamless vernacular framing of these utterances constitutes an inescapable linguistic orientation. The Compson children grow up in a world saturated in repressive norms of physical decorum and all-too-certain forms of punishment for infraction. Looking down at the violation done to his body, ignorant of what he has done to bring on this inscription – a brand wrought into his bodily core, ensuring obedience to sexual norms – Benjy epitomizes a general fate. Your body is not your own, it lives within a network of cultural sanctions, the stresses to which it is subjected are beyond individual mastery.

If Benjy's somatic life registers as a form of continuous alienation – he is clothed, fed, seated, kept in or out of the house, summoned, concealed, according to social mores whose logic he ignores – he differs in this from the other male Compsons more in degree than in kind. Faulkner's text immerses the bodies of Benjy's two brothers and his father in frames of predication that, though consensual, they neither sought nor can escape. Quentin's virginal body embarrasses him. He passes his chapter teasing and attacking that body – trampling its shadow, denying himself meals, remembering his broken limb, suffocating on the smell of honeysuckle, imagining castration. His body is his Other. Brought up in such a way as to find an intolerable misfit between what he (impossibly) wants and what he (confusedly) is, he takes out upon the body (that of others at times, his own at all times) the aggression he cannot otherwise release. He delights in the imagery of its dissolution.

Jason rides daily in a car that brings on migraines, unable to forgo this replacement of his lost status symbol. If he seems the free-moving tracker of his niece, he is equally tracked by the racial/gender tropes and economic structures of his culture: a tracking that registers somatically in the antics of his stop-and-start gyrations. Blacks, women, drummers, Compsons, swallows, the stock market and its manipulative Jews: these unreliable phenomena (versions for Jason of the Other) impose upon him their own alien and hostile pace; his body dances in pain to what he takes to be their tune. His acts of aggression are essentially reactive. Faulkner shows him in the grip of forces and figures he detests but cannot master, heading unerringly toward his encounter with the little old man with the butcher knife. In the pleasure he gets in contemplating his body's present and future pain – its subjection to inescapable practices – Jason is only a shade less eager than Quentin for his own crucifixion.

As for Mr. Compson, he is patiently drinking himself to death, wounded beyond saying (despite his saying) by his daughter's non-virginal body, seeking refuge in the generations-sanctioned ritual of male boozing. (Faulkner knew intimately this consensual form of marking the male body. He fully joined the self-destructive drinking rituals legitimized generally for Southern men and specifically for the three generations of male Falkners who had been long preparing his entry: avatars indeed.) The text's phrase for the power threatening these males and requiring such "cures" is "nature" – "it's nature is hurting you" (132), Mr. Compson tells his anguished son – but what we see is a cluster of cultural roles (gender-specific attitudes toward one's own and other bodies) that make adaptation to natural process impossible, that insist upon tragic alternatives.[8]

If the bodies of the Compson males enter Faulkner's text thus programmed, those of the Compson females run an even tighter gauntlet, and this regardless of their position vis-à-vis the operative norms. Mrs. Compson who does everything "right" suffers as much as her daughter and grand-daughter who do it all "wrong." In a culture that hystericizes the female body none can escape mangling.[9] Lacking models that might fuse the roles of motherhood and adult sexuality, Mrs. Compson lives out her life as an arrested virgin, perpetually shocked by the stir of desire. Her marriage bed has regressively become her sickbed, her husband has been regressively replaced by her brother and her second son. Behind her willed ignorance ("Thank God I dont know about such wickedness" [323]), we glimpse a woman – as I explored in the first chapter – whose body has been socially constructed for disaster.

The bodies of Caddy and her daughter Quentin are narratively tracked from start to finish in sexual terms. These two women are constantly under surveillance and pressed to confess. The text (through the lenses of the three Compson brothers) dilates upon their gestures, noting how they look, move, and smell, what perfume they wear, what clothes they put on and take off, the way water silhouettes their limbs. Indeed, a

---

[8] Wadlington pursues this oppositional logic of tragedy: "Quentin and his father tend to experience difference as contradiction, multiplicity as a stalemated war between 'impure properties.' The whole novel traces the fault lines of this mental set. A universe of antagonisms is formed, all divided and subdivided, as awareness focuses on each, into further bifurcations of A and not-A" (69).

[9] Foucault argues that Western European thought embarked throughout the nineteenth century upon an hystericization of women's bodies: "a threefold process whereby the feminine body was analyzed . . . as being thoroughly saturated with sexuality, whereby it was integrated into the sphere of medical practices, by reason of a pathology intrinsic to it; whereby, finally, it was placed in organic communication with the social body (whose regulated fecundity it was supposed to ensure), the family space . . . and the life of children (which it produced and had to guarantee, by virtue of a biologico-moral responsibility lasting through the entire period of the children's education): the Mother, with her negative image of 'nervous woman,' constituted the most visible form of this hysterization" (*Sexuality* 104). Although Foucault never mentions Faulkner, it would be difficult to describe more acutely the dilemma of Mrs. Compson.

young girl's muddy drawers has the entire text in thrall. The sign of her coming menses commands the attention of everyone (writer, characters, reader), as though the monthly behavior of this particular organ, by some synecdochic madness, signaled the masterplot of every female drama.[10] Such bodily notation is energized by the brothers' affective investment to be sure, but more profoundly shaped according to a cultural trope that equates menstruation with death, leakage, and engulfment: the woman's all-threatening otherness.

These last two portraits support Foucault's claim that sexuality has been the essential element in Western female identity: sexuality "as that which by itself constitutes woman's body, ordering it wholly in terms of the functions of reproduction and keeping it in constant agitation through the effects of that very function" (*Sexuality* 153). Patriarchal insistence upon mastering female sexuality shapes a discursive practice in which women enter the male gaze only as creatures of their own bodies. The culture-constructed clock they follow in Faulknerian narrative (as in most Western narrative) is the clock of their sex-coded bodies: virginity, menstruation, intercourse, childbearing, menopause, sexless old age. Given this representational founding of women's identity upon their sexual liabilities/possibilities, it follows that surveillance, judgment, and the need to make them confess are the narrative activities that accompany their moves. Women are the heart of the mystery – a mystery wrought into their material being, a mystery that veils as it models male mastery. We as readers have access to them as lovingly and/or unforgivingly charted bodies, involuntarily wreaking misery upon both their men and themselves through their inability to affirm or escape this ideological frame.

Finally, social norms are most massively and painfully imposed upon bodies in this novel within the ideologeme of *home*. "One day we should show," Foucault writes, "how intra-familial relations, essentially in the parents–children cell, have become 'disciplined,' absorbing since the classical age external schemata . . . which have made the family the privileged locus of emergence for the disciplinary question of the normal and the abnormal" (*Discipline* 215–16). Home is the baleful magnet that Benjy revolves around, that Jason returns to (with pounding head) for his daily lunch, that Mrs. Compson suffers in the name of, that Caddy cannot forgive herself for betraying, that is systematically driving her daughter Quentin crazy. Home (despite its remaining a totem concept for

---

[10] Thomas Laqueur writes of the extraordinary hold that the activity of menstruation has exercised upon the Western male imagination: "The silent workings of a tiny organ weighing on the average seven grams in humans, some two to four centimeters long, and the swelling and subsequent rupture of the follicles within it, came to represent synecdochically what it was to be a woman" (28).

all the Compsons) is a misnomer for a prisonlike space in which the warring and undomesticated injunctions of the larger culture are not only not kept at bay but focused for maximum injury: where racial and gender abuse is released every day, where bogus checks are sadistically burned and stolen money is restolen, where meals are the site of fierce generational attack. Home is where the cacophonies of the culture scream loudest, where its most destructive norms effectively seize upon subjective bodies. (Ostensibly the reverse of Parchman and Jackson – those overt sites of enforced training – home acts in early Faulkner as more nearly their equivalent: a space of inescapable subject (de)formation.) It is where this text most registers the body as "the inscribed surface of events (traced by language and dissolved by ideas), the locus of a dissociated Self (adopting the illusion of a substantial unity), and a volume in perpetual disintegration" (Foucault, "Nietzsche" 148): the locus, indeed, of sound and fury.

Bodies within this novel submit in a myriad deforming ways to the behavioral codes of the larger culture. At the level of Faulkner's story there is no escape. At the level of his form, however, and especially in the deployment of narrative voice, this text enacts upon the reader its subversive – and Modernist – countermoves. *The Sound and the Fury* refuses to conduct the business of the novel-as-institution: to pass on to the reader, within the compass of a coherent narrative voice, the wisdom gleaned from a subjective selection and harnessing of cultural codes. Instead, all ideological assertions in this novel (insofar as they must move through the filter of conflicting narrative voices) shatter. *The Sound and the Fury* unforgettably produces the static of voices competing against – and even more within – each other. Ideology emerges through such double-voiced cacophony not as a subjectively empowering set of beliefs and behaviors but (*pace* Althusser) as a disabling interference: as what separates characters in the very moment that it yokes them together.

"The speaking person in the novel is always, to one degree or another, an *ideologue,* and his words are always *ideologemes.* A particular language in a novel is always a particular way of viewing the world, one that strives for a social significance" (Bakhtin 333). In *The Sound and the Fury* such striving for larger ideological validity – as in the declaiming of Mr. Compson, Mrs. Compson, and Jason (three who know, who would instruct others) – only guarantees disaster. No one's words take on general authority; no one's words manage to retain their "original" charge. Phrases become slippery, lose their pedagogic import as they get revoiced (Mr. Compson's consolatory "temporary" becomes Quentin's suicidal "temporary"). Although all are taught, trained within an inch of their life, none is educated. No one's spirit has been led out by the words of another into larger life. No discourse succeeds in colonizing any other discourse and establishing itself as a norm for subjectivity.[11]

By beginning with Benjy's narrative voice, Faulkner seems to be seeking a Barthesian *écriture degré zéro*: writing without *parti pris*, free of social orientation.[12] Benjy's voice fails to understand, and through him we (especially as first readers) arduously suspend the grids of our own conditioned understanding. We teeter on the verge of what feels like a noncultural space. It is as though (in an essential Modernist paradigm) we were being de-ideologized, stripped of our habitual sense-making tropes (this is why so many readers put the book down after a few pages). As though beyond the inflections of class, race, and gender, Benjy's unmapped voice, without the hint of a project, seems to register within the reader with a kind of pre-Oedipal immediacy, as the voice of the infant prior to entry into the Symbolic order.

Yet his unspoken voice serves also as the recording frame for a whole range of spoken vernacular voices, voices saturated in the cultural code (shared by parents and children, Compson whites and blacks, alike) of "what everyone knows," the common domestic language of cajolery, threat, and promise. Benjy lives silently amid such language; "surrounded by words he cannot use, he is used by words" (Morris 136). Such incapacitation notwithstanding, insofar as this chapter has its way with us (and I have never known a lover of the novel who did not prize the first chapter), it seduces through the twin pleasures of childhood imaginatively revisited (the play, pastoral even when painful, of children's vernacular voices) and infancy radically invented (the project-free poetry of Benjy's own voice). I return to the Modernist implications of such seduction later.

Quentin's voice lacks innocence. He is nothing if not inscribed in the

---

[11] Ross briefly but aptly characterizes the violence rather than resolution that occurs in Faulknerian dialogic encounters (*Fiction* 81–3), concluding that "Dialogue in Faulkner becomes emblematic of all differentiation" (83). I explore more fully in the Conclusion the ways in which *The Sound and the Fury* owes its canonical status to its apparent refusal of ideological resolution.

[12] Barthes claims that "when poetic language radically questions Nature by virtue of its very structure, without any resort to the content of the discourse and without falling back on some ideology, there is no mode of writing left, there are only styles, thanks to which man turns his back on society and confronts the world of objects without going through any of the forms of History of social life" (*Reader* 60–1). He is here describing the legacy of French Symbolism, precisely the legacy that nourishes the early Faulkner's Modernist conviction that Art abides only in the sacral realm of the unsocialized, the unspeakable. Such a legacy leads directly to Benjy. Bakhtin discusses the verbal role of the fool and the rogue in terms equally pertinent to Faulkner's strategy in creating Benjy: "All the old links between a man and his act, between an event and those who participate in it, fall apart. A sharp gap now opens between a man and the external position he occupies – his rank, his public worth, his social class" (408).

Symbolic; its commands and references careen crazily within his head. At best he manages a feeble rewriting of its injunctions. He inwardly cites the sayings of Saint Francis and Christ in such a way as to reverse their import: Saint Francis who had it wrong since he never had a sister, Christ who was worn down by the wheels of a watch rather than crucified, who "not for me died not." In like manner Hell may genuinely menace Quentin yet not without his creatively reversing its force. Heaven becomes, in Quentin's private eschatology, the place where only the flatirons will go when He says Rise. Quentin himself will remain satisfyingly undiscovered, ensconced with Caddy in his reconstructed corner of the underworld.

These metaphysical maneuvers hardly liberate. Whatever his revisionary schemes, Quentin descends to his death a prisoner of his once-aristocratic Southern culture's codes: guilt-ridden by his own desires, incapable of turning his father's skepticism into a life-philosophy, deafened by the silent, exterior voices that have penetrated within and indicted him for being an inadequate son, brother, and gentleman.[13] If a coherent voice is a protective skin – protective because it subjectifies and makes instrumental some of the sayings of a culture while resisting others – Benjy and Quentin emerge naked. In their different ways they have no filters, can do little but suffer or die. Quentin's silent voice compels us, like Benjy's, in its radical undefensiveness. Faulkner proposes through such candor a uniquely intimate relationship with the reader. Benjy's lack of project and Quentin's desperately confused project disarm our own project, and we enter – as it were, naked ourselves – into the pathos of their lives.[14]

This intimacy abruptly ends with Jason's opening words. There ideology reconstitutes itself, registering as the exclusionary weapon and armor of one who thinks he knows. (His recurrent "I says" occupies the

[13] Cf. Ross: "Like a listener, Quentin allows others' words to formulate his subjective life for him, passively absorbing experiences that he should actively engage in" (*Fiction* 181).

[14] This is a moment in my argument when the inclusive "we" must be problematized. Gender, race, and the class equivalent of educational training affect our response to these two narrative voices. Broadly read, college-educated white males are likely to respond most passionately. White females with the same other characteristics also seem to participate in this reading experience (although a feminist orientation increasingly complicates the emotional agenda of Quentin's chapter). But I have rarely known a black student to enter uncritically into this text's morass of white male subjectivity. And no reader without a college education is likely to penetrate Faulkner's daunting linguistic experiments in order to take to heart the models of subjectivity so powerfully offered here. (The categories I have just sketched are of course cultural positions, not biological essences, and any reader *could* occupy any position.) I speculate later, and especially in the Conclusion, on the particular audience of *The Sound and the Fury*. I should note here, though, that the binary opposition between High Art and popular culture operative in this rhetorical strategy is of course characteristic of Modernism itself. Indeed, the desire for a project-free plot and the strenuous refusal of a broadly shared rhetoric not only dominate the fiction of Proust, Joyce, and Woolf (to name three of Faulkner's greatest near-contemporaries) but constitute perhaps the central "project" of that fiction.

least reflective of present moments. Such a rhetorical structure not only isolates him from his grammatically correct family but gives a class coloration to his search to repress the unfolding of time itself, a project self-evidently doomed in this novel.) Blindly imbued with the binary prejudices of his culture, Jason offends with a trenchancy made all the sharper by the reader's earlier exposure to Benjy and Quentin. Moreover, he seems to speak directly to us, virtually daring us to be for or against him. He continues thus the futile family trait of seeking through voice alone, through verbal defiance, to shape his world by aggressively *naming* it. Jason's need to polarize is uncontrollable. Women, blacks, and Jews converge in his discursive world as cunning figures of betrayal: essentialized, other, subhuman, yet diabolically capable of thwarting him. We join this group. Ironizing our relation to him (seeing around him), we reassert our suspended values, pit our subjectivity against his, and come down on Jason in what is a much simpler reading experience.

Or do we? The irrepressible energy of Jason compels even as if offends. Beneath his obvious role as tyrant-about-to-become-scapegoat, he elicits (though rarely for first-time readers) a throb of complicity with his plight. In him Faulkner has joined a cluster of repulsive clichés, preparing for the scapegoating that follows: the poetic justice (foiling Jason) that the plot must substitute for the authentic justice (redeeming Benjy's and Quentin's and Caddy's pain) that it cannot deliver. At the same time Faulkner's text is genuinely under the spell of Jason's discourse. His utterance dominates the last half of the book. His biting humor, bracing and vicious in about equal proportions, leavens a portrait that is resolutely mean-spirited. Yet Jason's is the only adult voice, the only grown-up subjectivity, that Faulkner delights in unfolding in a sustained way in this book. Is this what he imagines you have to sound like if you are white, adult, and wish to survive in that family?

In the last chapter the vocal strategy shifts yet again, the new arrangements of syntax, vocabulary, and distance requiring yet another readerly orientation. The descriptions of Dilsey and of the Reverend Shegog proceed with a deliberateness of pace, celebratory focus, and polysyl-labic/Latinate dignity unthinkable, elsewhere. Shegog is even entrusted with the narrative itself. Virtue (black) may now emerge; skulduggery (white) gets some comeuppance. These moves generate a welcome measure of catharsis. Yet, despite the gratifying sense of space, time, and narrative logic once more in conventional order, the conclusion of the novel is scrupulously inconclusive. It remains now to delineate some of the social roles and ideological positions implied by such insistent non-resolution.

This novel, usually selected as his favorite as Faulkner reflected back upon his career, seems most purely to emancipate itself from his surrounding culture's traditional pieties, pieties less of theme than of procedure. Like that of *As I Lay Dying,* the narratorial strategy of *The Sound and the Fury* manages to exploit yet remain unco-opted by the conventional, the vernacular, and what would later become Faulkner's high rhetorical voice. Eluding the social/intellectual assumptions and allegiances associated with each of these discourses when hegemonic – the sober, commonsensical reliability of Western realism, the cozy familiarity of Southern rhythms and reference, the authority of oratorical declamation – Faulkner's texts of 1929 and 1930 move by way of startlingly vivid idiolects, and permit seemingly unmediated access to psyches damaged beyond repair, articulated each within its own virginal language and offered to us as an all-absorbing spectacle. To be sure, Faulkner cites generously the spoken country rhythms of his figures, yet he engenders for Benjy and Quentin's silent self-communing – and thus for the reader's relation to them – a language all its own: as if no one before him had ever heard the voice of solitary consciousness.[15]

Faulkner himself seems to have disappeared.[16] Not only does he successfully "ventriloquate" (Bakhtin 299) the inner speech of his three narrators, but that speech (for the first two of the narrators) seems to float free of secure ideological alignment – of "what everyone knows." It is as though Faulkner found his way into that inchoate portion of his characters' being that is prior (though not immune) to ideological shaping. (Thus I speak of these texts as spectacle. Even though *As I Lay Dying* unfolds a story saturated in ideological givens, we remain drawn to these figures as stricken consciousnesses, arrested in astonishment and offered to our gaze.)[17]

In *Light in August* Faulkner was already abandoning such a narrative procedure, and by the time of *Absalom, Absalom!* and its spinoff *Pylon* he had found his way into (or been found by) a narrative voice whose syntax and assumptions he might richly modify over the next twenty-five years

[15] This sense of a purely private language is of course illusory: "Private property, in the domain of language, does not exist: everything is socialized. The verbal exchange, like every form of human relation, requires at least two interlocutors; an idiolect, in the final analysis, therefore can only be a slightly perverse fiction" (Roman Jakobson, *Essai de linguistique générale,* cited by Nancy Miller, 351). Slightly perverse, perhaps, but it takes remarkable writing to generate such a fiction.

[16] Of course his seeming to disappear is a powerful way of being present. Bakhtin writes: "Behind the narrator's story we read a second story, the author's story; he is the one who tells us how the narrator tells stories, and also tells us about the narrator himself. We acutely sense two levels at each moment in the story; one, the level of the narrator, a belief system filled with his objects, meanings and emotional expressions, and the other, the level of the author, who speaks (albeit in a refracted way) by means of this story and through this story" (314). My point is that in the fiction that begins with *Pylon* the author is rhetorically present in a characteristically different, overt way.

[17] For a full discussion of astonishment as form and theme in *As I Lay Dying,* see Bleikasten's chapter in *The Ink of Melancholy.*

but would never wholly abandon. This later voice is of course the one we call "Faulkner," and once we concede that it is more capacious than any summary of it suggests, it remains recognizably a *voice:* "Faulkner." Unlike the writer of those two texts of 1929 and 1930, "Faulkner" (I insist on the quotation marks: I am speaking of an identity limned by a certain deployment of language) is openly immersed in ideology – his vocal performance cries out its range of reference, its orientations, its difference from the characters it produces – and thus a later text like *Go Down, Moses* (to take a successful example) continuously suggests its ideological frame as a kind of epiphenomenon of the narrative voice itself.[18]

The necessary corollary, of course, is that, despite their apparent refusal of cultural alignment, the produced voices of the texts of 1929 and 1930 very much imply an ideological orientation as well. An aesthetics of shock, a fiction of interior spectacle unmoored from conventional plot-maneuvers, a focus on outraged individual consciousness, a lyrical narrative voice that lives in the moment-by-moment poetry of the deracinated ego: these are recognizable attributes of the alienated high-culture text of Western Modernism. Premonitions in the work of Conrad and Anderson, theoretical underpinnings in the work of Freud, substantial parallels in the work of Joyce and Woolf could easily be adduced. Their texts also exoticize (render as strange and unavailing spectacle) the local culture from which their materials originally derived. Readers of such texts enact many subjective roles, but a central one is their performance (while experiencing Benjy and Quentin's voices) of their own authentic and privileged alienation, their sense of individual identity as fractured, in shards, paralyzingly at odds with the directives of any hegemonic ideology.[19]

The Sound and the Fury's Modernist art of trauma and discontinuity holds us not least – we, its college-trained, "elite" readership – by touching the infinitely precious, socially inconsolable Benjy deep within us, that inner core of our being that we insist upon as unteachable and that (so we want to believe) exquisitely fails to come to terms with the discur-

---

18 Stonum reads the increasingly overt ideological alignment in Faulkner's later work more sympathetically than I do: "The subject there is always already in a world and constituted by his relation to it" (154). I agree, but I believe as well that as Faulkner's cultural allegiances took on weight and conscious precision, his rhetoric became more hospitable to traditional discourses and began to lose its power to disturb.
19 The classic account of Modernist texts' refusal of ideological coordinates – indeed, their rejection of the norms of representation itself – is Lukacs's "Ideology of Modernism." Jameson shares many of Lukacs's strictures, but he also perceptively acknowledges the Utopian energy that fuels these experimental departures from habitual (read: hegemonic) description and response (*Political* 219–38). Moreland (in the first full-length study of Faulkner's relation to Modernism) tends to read that relation as monolithically impoverishing. For him, the texts after *Absalom, Absalom!* indicate a way out, not a collapse.

sive practices that enable our subjectivity. As its readers we seem to transcend our own ideological harness, abandoning our mundane complicities for the rarefied poetics – satisfyingly tragic – of idiocy and suicide. A text whose voices thus produce in us a sense of inexpressible loss, of that pre-Oedipal wholeness which social life necessarily despoils, seduces by its very illusion of spent freedom. Such perfection could be varied and extended in *As I Lay Dying* but not otherwise repeated. Faulkner completes here "the change from a 'lyric' persona dichotomously separated from others, as in the early poems, to a writer who knows that his door had to be opened" (Wadlington 98). Henceforth Faulknerian voice would typically live immersed, as Faulknerian body always lives immersed, within the generations-thickened weave of the Symbolic. I turn to *Light in August*.

&

> Then Grimm too sprang back, flinging behind him the bloody butcher knife. "Now you'll let white women alone, even in hell," he said. But the man on the floor had not moved. He just lay there, with his eyes open and empty of everything save consciousness, and with something, a shadow, about his mouth. For a long moment he looked up at them with peaceful and unfathomable and unbearable eyes. Then his face, body, all, seemed to collapse, to fall in upon itself, and from out the slashed garments about his hips and loins the pent black blood seemed to rush like a released breath. (512–13)

The elided castration of *The Sound and the Fury* bursts upon us here; *Light in August* has been preparing this moment for hundreds of pages. Joe Christmas's body an enigma, concealing a racial identity he can never be sure of, he moves through his life obsessed with the blood (his own and others) that he can make flow. There can be no peace until he has finally summoned and spilled all the liquid in him. Percy Grimm gives him the literal release he has been seeking.

Grimm gives it, yet we see Grimm as merely the last in a series of men and women whose encounter with Christmas erupts as a bloodletting. There is no body in Faulkner's work more patiently depicted, none more variously abused, than Joe Christmas's. Through Christmas's overcharted body Faulkner renders somatic the crossed circuitry of a culture. The dietitian, Doc Hines, and McEachern each deform his consciousness by co-opting – making alien to Christmas himself – some exposable region of his body, marking it out as the suffocating, toothpaste site of intercourse, as the "face . . . eyes and hair" (148) of Nigger, as the chastisable mirror in which Calvinist fanaticism can play out its fantasies of omnipotence and revenge. Later, with Bobbie and with Joanna, he again encounters not so much single human beings as ideological sites in which certain stances toward the body appear incarnate: Bobbie who is never his woman alone but always brings with her Max, Mame, and the numberless men she has professionally slept with; Joanna whose alternately frigid or writhing body carries within it the converging neuroses of four generations of male Burden Calvinism. His body and those of the women he loves lose their singularity, become sites that bespeak nothing so much as the tracking of those who have been there before.

"Memory believes before knowing remembers" (111). The body in *Light in August* is a memory trap, stained sooner and longer than the mind, incapable of forgetting its traces. In Christmas's body especially we see the accumulation of this damage, and in his dealings with that damaged body we see as well a corresponding counterurge: the urge to master (by bodily absorption or transcendent escape) those unwanted traces. This urge is so often associated with Faulkner's males as to appear a certain dimension of their masculinity itself. Donald Mahon, Bayard, Quentin, Joe Christmas, the reporter of *Pylon*, Sutpen and Charles Bon's son, Harry Wilbourne, Labove and Mink, Rider, Chick in *Intruder:* these figures share what Faulkner calls in *A Fable* "a passion, an immolation, an apotheosis" (153). They move single-mindedly toward (or remain arrested within) some scene of incandescent disaster, a scene in which normal bodily activities are suspended. Such men cease to eat and to sleep (women surrounding them often press both these activities upon them). They have entered instead upon a collision course with that outside them (or within) which they most fear and desire, thus bringing on a conflagration, an essentializing agon of the self.[20]

This agon is always dangerous and usually fatal. The male seeks to center on his essential identity by refusing to truck with his passion, to be deflected into civility. He would remain unadulterate, untamed. The ordeal of self-focusing is insistently punitive, as if for Faulkner the entry into male selfhood were inseparable from aggression against the body, disgust with its requirements. Eating, sleeping, and talking become (female) distractions. The promiscuous body must suffer, risking destruction to attest to its submission to the soul's integrity. Is it too much to say that this male quest for immolation is at heart a lust for virginity, a desire to transform (by discipline or abuse) one's own motley body into a self-owned space that would fantastically command or refuse all trace of the Other? For the poetics of virginity is thoroughly male: a boundary-sustained immaculateness, an anxiety bordering on hysteria at the thought of transgression, an insistence on culturally rewriting the body's natural propensities.[21]

Light in August is Faulkner's text that (after *As I Lay Dying*) plays out

---

[20] Bleikasten (in "Figures de la mort") explores as a kind of death urge the need of the Faulknerian hero to rise into transcendence. His argument, although not gender-focused, is related to mine in its emphasis upon this "heroic" passion.

[21] See the second half of Chapter 1 for fuller discussion of the construction of gender within both Faulkner's texts and the broader history of Western representational habits.

the male lust for virginity in the most explosive physical terms. On the one hand, the individual body unforgivingly registers every last mark of the larger culture's mapping. On the other, the individual body is the untamable, uncrossable border of selfhood, *"the citadel of the central I-Am's private own"* (*AA* 173). Simultaneously adulterate in fact and virginal in need, the body emerges as an intolerable contradiction that fuels this novel's acts of violence.

"Something is going to happen to me" (114), Joe thinks to himself just before murdering Joanna, and the phrasing is suggestive. The body, overloaded with cultural tracking, is about to explode from abuse. Yet this tracking has remained unconscious, securing for Joe no useful mental orientation. Still innocent, he has "learned" nothing, not even that he is on the edge of murder. Further, Joanna is hardly in this scene. The phrasing tells us that the coming act will be reflexive, bubbling up within Joe himself. So highly wrought is the discontinuity between his conscious mind and his offended body, so contradictory his mix of virginity and adulteration, that the social bearing of his act, its ideological resonance, remains hidden from him.[22]

Finally, the phrasing inserts us, as readers, into a subjective space of considerable anxiety: seconds before an explosion is to occur, within the body/mind of one who will undergo this explosion without understanding it. Faulkner has Temple Drake and Harry Wilbourne think exactly the same thought in *Sanctuary* and *The Wild Palms*. In each case he places us uncomfortably near an embodied psyche under unbearable pressure. As opposed to the more pedagogic crises of Faulkner's later fiction – scenes where Gavin or Ratliff or Chick finds the normative formulas to pacify the urgency – these are scenes in which the character's unframed disorientation passes directly into a disquieted reader. At such heightened transferential moments no one's sense-making framework operates to contain the unleashed energy; we become immersed in a cosmos no one owns.

Before moving to the representation of the female body in *Light in August* I want to reemphasize the gender dimension of this "syndrome." It is very much a male complex, a sequence whose emotional force is founded on loss of mastery, orientational collapse. Within this economy women, by contrast, are figured as less menaced by the adulterations of daily life, and they are correspondingly less intent upon either virginity (the refusal of all alien scripts) or mastery (the conversion of every externally imposed trace into a signature of the self). Faulkner's women, it

---

22 Duvall ("Critics"), following Meats, spells out the ideological dimension of our repeating the town's judgment by referring to Joe's act as a murder. Faulkner deliberately leaves the physical event shrouded, so that its ideological repercussions (its alignment within a racist discourse) can operate more visibly.

turns out, do indeed share a gender scripting of nonvirginity ("Because it means less to women, Father said" [SF 89]). Drawing on a discursive practice at least as old as Milton and as recent as Freud, Faulkner imagines them to be born adulterate (Liliths at their core), beneficently so if not tampered with by the constrictive anxiety of their fathers, brothers, and lovers. Such a frame allows us now to discuss Faulkner's representation of Lena Grove and Joanna Burden.

Lena Grove is as immersed within a cyclical schema of nature as Joanna Burden has been uprooted from such a schema and plunged instead into a linear (multigenerational) schema of culture.[23] Lena's "natural" rendering answers to the male culture's normative model of woman as, precisely, the one beneath and beyond humanity (which in its cultural capacity for outrage – for values held deeply enough to *be* outraged, for souls irreducible to bodily realities – is recognizably male), the one who through her womb touches down to the ground of nature, a sanctuary beyond ideological tracking. All males in this novel who graze against her penetrate the surface alone of her being; deeper down she is in uninterrupted communion with her burgeoning infant. The cultural trope operative here underwrites Lena's appeal by effacing her desire. Thus "unburdened," Lena yields herself fully to the needs of maternity. Faulkner's imaginative investment in "the sanctity of motherhood" explains not only the relative unimportance of Burch or Bunch to her (her untroubled focus is elsewhere). It sheds light as well on the corrosive counterportrait of Joanna Burden, a woman incapable of sustaining her "natural" identity, producing an infant, and thus achieving that deep, quiet center supposedly beyond ideology.

Yet the cumulative deformities wrought into Joanna fascinate Faulkner, and for pages on end she achieves what no one else in this text can achieve: she takes our attention away from Joe Christmas when he is likewise on scene. Seeking to clock the periodicity of her phases, to bring her unpredictable energies into the narrative coherence of a male taxonomy, Faulkner so loses sight of Joe's own peculiarities that he writes: "His [Joe's] own life, for all its anonymous promiscuity, had been conventional enough, as a life of healthy and normal sin usually is" (285). No reader of the previous 175 pages – the dietitian, the young black girl, Bobbie, the prostitute Joe almost murders – should accept the normative blandness of this summary sentence, but we let it pass, so caught up are we (along with Faulkner) with the eccentricities of Joanna's sexual liabilities/possibilities.

Sexuality is hystericized here. We are not far from that repellent defini-

---

23 Bleikasten explores fully the novel's contradictory views of women, as polarized into Lena and Joanna (*The Ink of Melancholy*).

tion of women in *Mosquitoes* as "merely articulated genital organs" (199). Now, though, the woman's "natural" identity has been trucked with by her patriarchal fathers, denaturing her into a figure half-Medusa, half-victim. Faulkner certainly gives us a compelling analysis of a woman's sexual energies deformed by her forbears – so imbued with their Calvinistic harshness that her escape into womanhood can only be through the counterextreme of nymphomania. Yet he gives us little other than this analysis. Joanna emerges in the text as a sort of appalling case study, her sexual instincts and ideological convictions inextricably contaminating each other. Of a Joanna as something more than the battleground where these forces neurotically clash, a Joanna who is more than the spectacular narrative of the culture-nature battle raging through her body, Faulkner tells us very little. A victim as much as Joe is, she is only a victim. Her creator can relate the essence, but not the accidents, of her life. This is so, one surmises, because the tropes through which Faulkner produces Joanna essentialize her. They limn her as, precisely, the creature of her own body. It follows (all too smoothly) that to deflect her from her bodily "requirements" is to unleash the narrative extremes of frigidity, nymphomania, and suicidal resentment.

If we move from the deployment of the body to the range of narrative voices in *Light in August,* we find not the sharp-edged juxtaposition of *The Sound and the Fury*'s discontinuous chapters, but instead the richer medley of voices that make up a town. A community, not a family, occupies the canvas here; and characters of considerable variety – Armstids, Mooney, Burch, Bunch, the Burdens, the Hightowers, the Hineses, a traveling salesman – are permitted to enter and speak/narrate in their own voices.[24] This novel manages imaginatively both to give voice to the outsider and to underwrite the value of common vocabulary, convictions, and procedures, without scanting the murderous scapegoating that can be the price of such a hegemonic discursive practice.

Faulkner so generously entrusts the vernacular voice to focalize his narrative here that the wonder is how the novel escapes becoming a prisoner of the subjective norms often implicit in that voice. Byron Bunch performs this role most often (remove him from *Light in August* and its narrative/normative coherence would collapse as swiftly as its story would collapse without Joe or Lena). Doc Hines and his wife in chapter 16, the traveling salesman in this last chapter, and unidentified rural voices elsewhere are likewise critical to the text's unfolding as a

[24] Ross rightly notes the ubiquity of talk in this novel, in its full range from unspoken and unconscious to communal and gossipy: "The town's attitudes are figured in its talk, in a communal voice that carries with it the quality of something ineffably given, something literally 'in the air,' as integral a part of the environment as the buildings, roads, businesses, vehicles, and other trappings of communal life" (*Fiction* 52).

vernacular experience. An irreplaceable passage like the following comes
to us from an anonymous Mottstown narrator:

> . . . until Halliday saw him and ran up and grabbed him and said, "Aint
> your name Christmas?" and the nigger said that it was. He never denied
> it. He never did anything. He never acted like either a nigger or a white
> man. That was it. That was what made the folks so mad. For him to be a
> murderer and all dressed up and walking the town like he dared them to
> touch him, when he ought to have been skulking and hiding in the
> woods, muddy and dirty and running. It was like he never even knew he
> was a murderer, let alone a nigger too. (386)

This voice (which narrates the twelve pages that follow my quotation as
well) conveys the community's racial brutality with a force that no liberal
voice could achieve through indignation. You have to know in your
bones (that is, to have been taught since infancy) what a "nigger" is –
how he moves, dresses, acts, schemes: the whole cluster of tropes that
textually constitute him – to narrate like this. The town speaks its cate-
gorical judgment in such a passage; it produces unhesitatingly its version
of the black body. Such narration is so cleanly achieved that liberal white
readers (such as myself) momentarily identify with its vigorous racism,
voice it within ourselves and recognize it as real, even as (recoiling) we
immediately repudiate that identification.[25]

Light in August best escapes the limitation of such vernacular norms by
its invention of other and quite different narrative voices: for example, the
lyrical voice that produces Lena for us, or Hightower's musing and
learned voice, or – perhaps most arrestingly – the voice that gives us Joe
Christmas's childhood and adolescence (chapters 6–10). The following
passage comes from chapter 10:

> Perhaps he heard only the long wind, as, swinging his hand as though it
> still clutched the chair, he sprang forward upon the two men. Very
> likely he did not even know that they were already moving toward him.
> Because with something of the exaltation of his adopted father he
> sprang full and of his own accord into the stranger's fist. Perhaps he did
> not feel either blow, though the stranger struck him twice in the face
> before he reached the floor, where like the man whom he had struck
> down, he lay upon his back, quite still. But he was not out because his
> eyes were still open, looking quietly up at them. There was nothing in
> his eyes at all, no pain, no surprise. But apparently he could not move;
> he just lay there with a profoundly contemplative expression. . . .
> Lying peaceful and still Joe watched the stranger lean down and lift his

---

[25] Wadlington, exploring our enactment of the roles scripted in Faulkner's texts by sub-
vocally sounding them, makes a kindred point about Jason's compelling voice: "When
we despise Jason, it is nevertheless the Jason we are performing and helping to give
imaginative life; in a sense it is our voice speaking the 'Jason script' that we despise"
(91).

head from the floor and strike him again in the face, this time with a short slashing blow. After a moment he licked his lip a little, somewhat as a child might lick a cooking spoon. He watched the stranger's hand go back. . . . (240–1)

To compare this beating with that narrated in the vernacular is to see what a different kind of intensity Faulkner can generate out of an unknowing voice.[26] This scene is hallucinatorily clear yet ideologically unframed – to Joe, to the narrator, to the reader. (Ideology is of course at the heart of this encounter, but vertiginously rather than clarifyingly so: crossed ideological circuitry releases the violence, no encompassing paradigm is there to recontain it.) "Something is going to happen to me" the reader thus invaded might feel. Time goes awry, space begins to loom, the body hurls into the Other and finds itself on the floor, conscious, lucid, immobile. Thought and matter become unhinged as this sentient being that is Joe Christmas encounters shock. The narrative voice's repeated "perhaps" loosens the action from any secure interpretive frame, producing the sense that we are undergoing an event before it has been processed into significance. The narrative voice in these "formative" chapters renders a young man's embodied psyche in such a way as seemingly to elude interpretational focus even as it never wavers from the moment-by-moment phenomenon of Joe Christmas's vulnerability.

I have of course been interpreting it all the time – as an experience of psychic–somatic exposure outside the knowing range of the vernacular voice – and the discursive practice Faulkner draws on here is the defamiliarization technique of Modernism itself. This technique, so crucial to the shock effects of Faulkner's great scenes of unprocessed outrage, is generalized by Roland Barthes as follows: "The pure and simple 'representation' of the 'real,' the naked account of 'what is' . . . thus proves to resist meaning; such resistance reconfirms the great mythic opposition between the *vécu* . . . and the intelligible; we have only to recall how, in the ideology of our time, the obsessional evocation of the 'concrete' . . . is always staged as an aggressive arm against meaning, as though . . . what lives is structurally incapable of carrying a meaning – and vice versa." ("L'effet du réel," as cited in Jameson, *Political* 233).

Barthes's formulation shrewdly identifies the space between Faulkner's Modernist practice and our Postmodernist perspective upon it. Whereas

26 *As I Lay Dying* embarrasses this generalization about the vernacular voice as comfortably inscribed within the Symbolic order. Consider Cash responding to Darl: "But I aint so sho that ere a man has the right to say what is crazy and what aint. It's like there was a fellow in every man that's done a-past the sanity or the insanity . . ." (228). Indeed, *Light in August*'s vernacular voices (especially Mrs. Hines's and Byron's near the end) are capable at times of remarkable freshness and surprise. The vernacular voice in later texts, however, tends to be cushioned more securely within the commonplace tropes of the regional culture.

Faulkner's experimental early novels reveal a desire to undo ideology – to generate scenes that resist ideological coherence or that reveal ideological vertigo, scenes whose brute power seems to touch down on the real itself (a domain deeper than ideology) – we may now see that posture as itself invested in Modernist ideology. In this current Postmodernist view, ideological inflections do not superficially distort some deeper reality; one does not dig beneath them to a nonideological core. More disturbingly, they create the real. "Power produces," Foucault claims in an argument that takes this insight to its limit, "it produces reality; it produces domains of objects and rituals of truth. The individual and the knowledge that may be gained of him belong to this production" (*Discipline* 194). If this is so, then the most elusive practices (and therefore the ones most in need of identification) may be less those that Faulkner's texts challenge than those with which his work (in its very act of challenge) is unknowingly complicit.

With this aim in mind I have sought to identify some of the culture's racial and gender tropes that "produce [the body's] reality" in *Light in August,* and I turn in a moment to a kindred exploration of the problematics of voice in *Absalom, Absalom!* Before leaving this text, though, I would like to claim for it a unique capaciousness within the Faulknerian oeuvre. In it he sounded his meanings in the richest, most dialogic range of voices, none of them escaping ideological coordinates, all of them mutually implicated in each other. Less a tour de force than *The Sound and the Fury* or *As I Lay Dying,* it is Faulkner's first major exploration of his own territory: its Modernist estrangement everywhere counterpointed by its colloquial power. An exploration, yes, but also a kind of finale. The writer who emerges three years later in *Pylon* has found his "own" gorgeously excessive voice, and for better and worse he will only intermittently thereafter lose it.[27]

> And then in the attic, the cot moved there, the few garments (the rags of the silk and the broadcloth in which he had arrived, the harsh jeans and homespun which the two women bought and made for him, he accepting them with no thanks, no comment, accepting his garret room in the same way, asking for and making no alteration in its spartan arrange-

---

27 It should be clear that I am not claiming that Faulkner "found his voice" only in 1935, in *Pylon.* Rather, I am arguing that Faulkner's extraordinary novels written between 1929 and 1932 establish his identity without settling into a (more or less unified) gorgeous rhetoric that we will henceforth think of as "Faulkner." That rhetoric, of course, is not monolithic; and texts such as the Snopes trilogy and *The Reivers* are written largely in another, more vernacular discourse. But to move from *Pylon* to *A Fable* – by way of *Absalom, Go Down Moses, Intruder,* and *Requiem* – is to encounter a rhetoric whose syntactic intricacy and polysyllabic intensity mount toward a discursive insistence almost beyond bearing.

ments that they knew of until that second year when he was fourteen and one of them, Clytie or Judith, found hidden beneath his mattress the shard of broken mirror: and who to know what hours of amazed and tearless grief he might have spent before it, examining himself in the delicate and outgrown tatters in which he perhaps could not even re-member himself, with quiet and incredulous incomprehension) hanging behind a curtain contrived of a piece of old carpet nailed across a corner. (*AA* 249–50)

The body's clothing in *Absalom, Absalom!* participates in a densely woven sign system, radiating a larger culture's network of religious and racial values. This poignant moment reveals Charles Bon's son caught incredulous between two such networks: his "silken . . . clothes, his delicate shirt and stockings and shoes" (247) that caress the body and delight in its possibilities, on the one hand, the "harsh jeans and home-spun" that cramp the body and testify to its need to be first covered and then put to work, on the other. In the former network the body is conceived as a pleasure zone – its pigment, its texture, its balletlike prowess so much potential for amoral delectation. In the latter, the body obtrudes to embarrass an austere soul that justifies itself by disciplining its wayward instrument.

Absalom, Absalom! tracks the body most powerfully by showing it as regulated by the norms of one culture while under the siege of another. The New Orleans of *Mosquitoes* has here become New Orleans jux-taposed against Jefferson, and this book negotiates a range of traumatic journeys from the one site to the other. Charles Etienne de St. Valery Bon, the tragic octoroon, Charles Bon himself: these are creatures of a New Orleans dispensation, irremediably exotic when on a Jefferson stage, and physically untransplantable. The body's character emerges in these failed graftings not as innate but as culturally produced. Physical proclivities inculcated in the first setting have become taboo in the second setting. The characters thus entrapped either wither or suicidally revolt rather than adapt.

In like manner Sutpen himself is somatically imagined as a mountain man, with a mountain man's race-free and class-free modes of physically engaging others. This body script lies like a palimpsest beneath Rosa's representation of him and his own self-reconception, waiting to reimpose itself. Deep within (beneath the willed change of voice, the adoption of a design), his body harbors a mountaineer's trust in physical strength alone, a mountaineer's indifference to color. Sutpen's blacks never learn English, neither does Charles Etienne's wife. This book is rife with a physico-cultural unadaptability that accompanies and belies its dizzying geographic shifts and narratorial double-jointedness. Quentin's inability to reroot himself at Harvard – his clothes are all wrong, Harvard is a

passive backdrop producing Shreve and a dormitory but little else –
underscores *Absalom's* insistence on placing its intransigent figures upon
multiple scenes and recording the anguish of their unavailing moves.

Their culturally shaped identity has already "taken"; its imprint is
deepest upon the body. No one better articulates this status of the body as
authentic register of the cultural imprinting that constitutes identity
(whatever contrary signals the mystified mind may insist on sending)
than Rosa Coldfield in Chapter 5. There she speaks of the touch of flesh
with flesh as a primordial and code-shattering impact: the encounter
between the body of the Other and that *"citadel of the central I-Am's private
own"* (173) which is one's own body. Yet, with the significant exception
of Rosa's encounter with Clytie, this text rarely depicts the career of the
body and its transgressed boundaries with such naked and disorienting
immediacy. Such transgressions are of course at the thematic heart of
Absalom, Absalom! I am concerned less with *récit* than with *discours*, however, and at this level of interaction – the relation between narrative voice
and reader, the way in which narrative voice produces body – all is
strenuously mediated.

The deployment of the body tends to be more specular and detached
than in *The Sound and the Fury* or *Light in August*. As readers we rarely
undergo the quasi-somatic unease of "Something is going to happen to
me." Instead, bodies are presented to us either elaborately clothed within
cultural sign systems or by way of self-conscious narratorial intervention.
Consider the metaphoric insistence of Ellen's physical career likened by
the narrator to a butterfly's transformations, or of Rosa in the chair
compared with a crucified child, or of Sutpen's face suggesting some
earlier "solitary furnace experience" (36), or of his body imagined as
something between the skin and the skeleton that somehow had gone
fluid and waste, or of the black figures recurrently seen as laughing
balloon faces. These elaborate similes tease the mind into flights of
thought by mediating the body, enmeshing it for our contemplation
within the highly wrought discourse of an indefatigable narrative voice.
The body in *Absalom, Absalom!* tends to emerge as a fascinating object
kept by the density of the narrator's rhetoric at a certain distance: a cameo
brilliantly displayed for us rather than unsettlingly projected within us.[28]

---

[28] I focus in this chapter on characters' bodies rather than narrators' bodies. A good
argument could be made (and by Wadlington has been made) that the "speaking reader"
(Wadlington's term) experiences as well the narrators' bodies (especially Rosa's and
Quentin's: spoken, fissured, doubled) through the narrators' extraordinary rhetorical
practice. Such an argument may do more justice to the reader's complex reception of
this novel's passionate outburst of language. I tend to read that outburst more skep-
tically, inasmuch as it draws for its authority (as Ross has shown) upon Southern
oratorical tradition. In any case, leaving aside the narrator bodies, the character bodies in
Absalom, Absalom! are produced in their own remarkable way and repay critical
attention.

Such display takes the form of tableaux, of scenes set out upon a stage. The narratorial voice of *Absalom, Absalom!* (especially when it is Mr. Compson's, or his as mediated by Quentin's or Shreve's) produces bodies in terms of culturally laden friezes:

> . . . a young man of a worldly elegance and assurance beyond his years, handsome, apparently wealthy and with for background the shadowy figure of a legal guardian rather than any parents – a personage who in the remote Mississippi of that time, must have appeared almost phoenix-like, full-sprung from no childhood, born of no bones nor dust anywhere – a man with an ease of manner and a swaggering gallant air in comparison with which Sutpen's pompous arrogance was clumsy bluff and Henry actually a hobble-de-hoy. Miss Rosa never saw him; this was a picture, an image. (90)

"A picture, an image": how richly *Absalom* produces these, giving us not the "bones" and "dust" to which it has no access, but (by way of the repercussion that is language) the tropes that follow and figure the departed Real: Sutpen as demon juxtaposed against Sutpen as Greek antagonist, Rosa as old maid against Rosa as defrauded youth, Charles Bon as weary sybarite against Charles Bon as anguished son, the old South of 1833 "when ladies did not walk but floated" (35) against the juggernaut of Sutpen already burst upon their scene, "the deep shaggy lawn" of Jefferson in September against "the long iron New England snow" (34) of Harvard in January. This book tirelessly proliferates such symbolic image-clusters, suggesting less the physical "object" itself – Sutpen or Rosa or Bon or Jefferson or Cambridge – than the matrical culture's available tropes, its discursive field within which the "object" receives its charge and becomes a signifier.[29] This is why the novel is so adjectivally insistent, also why (among other reasons) it exhausts its reader.

We might expect a text that draws so heavily upon the already-said to engage us smoothly, easily dispersing its materials into our repertory of familiar discourse. *Absalom* avoids this cliché effect by means of syntax and overflow: less a proffering of unknown items than an onslaught of known ones, too many to digest, within sentences too sinuous and multifocused to track easily. Objects become immersed within webs of cultural reference, always on the edge of becoming typical, if not archetypical. The fact that Faulkner's text distrusts its referential network – recurrently overturning its "pictures," its "images," once it has estab-

---

[29] Bleikasten stresses that "Faulknerian description is never just a mere display of objects in space; it digs and delves, explores their past, exhumes their secrets, and so provides them with a measure of temporal depth. Objects in Faulkner appear to absorb temporality like sponges" ("Paradoxes" 173). Referring specifically to *Absalom*, Morris points to this "incorporeality" in Quentin's narrational imagination: "What Quentin sees is not 'substance' but narrative as explanation, legitimacy; he perceives nothing; he comprehends" (187).

lished them – should not blind us to the text's dependence upon such reference in the first place. Objects within such a representational practice tend toward a certain excess of point:

> . . . the magnolia-faced woman a little plumper now, a woman created of by and for darkness whom the artist Beardsley might have dressed, in a soft flowing gown designed not to infer bereavement or widowhood but to dress some interlude of slumbrous and fatal insatiation, of passionate and inexorable hunger of the flesh, walking beneath a lace parasol and followed by a bright gigantic negress carrying a silk cushion and leading by the hand the little boy whom Beardsley might not only have dressed but drawn . . . (242)

One could never mistake this cluster of figures for any group of characters in *The Sound and the Fury* or *Light in August*. The octoroon's clothes, her habits, her setting, her painter, in a word, her aura: these dominate the portrait, putting us in the presence less of a figure than of a set of cultural alignments. We see not a person but a way of life (the octoroon has, and needs, no individualizing name): New Orleans sensual satiety, late-Victorian swooning over the voluptuous female principle, studied indifference to male moral rectitude. This woman may weep (like Ellen), but we do not respond to her painterly presence with anything like the urgency or vertigo that accompanies our encounter with Benjy or Quentin or the adolescent Joe Christmas. Generated from a vocabulary of *fin-de-siècle* lushness that neither Faulkner nor his reader accesses unselfconsciously, she remains exotic and complete, standing at a distance from us, whereas they – motley and unfinished – penetrate disturbingly within.[30]

The octoroon is clothed in the attributes of a specific culture. She is also (though silent herself) clothed in the syntax and vocabulary of a remarkable narrative voice. Much has been rightly said about the capacities of this voice – its range of reference, its sinuous flexibility, its hospitality to different speakers and space/time frames – but I would like here to explore some of the defects of its virtues, the poverty entailed by its richness. For it does remain an imperial voice, subsuming the entire

---

[30] Carolyn Porter provocatively explores the visual and vocal fields of *Absalom, Absalom!* She argues that the narrators' deployment of detached tableaux seeks to shore up a Sutpenian (and all too American) relation to experience: as something "out there," separate from its perceiver, thus leaving the perceiver's illusion of innocence intact. By contrast, the sense of being immersed in "history as stream of event" (60) is mainly conveyed vocally. The reader's participation takes place through a kind of metonymic immersion in voices and events that remain cryptic, unfinished, still alive with their becoming. My argument in this chapter reads the visual field much as Porter does, but I read the vocal performances of *Absalom* as more oratorically "finished" and authoritative than she does. (My commentary on this novel in the previous chapter argues, I hope not perversely, the other side of this same issue, finding in *Absalom*'s narrative strategies a compelling admission of temporal contingency.)

narrative enterprise (whoever the speaker) within its hypnotic rhythms. Such an all-embracing voice systematically scants the sociolinguistics of utterance, the localized encounter of differing orientations potentially at issue in any verbal exchange.[31] When Quentin internalizes his parents' voices, when Hightower and Byron sound their different world views through their differences of syntax and vocabulary, we engage in a dialogic clash of feelings and beliefs wrought into the most minute linguistic usages. In *Absalom* the drama of class and race inequalities is conducted almost wholly outside this register, and we might briefly consider – with regard to Clytie, Wash Jones, Sutpen's father, and Sutpen – the consequences of Faulkner's treatment.

Silent Clytie was not always silent. In "Evangeline," a 1931 version of the *Absalom* materials, the Clytie figure – named 'Raby – unfolds crucial elements of the plot, gradually revealing the miscegenation at its center. Within *Absalom,* however, she has become silenced. Despite Rosa's brief but intense speculations about her, the text offers no direct (and little indirect) experience of her subjectivity. Even Rosa's powerful "address to Clytie" centers on her status as Sutpen's agent, not as a principal actor/sufferer in her own right. Rosa "remembers" her only to the extent of knocking her down during that last visit to Sutpen's Hundred. The text "remembers" her even less generously, telling us nothing of her mental/emotional life, displaying no interest in any self-shaping moves she may have instigated from within. Or without: has she acquaintances? a mate? offspring? What does *she* think of her progenitor (we know at great length what everyone else thinks of him)? Hers is a role no reader is asked to internalize, and her muteness is in keeping with the larger absence of black speech within the novel. (We may of course internalize her nevertheless, as we may internalize any character, but my point is that Faulkner's textual strategy of selective attentiveness scants her.) In this sense she joins the inarticulate ranks of Sutpen's savage blacks and of Charles Etienne's speechless wife: creatures to whom things are done rather than characters the contours of whose subjectivity we are invited to imagine as sentient, reflective, like our own.

Wash Jones is by contrast textually produced through his class–saturated speech. Faulkner registers the status–charged relations in this novel

---

[31] Cf. Bakhtin: "the novelistic hybrid . . . is double-languaged; for in it there are . . . two socio–linguistic consciousnesses, two epochs, that . . . come together and consciously fight it out on the territory of the utterance" (360). I stand behind the criticism of *Absalom*'s imperial voice implicit in Bakhtin's point, yet I should note that the dialogism of *Absalom*'s voice(s) has been compellingly argued. Matthews (*Play*) and Wadlington make, to my mind, the most persuasive cases for voice's unharnessed richness in this text. More recently, Morris has refocused such vocal restlessness in terms of an interruptive, parenthetic energy: "This model of interruptive hearing dominates *Absalom, Absalom!* and it never results in either the production of mere noise or the reduction of several voices to a single voice" (203).

through Rosa's detestation of that "animal who could stand in the street before my house and bellow placidly" (168). Jones's strategically placed "Air you Rosie Coldfield?" lingers in both Rosa's and the reader's mind, underscoring by its very vulgarity the collapse of her dreams. Jones himself dreams poignantly within his vernacular idiom, but his language emerges more potently as that which dreams would put behind – as a poor-white earthiness which designs are meant to escape. Faulkner's text rhythmically sounds this voice at appropriate intervals, silhouetting others' airy dreams against its graininess. Perhaps Jones is so generously sounded because the two lower-class figures whom he must do linguistic duty for, Sutpen and his father, are virtually exempted from vernacular reality.

Sutpen's father is oddly silent in *Absalom*. Enmeshed within Quentin/Shreve/Mr. Compson's enriching weave, he utters only two phrases in his own voice, both of them class- and race-incensed: "'We whupped one of Pettibone's niggers tonight' . . . 'Hell fire, that goddamn son of a bitch Pettibone's nigger'" (289). If he were further vocalized, might not his accents penetrate, like Mr. Compson's into Quentin, more deeply into the mental fabric of his son? And if the text were to imagine (extensively rather than for just four pages: 293–4, 296–7) Thomas Sutpen's mental world as an idiolect shaped by the poor-white accents passed on by his father, might he not become to that extent less amenable to the all-co-opting, opulently class-transcending voice of his various narrators?

Sutpen's own rejection of a classed voice is of course motivated. Discussing Sutpen's need to throw off that voice, Wadlington has shown that "the sustained calm voice that subsequently emerges with Sutpen's epiphany will be forever innocent of such vocal, or other [class-oriented], indications of vulnerability" (200). Immunity at the level of voice, yes, but (as Wadlington also argues) the text's deployment of certain vignettes – Sutpen fighting with his blacks that harks back to his childhood training, Sutpen's careening carriage that echoes the carriage that nearly runs his sisters down – keeps reminding us of traumatic residues, of a poor-white fixation concealed (so to speak somatically) behind the voice's achieved transformation. Put otherwise, "memory believes before knowing remembers": the body has registered – and registered through touch: a slammed door – what it cannot erase. This registering takes place vocally only once, in those memorable four pages of the young Sutpen's significantly *vernacular* voice. In this encounter the citadel of the central I-Am has been gravely damaged, though the outraged will battles on. Writ large, this tension is enacted in the very form of *Absalom, Absalom!*: the attempt through creative voice (the twentieth-century narrators) to revise what has been inalterably imprinted upon suffering and class-inflected bodies (the nineteenth-century characters).

Sutpen's transformed voice (bookish, painfully achieved) is instrumental to the text's revisionary narrative design, permitting his consciousness to seem to break clear from the linguistic mold of his own formative space–time. Beyond this, his preponderant silence and lack of self-communing leave the delineation of his subjectivity open to the accents of his interpreters. Since these interpreters all speak variations on the same voice, Faulkner has removed unwanted static from the verbal field generating his central figure. Sutpen becomes available for representation as a djinn, an explorer, a gambler, an Agamemnon, a Faust: any role imaginable so long as it be mythic, larger than life, transcending the confines of class, time, and region. This novel so sensitive to the damage done to others by an "abrupting" figure enacts, at the level of rhetorical practice, a similar aggression. Its transforming voice tends to make spectacular (to turn into an image, a picture) the portrait of every character it invokes.

If *Absalom*'s narrative voice produces character in an unvarying way, that voice articulates time with another kind of insistence. Beyond the unpredictability of this or that time frame, the voice in general conveys a sense of time-as-overarching-continuum. Consider, for example, this unemphatic passage from the text:

> That was the summer following Henry's first year at the University, after he had brought Charles Bon home with him for Christmas and then again to spend a week or so of the summer vacation before Bon rode on to the River to take the steamboat home to New Orleans; the summer in which Sutpen himself went away, on business, Ellen said, doubtless unaware, such was her existence then, that she did not know where her husband had gone and not even conscious that she was not curious. (84–5)

This passage dramatizes ignorance in a way that typifies *Absalom*: characters immersed in a sequence of events whose implications they as yet (and perhaps forever) ignore.[32] Yet one may hear in the passage an extraordinary knowingness as well, the knowingness of a narrative voice that doesn't so much inform us of what is at stake here as intimate its possession of a space of knowledge beyond that of the characters. Ellen may not know, but this voice knows that she does not know. It knows because, unlike Ellen – unlike all the nineteenth-century actors in this story – it enjoys the cumulative perspective afforded by time. The narrative voice in *Absalom* lives in a three-dimensional time, as it meditates upon its figures caught up in a two-dimensional time. The sentence that we think of as "Faulknerian" – a sentence whose supreme arena is this novel – is suffused with the resonant authority of time long endured and

---

[32] Moreland (41–4) suggests a motive for the community's insistent "not-knowing": they cannot afford to acknowledge the light that Sutpen's blatant transgression of the law sheds upon their latent abuse of it.

at least partially mastered. Not that it is an all-informing voice; there remain in *Absalom* disturbing lacunae beyond our power to fill.[33] Yet is the narrative voice's rhetorical authority ever concealed or placed in doubt? If we as readers feel overwhelmed by this text, it is surely because the voice that produces the text is calculated – through its rhythmic power, its gorgeous vocabulary, its perceptual vividness, its emotional depth, intellectual range, and temporal sweep – to overwhelm us. How shall we characterize, then, the ways in which *Absalom*'s specific rhetorical strategy – its way of producing voice and body – both engages and rewrites the larger cultures' (both Southern and American) discursive practices?

To attempt to answer that question is to begin to close my discussion of this novel as a cosmos no one owns. The distancing of figures, the elaborate tracking of the body within a network of cultural tropes, the proliferation of events in the form of images and pictures, the penchant for larger-than-life portraits, the vocal authority deriving from an immersion in, and partial mastery of, the movement of time from 1808 until 1910: these are the givens of *Absalom, Absalom!*'s form. They are also means that enable, by at the same time disabling, this novel's poignant dreams still to be dreamed. On the one hand, the novel summons up the codes of its antebellum culture – its gestures, clothes, projects, fears – in their most opulently scripted guise. (I say "antebellum" though these codes are generated only after the war, as a way of rewriting what had been lost.)[34] On the other hand, it dizzyingly scrambles these coded materials, arresting and rearranging them at will, depriving them in advance of the "innocence" of their own narrative unfolding.

The actors caught up in such tableaux seem doomed beforehand to defeat. Such doom is wrought into both the finer knowledge of the narrative voice and the presentation of collapsed effects before swelling causes. Cleansed thus, struck down before they even rise, they open up to unsentimental treatment, and their ideological dilemma takes on its foreclosed grandeur. The defeated Southern planter dream (Sutpen's design) joins with the threatened American dream of self-creation (Sutpen's desire). These merge, rise into a credibility all the more touching for our

---

33 Peter Brooks ("Incredulous Narration") makes the best case, *pace* Cleanth Brooks and others, that *Absalom* is constitutively gapped, not a potential plenitude awaiting our response to all the coded hints.

34 Matthews's most recent work ("Rhetoric of Containment," "Modernization and Modernism") explores this apparent nostalgia/actual exploitation wrought into the elusive relation between the rhetoric of the Lost Cause and the economic practices of the New South. Morris is also attentive to the "matter" of *Absalom, Absalom!* as fully textualized. He reads Sutpen "as a projection of the 30s, of that southern project to rewrite the history of the South in order to sustain or recreate a myth" (22). For a persuasive account of the Southern recontainment of supposedly liberated blacks during the fifty years after the war, see Steinberg.

foreknowledge of disaster, and collapse of their intrinsic flaws. The pathos of their undermining, repercussive, played out again and again, emerges as High Tragedy.

Such High Tragedy has its own relevant chronological context. This text written in the 1930s scrupulously refrains from passing 1910, yet the defeat of aspirations that it explores answers indirectly to the silenced intervening years. Sutpen's "innocent" dream, his attempt to fashion a dynasty, his resonating failure: these have an intensified pathos in the Depression-ridden 1930s, when the meanings of that dream of limitless free will underwent perhaps their acutest period of stress. The liberal voices of the industrialized New South of the 1910s and 1920s, moreover, had been engaged less in challenging antebellum dreams than in burying them, underscoring their obsolescence. Thus the Southern agrarian myth – more than ever insolvent, more than ever in demand – required defenders and found them in the emergence of the Fugitives and the publication of *I'll Take My Stand*.[35] Within such a wider frame of cultural contestation Faulkner's rhetorical practice in *Absalom, Absalom!* reveals, I think, its own divided allegiance.

For if, on the one hand, the text reveals those dreams to be doomed through a misconception of individual power and a blindness to the traumas inflicted by the prejudices of race and class, it also (re)produces, on the other, the passionate aspiration with which such flawed dreams could once be invested. The plot of this novel depicts defeat, the form decapitates aspiration before it can flower. Yet, above all, *Absalom, Absalom!*'s declamatory rhetoric insists upon the *importance* of the ordeal it goes to such pains to narrate.

This novel insists as no novel of Faulkner's had ever insisted before. One could even say that the central drama of reading *Absalom* is our attending to the intricacies of that narrative insistence. Its nineteenth-century characters recede into the rhetoric, becoming the objects rather than the subjects of narratorial urgency. Shaped to their cultural roles and conflicts by the overarching narrative voice, they do not enter – like Benjy, Quentin, and Joe Christmas – into a disturbing relation (quasi-somatic, shock-filled, ideologically untracked) with the reader. Rather, they are movable creatures, somatically maladaptive but psychically reconceivable according to different perspectives. They relate most intensely not to the reader but to altering narrators' projects. And insofar as all the narrators compose together the refracted voice of "Faulkner himself" – the writer in quest of his cultural origins, their victim and their survivor, intent upon exhuming their tragic importance – reasons for such stylized portraiture begin to emerge.

---

[35] Woodward's *The Burden of Southern History* is the locus classicus for discussion of this phenomenon. See also Cash, Cowan, Tindall, O'Brien, and King (*A Southern Renaissance*), as well as Porter, Matthews ("Modernism" and "Rhetoric"), and Morris.

The critical issue becomes narratorial access to a vanished and increasingly irrelevant regional past: access founded upon acts of speaking and hearing, upon elaborate rehearsal of shared Southern tropes.[36] The South of his earlier fiction had not receded enough to require self-conscious lambasting or lamenting; it was the unthinkingly present context of his materials. Only in *Absalom* (in however tortuous a way) does Faulkner deliberately claim the full temporality of his inheritance, an inheritance he would be less likely to dress in such Sunday finery if he still had everyday commerce with it. A gorgeous and unmistakably Southern rhetoric emerges here, proclaiming the writer's voice in a new way as regional, proclaiming it, further, as *his own*.

Deconstructive logic notwithstanding, our stubborn (though illusory) sense that we are hearing the writer himself, hearing his own voice, shapes decisively our reading of this novel, establishing it thus as the pivotal novel in Faulkner's career, the one in which his "signature" emerges as a rhetoric: a distinctive use of syntax and vocabulary that we are invited to take as an originating power. Yet this moment when he first urges the authority of his "own" voice is precisely the moment when he enters the oratorical discourse of his Southern culture. With whatever gorgeous flourishes and fiendish hedging, he signs on. The unmistakable accent that ensues is the index of his vocal acculturation, his fatefully "assimilating the words of others" so as to achieve his own "ideological becoming" (Bakhtin 341). It is this aggressively Southern voice that saturates the actors in their cultural traditions and tropes them as players within the pageant.[37]

Not that this pageant unfolds in such a way as to yield any simple pleasures to the reader first encountering it. The pageant does not unfold at all; it abrupts, repercusses, moves discontinuously, cryptically. The

---

[36] Gresset posits also that *Absalom* marks the turn from a fiction centered on the gaze to one centered on the word: "Car le 30 mars 1935, quand il (re)commence *Absalom, Absalom!*, Faulkner met en oeuvre une tout autre stratégie que celle, désastreuse, du regard. C'est le verbe, cette fois, qui va servir à tenter l'impossible. . . . Avec *Absalom*, donc, commence une phase . . . qui ouvre tout grand sur une ontologie du discours. Un passage se fait du sujet singulier au sujet pluriel" (*Fascination* 279).

[37] Drawing on Southern historians as well as theories of rhetoric, Ross places Faulkner's texts (notably *Absalom, Absalom!*) within the tradition of Southern oratory (*Fiction* 185–233). Ross recurs to the authority lodged within this rhetorical model – "Oratory is inherently monological in both form and intent, for it articulates certainty" (213) – but he ends by arguing for *Absalom*'s reliance on dialogic scenes as an effective undermining of its own oratorical power. In my reading, the text remains more disturbingly complicit with the oratorical (ultimately monologic) authority proclaimed in its rhetorical stance. Wadlington reads the struggle between monologic and dialogic impulses – "*Absalom, Absalom!*'s murmurous . . . ventriloquial voices" (213) – as taking place in the theater of the reader as s/he performs the text (172–219). The invention of this oratorical voice is in any event decisive for Faulkner's career. Its teeming adjectival insistence fills the overheated canvases of *Pylon* and *Intruder in the Dust*, and its authoritative scope generates the history-laden sequences of *Go Down, Moses* and *Requiem for a Nun*, as well as the near-cosmic arrogations of *A Fable*.

intellectual and analytic demands imposed by the novel's unrecuperable form remove all complacency from the narrative contract. This most Modernistic of Faulkner's texts is stunningly subversive in other ways as well, as indicated elsewhere in this study and more amply by other critics (*Absalom*'s experimental brilliance does not lack supporters). Racial prejudice, class and gender norms, and narrative expectations undergo a seismic disturbance within its corrosive pages. Those earlier dreams cannot here be dreamed again with impunity. Indeed, no nostalgic Southerner is likely to put up for long with Faulkner's astonishing procedures.

Yet, as I have been arguing, *Absalom*'s structural iconoclasm screens a complex rapprochement with the tropes and rhythms of traditional Southern oratory. The novel's fierce refusal of readerly orientation is compatible with a resonant homecoming. *Absalom*'s "illimitable courage for rhetoric" (*Selected Letters* 188) registers less the subject-altering encounter with the voice and body of the Other than the subject-constituting drama of "Faulkner" (through his various but kindred-voiced narrators) quarreling with – but more deeply insisting upon – the terrible beauty of his trope-saturated inheritance. Doubtless it can't matter; more urgently it must matter: to him, then through him to us. (The "us" of this claim is not offered as prescriptive: the text is open to other powerful and empowering readings. I am identifying what I take to be its deepest invitations, the relation to the reader that its narratorial negotiation of voice and body imply.) The matter of Sutpen is proposed, from the first word of the text until its last, as deathlessly significant. The voice proposing it (whoever the ostensible speaker) emerges as defiantly, fatally Southern.

It is satisfying to claim that *Absalom, Absalom!* rehearses antebellum dreams in order to imagine their revision and to reenact their collapse. It is more disturbing to suggest that it reenacts their collapse as the necessary condition for legitimating their passionate rehearsal. When they collapse yet again, their repercussive thunder sounds not just a local defeat but checkmate, not just the end of a story but the end (at least for Quentin Compson) of the Southern clock.

꙳

In Chapter 2 I followed the vicissitudes of Lucas Beauchamp's representation, claiming that as he moves from a comic figure in the short stories to a protagonist in *Go Down, Moses*, he takes on unprecedented dignity and lineage. In so doing, he exemplifies what I want to stress in this chapter: *Go Down, Moses*'s normative focus upon the body as a lens through which genealogical descent can become visible and resonant. The text insistently inscribes the body within a structure that we might define (horizontally and vertically) as the history of a patriarchal family over time: seven generations of whites and blacks each of whose identity is textually produced, precisely, through kinship with each other.[38]

The coherence of *Go Down, Moses* not only depends upon this ubiquitous pattern but, as Michael Grimwood has persuasively shown, it is a coherence arrived at only late in Faulkner's crafting of his materials, and arrived at through crisis. The crisis concerns Faulkner's racial and cultural views and can be localized in the genesis of "Pantaloon in Black" and "Delta Autumn." Writing these two stories compels him, first, to refashion his facile black portraits in "The Fire and the Hearth" (what he at first referred to as his "stories about niggers" [Grimwood 228]) so that they not shame the tragic understanding of racial stereotype in "Pantaloon" and, second, to extend all the stories in such a way that, echoing each other, they illuminate the descent of the larger Southern culture into exhaustion. The strategy for accomplishing this dual purpose is itself single: a reconceiving of all the novel's principal actors, black and white, as members of the same family during its tumultuous 150-year history.

"Delta Autumn" contains the germ of this novelistic vision. Earlier stories are rewritten with its radiating insight in mind, just as "The Bear," the only narrative in the novel to be made up mainly of new materials, takes conceptual shape as a nineteenth-century exploration (half retrospective, half ongoing) of motives and events whose twilight consequences occur in "Delta Autumn." Ike McCaslin, a minor figure in earlier tales but essentially produced – born old – in "Delta Autumn," becomes the ghostly presence tangential to "Was," as well as the childhood center of "The Old People" and the young man finding and defending his identity in "The Bear." Carothers McCaslin, unthought-of until Faulkner began his revisions but now needing to be invented as old Ike McCaslin's dead ancestor, is installed at this late moment of textual genesis as the tyrannical source of all subsequent McCaslin destinies (a compelling instance, this, of the belated invention of one's origins). Cass, Zack, and Roth then take on as though magically their fated family identities. So likewise comes into being the axis founded on the abuse of Eunice and Tomasina and the dispersion of their offspring. Both these strands coalesce one last time in the anonymous "doe" in "Delta Autumn," the "black" woman who can only be – Faulkner now sees in this eleventh-hour logic become irresistible – the grandchild of the long-lost Tennie's Jim.

---

[38] Kenner, who denies many of Faulkner's effects, shrewdly notes that the expansive urge within his narratives virtually demands family ties: "to commence with the merest glimpse and by way of wringing out its significance arrange voices and viewpoints, interpolate past chronicles . . . and tie the persons together, for the sake of intimacy, intensity, plausibility, with ties of blood and community and heritage . . . [h]e needed inarticulate blood ties" (205–6).

Old Ike McCaslin touches her hand: "He didn't grasp it, he merely touched it – the gnarled, bloodless, bone-light bone-dry old man's fingers touching for a second the smooth young flesh where the strong old blood ran after its long lost journey back to home. 'Tennie's Jim,' he said. 'Tennie's Jim' " (362). I cannot read this passage without a flush of feeling, which is to say that if *Go Down, Moses* is to achieve its intended power, I must (and do) subscribe to the discursive premise wrought into its representation of body: the premise that individual trait and gesture play out at the same time a familial narrative that long predates the individual, that, in the mystique of blood descent, private telos recapitulates family arche. If we consider how explosive "touch" is in both *Light in August* and *Absalom, Absalom!* – cutting across ideological arrangements and maddening the private subject on whom it "abrupts" – we begin to see how much more gently the body transgressions in this later text can be imagined. More than an individual undoing, the touch of white upon black here signals a familial regrouping – one that seeks to temper (by echoing) the family-undoing touch of Old Carothers upon Eunice and Tomasina, of Roth upon the doe. I shall explore further the ideological implications of this premise, but not before attending briefly to the text's other ways of representing the body.

Ike is born old in *Go Down, Moses* in two senses. He is conceived late in the genetic process of the novel, and he is conceived as an old man. Rigorously deprived of the life of his own body (in earlier versions of this material and other references to it he is granted offspring: not so in the novel proper), Ike floats through much of the text as a disembodied witness.[39] He first appears (in "Was") as a sort of spectral consciousness not yet born, and this too early/too late dimension nicely points to his somatic weightlessness. His body's capacities emerge confidently only within a schema of nature (the wilderness stories). Within a schema of culture he lacks bodily assurance, seeing his wife's body only once, never siring a son. Like his uncle Hubert, he will die virginal, inviolate. Like Old Ben and Lion he is conceived with his end already in view – a doomed witness whose outpouring of spirit will be coeval with the final flourish of a vanishing way of life.[40]

Old Ben and Lion: only *The Hamlet* rivals *Go Down, Moses* as a text in which animals matter so much. The bear and the dog who tracks him

[39] In the magazine version of "Delta Autumn" (December 1940) Ike "had had a wife and children once though no more" (*Uncollected Stories* 274), and in *The Hamlet* (1940) reference is made to Ab Snopes having once "wintered his family in a old cottonhouse on Ike McCaslin's place" (9): both notations portray an Ike not yet unhoused and incapable of offspring.

[40] In the second part of Chapter 3, I probe in greater detail the implications of Faulkner's having established Ike's old age (and place in the Symbolic) before inventing his youth.

lavishly command their author's attention. Consider the implications of this portrait of Lion:

> . . . the big head, the chest almost as big as his own, the blue hide beneath which the muscles flinched or quivered to no touch since the heart which drove blood to them loved no man and no thing . . . Lion inferred not only courage and all else that went to make up the will and desire to pursue and kill, but endurance, the will and desire to endure beyond all imaginable limits of flesh in order to overtake and slay. Then the dog looked at him. . . . Then it blinked, and he knew it was not looking at him and never had been, without even bothering to turn its head away. (237–8)

This portrait seems steeped in a male fantasy of power joined with immunity. Accorded many of the later Faulkner's favorite virtues (courage and will and endurance), Lion embodies what I called earlier the male lust for virginity. He has completed his own circuit, is dauntingly whole unto himself (Boon, who is merely human, cannot resist such perfection). Lion lives within the precincts of his own body, and his desire – satisfyingly unlike human desire, which introduces lack and alterity into the one who desires – can be wholly slaked. The totem animals of this text are surpassingly male, a sign of the text's longing for nonrelational transcendence, for identity as pure, self-contained power, free of internal difference, free of the female inside and outside the (male) self.

For these reasons the portrait of Rider challenges the representational economy of the body within the larger novel. Rider is intolerably self-divided, in anguish because of the departed Mannie who is still within him, a figure whose physical strength gives the measure not of his immunity but of his invadedness. Faulkner writes "Pantaloon in Black" in such a way that Rider's moving body utterly compels the reader. We remain (until the chapter's final pages) immersed within that body, suffering its ordeal.[41] Rider's trajectory is narrated with a frame-shattering immediacy, which we share as we share the quasi-somatic vertigo of Benjy and Quentin and Joe Christmas. No extensive familial analogies intervene here. No time-generated patina mediates Rider's ordeal, no genealogical overview anneals it by supplying an ancestral blood transfusion. His fatal encounter with the boss-man explodes not with the patriarchal resonance

---

[41] I addressed in Chapter 2 the claim that an undeviating stress upon Rider's body constitutes in itself a racial trope, a figuring of the black as body. The attentiveness of Faulkner's bodily portrait transcends this critique, it seems to me; the representation of Rider's anguish-driven movement is saturated in authorial respect. Yet it must be conceded that the language to which Faulkner has access to "say" Rider is a language foreign to Rider's own terms for articulating his subjectivity. The same point could be made for Joe Christmas and, a fortiori, for Benjy. Its bearing remains, perhaps, disturbing, but not necessarily racist.

of Lucas's with Zack – a resonance in which individual telos satisfyingly touches ground upon family arche – but instead with the ungraced racist brutality of the 1940s: and it remains explosive.

Produced less by family than by history – a poor black man, working for next to nothing in a sawmill, illiterate, schooled in a religion meaningless to him in his crisis, immersed within racially abusive practices – Rider has none of the consolations of caste afforded others in this text. Exposed, inarticulate, crucified, the representation of Rider takes us back to Benjy's primordial "I was trying to say." His nakedness and penetrability reveal by contrast how many layers of clothes this text has managed to contrive for its other actors. These clothes – the culturally provided, familial accommodations that consolidate identity and allow outrage to be borne – take one metaphoric form as the text's way of furnishing its human bodies. The other form they take (and the one to which we now turn) is the text's way of furnishing its human voices.[42]

"All words have the 'taste' of a profession, a genre, a tendency, a party, a particular work, a particular person, a generation, an age group, the day and the hour," Bakhtin writes. "Each word tastes of the context and contexts in which it has lived its socially charged life" (293). Although I cannot fill in each of those slots for the typical sentence of *Go Down, Moses,* I would claim that its most memorable ones posit a certain age group (old age), a particular season (autumn), a special setting (woods if not wilderness), a recurrent mental/emotional field (lyrical recollection), a typical rhythm (incantatory), a given syntax and vocabulary (compound, polysyllabic, Latinate), a gendered subject (male), an assumed race (white), and a presumed class (Southern aristocracy – or as close as we get to it in America). The "socially charged" context they imply is a sort of privileged male retreat, a sanctuary of rare and sifted thoughts, within a sylvan space uncontaminated by present-day urban realities, dedicated to the sonorous poetry of reminiscence rather than open to the motley unpredictability of ongoing projects. These traits together make up a distinctive "taste," as the following passage (which could come only from this novel) reveals:

> . . . summer, and fall, and snow, and wet and saprife spring in their
> ordered immortal sequence, the deathless and immemorial phases of the
> mother [the wilderness] who had shaped him if any had toward the man

---

42 The merit of Wadlington's *Reading Faulknerian Tragedy* is that he focuses attention upon this issue of cultural furnishing or exposure. Shifting the critical emphasis from epistemology (how we interpret what we read) to acknowledgment (how we – like author and characters – secure our own human identity by engaging the cultural roles proposed within the activity of reading), he addresses a necessary yet hazardous process in which writer, characters, and reader are reciprocally implicated: "the process in which culturally furnished enactments and capabilities mutually enable as well as mutually subvert one another" (43).

he was, mother and father both to the old man born of a Negro slave and a Chickasaw chief who had been his spirit's father if any had, whom he had revered and harkened to and loved and lost and grieved: and he would marry someday they too would own for their brief while that brief unsubstanced glory which inherently of itself cannot last and hence why glory: and they would, might, carry even the remembrance of it into the time when flesh no longer talks to flesh because memory at least does last: but still the woods would be his mistress and his wife. (326)

The novel speaks of course in other tones. ("Was," "Pantaloon in Black," and "Go Down, Moses" wholly lack such sentences, as do the humorous sections of "The Fire and the Hearth"; and the dialogic encounter between Cass and Ike in the commissary moves according to a quite different vocal strategy.) But this remains the narrative voice's major chord, its most resonant note. Such a voice is sublimely unplaced, contemplating the human and natural scene from an immeasurable distance of time and space. From this vantage point the spectacle emerges, in its "ordered immortal sequence," its vicissitudes contained within a kind of retrospective pageant. Reprieved from the intrusions of the female (the disfiguring psychic scar that comes of maternal birthing, the wound inflicted by a failed marriage), secure even within the increasing frailty of his body, the autumnal subject of this prose (Ike McCaslin, mothered and wived by the woods rather than women) enjoys a rapt sense of belonging. Like a displaced pre-Oedipal bonding, the contemplated wilderness offers him food and activity, solitude and company. It is a structure for understanding space, time, race, gender, and memory, all within the governing trope of common blood, a single family.

Such vast sentences – with their periodic flow (their biblical continuities of "and" and "and" and "and") – dominate the matter they contain. Nothing jagged can enter their precincts and retain its power to upset. *Go Down, Moses* engages its materials through this voice in the form of immortal recollections – snapshots – that nourish now, whatever their earlier charge might have been. The earlier threat of Lucas's and Zack's nearly fatal struggle becomes narratively pacified and naturalized within the memory of the harvest ("That had been a good year . . . after the rains and flood" [57]) that follows and rounds it off. Boon's violent escapades in Memphis meld into Ike's later memories, with no disturbing consequences. (Memphis cannot otherwise enter this narrative. Its urban incoherence refuses the natural/genealogical/familial mold of *Go Down, Moses*.)[43] Dominate, contain, pacify, meld: the verbs I have employed chart the ideological work being performed by this dimension of the

---

[43] *Sanctuary* and *The Reivers*, respectively, accommodate a Beale Street/whorehouse Memphis of nightmarish or comic proportions, a Memphis troped compatibly with the other materials of these texts and not set in opposition to the pastoral big woods.

text. A time, a region, and a set of activities are being rendered sacred; and the text's repudiation of other times, regions, and activities is as unhesitating as its cherishing of what remains within its borders is tender. Beneath *Go Down, Moses*'s commitment to the quickness of wild things – "we dont want him tame," Sam says of Lion – one finds a discursive practice that tends, precisely, to tame its encounters, to enfold them in a rhetoric that softens as it distances, to dilate in the pathos of nostalgic rehearsal, of diminished yet dignified survival.

This elegiac voice is notably "wiser" than the voices that narrate the earlier novels. Here, for the first time, blacks and whites use the Bible alike – with little ironic double-voicing operative – to align their moves within long-established cultural norms.[44] Molly speaks scripture in "The Fire and the Hearth," announcing God's intent to have His earth properly worked, not treasure-plundered, and Lucas ends in submissive agreement: "Man has got three score and ten years on this earth, the Book says. . . . I am near to the end of my three score and ten, and I reckon to find that money aint for me" (131). In sanctioning a racially saturated practice – blacks faithfully working the land that belongs to whites, increasing the profit of the latter – "The Book" benevolently contains the threat of revolt that lurks in Lucas's antics. Ike, for his part, speaks God's word with sometimes alarming ease in "The Bear" and "Delta Autumn." We are far from Faulkner's ironizing of McEachern and Hines, far also from the speculative Mr. Compson in *Absalom* when he imagines God's mind musing on the eccentricities of human behavior. There the gap between God and his speakers was accented; here the divine intention has become more accessible and pacifying. It curbs excessive behavior, ratifies long-standing norms, speaks in the form of eternal verities.

This norm-weighted, often Bible-inflected voice has its blind spots. Although Ike's attempt to say "Negro" improves upon Cass's conventional definition, it will lead in *Intruder* to the suffocating righteousness of "Sambo." Even here Ike's ardor is articulated in the parental rhetoric of noblesse oblige: "I will have to find her. . . . We have already lost one of them" (277). "They" are figured as our helpless children; "we" cannot let "them" suffer further through wandering on their own; their wandering will lead only to further error without "our" guidance and support. In addition, this narrative voice so tender toward its own wayward wards turns away its face in predictable ways. Carpetbaggers ("that third race even more alien to the people whom they resembled in pigment and in whom even the same blood ran, than to the people whom they did not"

---

[44] Double-voicing is of course a close call; evidence for it, as for irony, may be invisible. Cf. Bakhtin: "Double-voiced discourse . . . serves two speakers at the same time and expresses simultaneously two different intentions: the direct intention of the character who is speaking, and the refracted intention of the author" (324).

[290]) take on the despicable form of the scapegoated Other: aliens whose progeny soon compete savagely with the blacks "they were supposed to have freed" (290) and who eventually lynch them. Such postbellum figures, originating from another time, place, and set of practices, are thus charged with the racial evil no longer assigned to "us," the true Southerners; and they are soon joined by others "who follow catastrophe and are their own protection as grasshoppers are and need no blessing and sweat no plow or axe-helve and batten and vanish and leave no bones" (291).

All of these foreigners, biblically summoned and dismissed by the narrative voice's uninterruptible pronouncements, are decisively separated from the subjects of this text: the whites and blacks whose common patriarchal source is Carothers McCaslin and whose suffering before and after the war is textually accessible.[45] An unbending conceptual binarism is at work here. These others (shiftless latecomers) have sinned against the reigning value of Go Down, Moses – the indigenous, agrarian, ancestral family – and their punishment is to be placed beyond the discursive pale. In like manner, Samuel Worsham Beauchamp, by abandoning the fire and the hearth rather than being deprived of it, like Rider, by bolting to the city and losing his McCaslin identity, forfeits his claim upon the narrative compassion that caresses this text's sacralized time, place, and traditions. It is as though, by deserting his family, he fell back into one of Faulkner's "stories about niggers." All that can be done for him is to restore his corpse to communal norms – to re-McCaslinize him – by the grace of a ritual funeral.

Not law but blooded family is Faulkner's credo here. "So a man's kin can't tell on him in court," (67) Lucas Beauchamp realizes. The binding power of family exceeds the power of law to pry apart. Such familial power can be radiant in this novel, as in the scene of Ike touching the hand of Tennie's Jim's granddaughter. Yet this power is never far from tyranny – family against law, us against them – as in several unintentionally disturbing passages of race representation in Intruder in the Dust. The care reserved for the tragically black and white family is also an arm raised against compulsory integration. For miscegenation (the transgression of sacred racial boundaries) remains at once the central abuse Go Down, Moses must atone for, the crossing it can never legitimize, the desire it keeps recording, and the deepest threat it can envisage: the miscegenation of "Chinese and African and Aryan and Jew, all breed and spawn together until no man has time to say which one is which nor cares" (364).

Disgust fills this passage. Its image of the present as a subhuman

---

45 For a reading of Go Down, Moses's incapacity to engage Southern history except through mystified paradigms, see Godden.

gland-charged overriding of what should remain precious racial and na-
tional distinctions bespeaks a writer whose compassion is carefully ap-
portioned, whose discursive world has undergone a decisive binary mapping. Violation becomes, so to speak, what others do or what happens to
them (which we bemoan) rather than what we do or what happens to us.
It becomes his work's second premise rather than its first: a mistake to be
communally mourned rather than a code-transgressing subjective reality
to be passed (as though unmediated) directly into the reader's own subjectivity. In its focus upon the infringement of blood barriers, the passage
announces caste as the register of value. Its voice speaks from within
consensus, to those who already understand. Like Southern oratory it
addresses "the converted in discourse that was already internally persuasive" (Ross, *Fiction* 192). Henceforth, Faulkner's representation of
voice and body will increasingly return to the oratorical tropes – the inert
sonorous nouns – elegiacally preserved within these boundaries.[46] Increasingly the boundaries keep out more of the quick and untamed than
they let in.

To say that the cosmos Faulkner sought to make his own becomes
more nostalgic, kin-centered, Southern, is to say that his texts align
themselves more hospitably within the ideological frame of an older and
increasingly beleaguered rhetoric. During his last twenty years Faulkner
exhausts his (Modernism-inspired) capacity to invent new fictional
voices, to see and vocalize the Other within the Self, the Self within the
Other, in ways sufficiently disorienting that the reader undergoes as well
an experience of alterity coiling within the precincts of the "same."
Rather, his work tends toward the two poles of low-current vernacular
ease or high-current oracular prophecy. Both poles make a kind of peace
with previous practices. He either reworks some of the regional discourses he has inherited, or he reproduces, with an insistence that can
border on the hysterical, vocal effects he had himself earlier produced.
Through such vocal insistence he tries, as Karl Zender puts it, "to outtalk
the world" (98), or, as Michel Gresset puts it, to "make God . . . close
His Eye" ("Faulkner's Voice" 193). His own previous fiction becomes one
more traditional resource.

Thus cushioned, his work moves into tameness: a preserve of older

---

[46] These complacent nouns do not disguise the specter of alienation and outdatedness that
stalks Faulkner's later texts, their marginalized awareness that the family values to be
defiantly proclaimed are already corrupted from within (cf. the Gowrys in *Intruder*).
Gresset proposes that the sonorities are set into place almost talismanically, to ward off
the darkness of Faulkner's fantasies: "Amour, compassion, courage, espoir, fierté, hon-
neur, pitié, sacrifice ne sont donc, aux mains de Faulkner devenu médecin malgré lui,
qu'autant d'instruments destinés à conjurer le mal de la vision pure. . . . Mettre en scène
des valeurs comme naguère des fantasmes, tel me paraît le rêve fou qui guide Faulkner
après la deuxième guerre mondiale" (*Fascination* 280–1).

values within the older tropes that sound them. It can still please, move, and exhaust its reader. Yet, despite the cosmic urgency of its occasional claims, it rarely startles. In ceasing to dramatize the culture's assault upon the subject or to contest the discursive practice that enabled his own eloquence, later Faulknerian subjectivity tends toward the flaccid and the oracular: as though "something between the shape of him that people knew and the uncompromising skeleton of what he actually was had gone fluid and, earthbound, had been snubbed up and restrained, balloonlike unstable and lifeless, by the envelope which it had betrayed" (*AA* 98). His rhetoric no longer engenders that body off-balance, no longer says that speechless and alienated being who is "trying to say." In their place is, more and more, an empowered, enculturated being whose prolific say is nourished by the accumulated resources of the already-said, whose somatic trajectory tends to be assured rather than exposed. *Go Down, Moses,* as the autumnal novel in which this transition announces itself, radiates thus a pathos beyond the pathos it knowingly espouses. [47]

&

I have urged throughout this chapter that Faulkner's representation of voice and body alters between 1929 and 1942, and that the ideological bearing of his work changes accordingly. I want to close by considering two objections to these claims. The first is that, by referring repeatedly to "Faulkner," I work within a normative definition of the author, what Foucault refers to as the author-function, "the principle of thrift in the proliferation of meaning" ("What Is an Author?" 159). Imposing this function upon the career risks presuming that "Faulkner's texts would be effectively limited to what is Faulknerian in them, the remainder being simply ignored or ascribed to confusion, posturing, or a falling away from his essential genius" (Stonum 199).

I do believe that the later work registers a "falling away," but not from some purely private resource that we could call "essential genius." Rather, Faulkner's ways of exercising his verbal energies, among the discursive resources open to him, shift decisively. He departs from a Modernist aesthetics of shock and ideological confounding, of fissured

---

[47] The pathos of rehearsing an obsolete genre – seeking to renew a discourse of the past – is discussed by Bakhtin in a way that suggests the Faulkner of *Intruder in the Dust, A Fable,* and the prose portions of *Requiem for a Nun:* "Such pathos is the discourse of a preacher who has lost his pulpit, a dreaded judge who no longer has any judicial or punitive powers, the prophet without a mission, the politician without political power, the believer without a church and so forth – everywhere, the discourse of pathos is connected with orientations and positions that are unavailable to the author as authentic expression for the seriousness and determination of his purpose, but which he must, all the same, conditionally reproduce by using his own discourse" (394–5). With specific respect to *Go Down, Moses,* Matthews reads the pathos more positively than I do, as an achieved ritual of mourning in which loss is pervasively conceded as the precondition of communal utterance (212–73).

subjectivity. He moves toward a conservative aesthetics of *Bildung,* of ideological bolstering. Critics who delight in a fiction centered upon man's enduring and prevailing have found much in the later fiction to admire, including subtleties that the fiction's detractors have overlooked. Its investment in dignified survival involves a rhetorical furnishing of bodies inscribed within tradition, voices possessed (or in pursuit) of wisdom. This fiction tends to speak of wounds annealed, trauma borne, orientation sought and achieved. It is not a question of wishing that the later novels continued the practices of the explosive earlier ones. As Stonum says, "the figure of [Faulkner's] authorship is the disciplined mobility inscribed within the transformations of his career" (201). He must change. My focus has been on the ideological alterations wrought into the change.

A second objection might be that attention to theme, rather than to the representation of voice and body, would better illuminate the texts' ideological alignment. My response is that the imprint of ideology emerges most tellingly in form rather than theme, and that the texts' ways of producing voice and body reveal Faulkner's figuring of the subject-in-the-world. As Jameson would say, the most telling ideology of the text is encoded in its form; it carries out its work upon us through form. For these texts' ways of figuring the subject in the fiction shape our way of being a subject in the reading. Our own subvocal and embodied activity of reading is critically implicated in this troping. Reading is less epistemological than performative: through reading (as well as other cultural activities) we daily enact our selves by trying out – shedding, refusing, reiterating, reshaping – the roles for subjectivity that our culture offers to us. Our own voices and bodies, like those within the texts, are never "givens," never unmediated, never simply ours. They become ours by way of role adaptation, renegotiated cultural inscription. They are continuously in need of – thus vulnerable to – externally provided paradigms of identity.

In the early Faulkner's Modernist experiments, this process of socially produced self-shaping is not only foregrounded and fraught with pain; it is, through the deployment of voice and body, dizzyingly passed on to us. Reading those texts involves a reexperiencing of the violence of the individual's entry into culture itself. As we read we "live" that entry as an internalized cacophony of bodies and voices suffering the impress of alien scripts. In so doing we undergo a sort of dispossession of our normal roles. We take on a measure of ideological vertigo; we become (for the time of the reading) a cosmos no one owns.

Faulkner in the late 1920s and early 1930s registers the acculturation of the subject as an assault. His texts speak of and enact the trauma of alienation. The South is where his people live, but it is hardly a resource for helping them to do so. Not surprisingly, these are the texts that won him lasting European praise, for such texts articulate his keenly Modernist and deracinated identity. Misread by American critics of the 1930s and 1940s as a regionalist, he yet became one in his later work. The region was the South, its oratorical tradition an increasing resource, its disappearing pieties an eloquent cause. Yes, he opens his world to accommodate Jews and Bohemians, but Mink Snopes and Chick Mallison remain his dearest voices, Gavin Stevens (with whatever qualifying touches) his troubled yet ceaseless translator. The later novels engage in an ideological work of recuperation, of placing the beleaguered subject in the right relation to traditional cultural values. They urge their reader to consider the issues and become wiser. They know what wise is.

The cosmos thus produced (in the reader, in the text) is culturally shaped in both early and later texts. Unlike the later texts, however, the early Modernist ones foreground their own artifice, display the waywardness of their composition, the penetrability of their juxtaposed bodies, the cacophony of their adulterate and unauthorized voices. Within these novels, within us while reading them, the culture abrupts relentlessly upon the self, turning it into a subject, furnishing it willy-nilly with its scripts. The pain of this ideological drama fuels Faulkner's supreme novels, propels into iconoclastic utterance all of their "raging and incredulous recounting" (*AA* 201), enters into and in its way decenters the reader.

Insofar as "the clotting which is [us]" (*AILD* 149) receives this charge and starts to unclot, we may glimpse the artifice of our own "clottedness," our unceasing and invisible alignment within the hegemonic practices of our culture. Such a (re)discovery of our constructedness – of the ways in which gender, race, and other cultural arrangements live unknowingly troped within us – is the first step toward our reconceiving (and potentially remapping) our roles within our worlds. Subjective wholeness may be a fiction but agency is not. For agency "mark[s] the idea of a form of subjectivity where, by virtue of the contradictions and disturbances in and among subject-positions, the possibility . . . of resistance to ideological pressure is allowed for (even though that resistance too must be produced in an ideological context)" (Smith xxxv). Contradiction and disturbance coiling within the subjectivity of a beleaguered protagonist: no writer has generated this drama more compellingly than the early Faulkner. The next step, resistance, is for his readers to take.

Conclusion

A cosmos no one owns: I have argued strenuously the ways in which Faulkner does not own his own work, and I am now in the difficult position of seeking, through a brief but answerable conclusion, to own my own. Rather than summarize the foregoing chapters, I shall begin by noting the perspectives (both limiting and enabling) without which this book could never have been written.

It is the work of a middle-aged white male; these are important facts. I came to Faulkner in the late 1950s, my university teachers were white and male, the reigning mode of study was New Critical. During the late 1970s and 1980s, however, the most stimulating work done on Faulkner departed decisively from the operative assumptions of my first Faulknerian readings. And this has meant that, insofar as I have responded to the newer work, my transferential engagement with the subjectivity of his beleaguered male protagonists has gradually taken on a different resonance. Awareness of the subject's immersion within gender, race, and other cultural constructs – all of these now seen to be wrought into a language problematic, a set of signifying economies – profoundly revises the critical landscape. We see a different writer, we see in a different way, writing (his and ours) becomes a different enterprise. Without these sea changes this book could not have been written. Without the previous engagement there would have been no commitment too deep to be discarded, too troubled to preserve without rethinking.

American academic, white and male: I write within Imaginaries that attach to those givens, even when I seek to think through a woman's and a black's perspective upon Faulkner's work. Henry Louis Gates has recently written that "No poet, ultimately, knows more than 'race'" ("Dis and Dat"), and I understand him to mean that our affiliatory limitations ground our insights. The reading of Faulkner's women and blacks proposed here is the reading of a white male. This condition obviously neither validates nor (less obviously) invalidates my arguments. White and black, male and female: these orientations are both biological and cultural, inescapable and aleatory. We can afford neither to essentialize them by reification nor to ignore them as inconsequential; and it may be appropriate, before closing this study, to speculate briefly as to how such other readings of Faulkner would differ from mine.

With respect to any specifics, a black reader's subjective experience of these texts is of course beyond my ken. I believe, though, that the art of "signifying" would emerge in such a reading as a widespread strategy operative in the behavior of Faulkner's blacks, thus denoting a greater empowerment of black lives than I have argued; black marginalization would also show up, probably strikingly, in ways I never noticed. More generally, the poetics of alienated Modernism might undergo a severer scrutiny, insofar as these texts' scrupulous refusal of a communal voice (a refusal I as a white male Modernist tend to celebrate) might well constitute for a black reader a major curtailment of the texts' community-invoking possibilities. As for a woman reader's take on Faulkner's achievement, we already have some examples (Wittenberg, Gwin, Sensibar, Fowler, among others) to judge from; these tend to probe Faulkner's rhetorical experiments with an eye to the emergent "semiotic." I expect a woman's reading to differ from mine in its more critical focus on the travails (a trifle comic perhaps to the female eye) of the urgent male ego at the heart of these texts' impassioned rhetoric and tortuous plotting. Perhaps the latent homosocial networking throughout the texts would achieve better focus as well, inasmuch as the male–female sexual problematic might emerge more clearly as a screen for concealing male–male fixations. Feminists and blacks might also, for reasons I respect but do not share, choose simply not to devote themselves in the 1990s to a book-length study of a white male writer who serves to ground the very canon they would destabilize. It seems imprudent to speculate further than this, but the general point remains in force: that such other perspectives will produce readings whose difference from mine is not only (not even mainly) personal but instead affiliatory, a function of group orientation.

The "we" that parades through this book seeks to remain self-aware of its conditional status, even though other readers (and not just women and blacks) will find it at times to be blindly universalizing. One cannot write simply as an I. The positions I urge are never mine alone, and I could not pursue them at such length if I did not want them to become yours too. As Wadlington has argued, and as I concur throughout this study, our identities are enacted in the risking of reciprocal acknowledgments, not in the reiteration of completed essences. Writing is inaugural – it is in search of its point, its reader – and I cannot know how much or how little I have inaugurated.

This study has focused on canonical texts, and it is time to ask more directly why these *are* canonical texts, as prelude to asking why we canonize Faulkner at all. I want to pursue this question speculatively, through an extended inquiry into the appeal of his most canonical text, *The Sound and the Fury.* In writing this novel, Faulkner was to say repeatedly over the years, he came upon his true vocation, recognizing his own deepest possibilities within the mirror of its emergent prose. What might it mean that he, and we following him, so value this text and make it our "heart's darling"? What larger cultural arrangements empower such an assessment?

&

"We must cease once and for all to describe the effects of power in negative terms: it 'excludes,' it 'represses,' it 'censors,' it 'abstracts,' it 'masks,' it 'conceals.' In fact, power produces; it produces reality; it produces domains of objects and rituals of truth. The individual and the knowledge that may be gained of him belong to this production" (*Discipline* 194). I begin with Foucault rather than Faulkner because our free assent to this as to the other texts we cherish comes triangulated, encouraged by others' voices, valorized by the culture's preexistent "rituals of truth." By circling Faulkner's text, seeking to identify some of the invisible "domains" and "rituals of truth" that make up its context and enable its canonical status, I hope to delineate that power-inflected space of hermeneutic norm within which we, its committed readers, are both produced and productive. What follows is an attempt both to narrate and to assess a fable of intersubjectivity in the Imaginary mode.

I say "we" and of course I mean "I." *The Sound and the Fury* has been for twenty years my "heart's darling" also, the text I manage every year to assign in one course or another. I want in this last commentary not just to reencounter it, but to probe the ideological postures I've been affirming during these years of praise (even though they've come under some suspicion in the foregoing pages). What scene of training have I been activating for twenty years – training my students to see in this text a supreme shaping of human experience, reconfirming the maps of my own subjectivity in the act of teaching it repeatedly?

I say "I" and of course I mean "we." My affair with this text is in some measure our affair, although the "our" in this claim is not inclusive but rather limited to white and male. Members of this group have canonized *The Sound and the Fury* – the period in which they began it is the 1950s – and it is in a certain measure their Imaginary identity that I and others (including women and blacks) reconfirm whenever we respond to the text along the lines I am going to describe. For if Foucault is right, my subjectivity cannot be mine alone. It too has been produced, and most potently so when I feel most myself – free, empowered, autonomous. We have, then, "freely" and "autonomously" come to see *The Sound and the Fury* as our "heart's darling" because it seems to touch something essential in our own inwardness – something untapped by our culture's proffered arrangements and discoverable only through the tortuous inventions of Faulkner's narrative form. It finds a space in us we did not know was there. More accurately, it produces in us the fantasy of a subjective space no cultural code can map. Perhaps the keynote to this space is *loss* or – to use Faulkner's obsessive term when describing this text – *failure*.

No reader of *Faulkner in the University* can fail to note the satisfaction with which he repeatedly links this word "failure" to his text. It is a failure so profound that it reveals the superficiality of others' success. Faulkner locates Wolfe's superiority to Hemingway precisely in failure: the "attempt to reach the unattainable dream, to accomplish more than flesh and blood could accomplish" (*FU* 206–7). The failure enacted in *The Sound and the Fury*'s story joins with the writer's own proclaimed failure of narrative form to suggest some ultimate domain of the unattainable. In such a poetics the satisfying of mere norms appears as a slavishly conventional move that any supreme venture will of course transcend.

Writing conventions can indeed be slavish. At the University of Virginia in 1957, one of Faulkner's students took umbrage at the writer's cavalier treatment of normative usage: "And another thing I noticed," the student said, "you don't advise that people have to have a subject and predicate for verbs and all those things." Faulkner backtracked, responding that Benjy "didn't know too much about grammar," but his critic was unappeased: "I'm referring mostly to Quentin and he certainly – he attended Harvard, he should have known" (*FU* 95). We smile at such obtuseness, think briefly of the norm–obsessed 1950s, and pass to other matters. But the text's bid for freedom is microscopically located in such an exchange. Neither Benjy nor Quentin can be contained within the proprieties taught at Harvard and elsewhere. They speak their liberation from grammar in "chanting measures beyond the need for words" (*SF* 340), and we participate in their apparently unco-opted idiolects.

These chanting measures are not only not normative but deeply confusing; and Eric Sundquist has rightly noted that this inaugurating masterpiece is, in an important measure, Faulkner's first incoherent text. "On turning from *Sartoris* to *The Sound and the Fury*," Sundquist writes, "one feels, in effect, that thought has been declared impossible and ideas irrelevant" (8). Thought impossible and ideas irrelevant: plunged within the minds of an idiot and his suicidal brother, we encounter failure as *their* tragedy and *our* transcendence. That is, their failure to sign on, to grow up, to assent to ideological alignment – their impossible thought and irrelevant ideas – these register in the *récit* as character tragedy, but in the *discours* as readerly transcendence. The reader's immersion within "a chaos freed of the falsifications of system" (Kartiganer 165) seems to delineate a space beyond ideology itself. Sundquist's concern is race relations, and he laments this early text's failure to coordinate its ideas, but critics with a different agenda might rewrite such refused coherence as achievement. As Eliot said of James, "He had a mind so fine that no idea could violate it."

With Eliot and James we enter a New Critical climate, and Lawrence Schwartz has recently shown how thoroughly a New Critical agenda ushered in Faulkner's canonization in the late 1940s and 1950s. For a generation James and Faulkner were twinned as our greatest American novelists – I was trained in the late 1950s and 1960s to regard them in those terms – and what they share (one of the few things they do share) is a formal complexity that seems to outstrip any systemic ideological tracking. Beyond ideology, detached visionaries, James and Faulkner were produced as star figures in a cold war politics of aesthetic vision and practice whose intricacies "do not submit to serve the ends of any one ideological group or tendency" (Trilling 7). No one put it better than Yeats (and we seemed twenty-five years ago to encounter this citation in every other critical essay we read):

> The rhetorician would deceive his neighbors,
> The sentimentalist himself; while art
> Is but a vision of reality.
> "Ego Dominus Tuus"

If the (triumphant) failure of system is the cardinal theme of this non-ideological art-domain, beyond rhetoric and sentiment, its narrative structure seems keyed – in the work of Faulkner – to another discourse that privileges failure: the discourse of psychoanalysis. Indeed, psychoanalysis provides us with the classic narrative form (and celebration) of subjective failure. A life in disarray (unable to align itself within cultural imperatives), a subjectivity blind to its own illness, a past traumatically alive in the irrational moves of the present: these ideologemes generate the narrative structure of *The Sound and the Fury* and *Light in August*. Such texts move through repetition, even as they may yearn for the more humanistic activities of recollection and working through. Sartre was the first (but hardly the last) to complain that time in such a structure is decapitated, severed from project, fruitless, in love with failure.

From Carvel Collins in the early 1950s through John Irwin and André Bleikasten in the late 1970s, our canonical readings of this text have leaned recurrently toward a psychoanalytic paradigm. What is at stake in such framing? Whatever their differences, such readings reconfirm the profundity of the anguished human subject, a profundity satisfyingly beyond ideological coherence. Jettisoning the coherent subject of liberal humanism, psychoanalysis yet retains – indeed enshrines – the category of the individual. Lacanian psychoanalysis may open up that category to a more systemic scrutiny of the Other ceaselessly affecting the subject, but even so, psychoanalysis continues to celebrate subjective depth and deviancy. It does so in the form of the subject's continuous, unwitting confession. As Foucault writes in *The History of Sexuality,* "we have passed from a pleasure to be recounted and heard, centering on the heroic or marvelous narration of 'trials' of bravery or sainthood, to a literature ordered according to the infinite task of extracting from the depths of oneself, in between the words, a truth which the very form of the confession holds out like a shimmering image" (59). Foucault goes on to propose that such a literature must be devious, and that its reading enacts "a ritual in which truth is corroborated by the obstacles and resistances it has had to surmount in order to be formulated" (62). Finally, he says, the secret being so arduously tracked in such texts is valuable not through any intrinsic worthiness but through "its obscure familiarity and its general baseness" (62). It would be hard to improve on this as one of the criteria of pleasure operating in our reading of *The Sound and the Fury.*

Subjective depth and inwardness, the obscure, well-nigh inaccessible secret beckoning to the avid reader: to narrate these materials requires, as the psychoanalytic plot requires, a subject in pain, stymied by repressive and immovable social norms. Until recently this drama of repression (a theme uniting Victorian and Modernist fiction) has been read within a single ideological schema: the social coercion of the subject, the unbearable constraint upon libidinal energies. From Blake through Freud and up to Marcuse and beyond, we have taken this story as our central one of hunger denied, of power opposing the subject. But John Kucich, in his *Repression in Victorian Fiction,* draws on Bataille and Foucault to turn this argument upside-down. The self-undoing of such repressed figures is an erotically charged spectacle, he proposes. Reader and character both wallow in "the luxuriant waste of emotional energy in self-conflict, the violation of self-coherence, and the emotionally extravagant sacrifice of the self" (23). Barthesian *jouissance,* Derridean *différance,* Kristevan "semiotic" – all these current terms of rupture privilege interior disturbance, self-fissuring, the transgression of internalized social codes. In their different ways, Maggie Tulliver, Raskolnikov, Stephen Dedalus, and Quentin Compson may live insufferably pinched lives in their texts' *récit,* but in the *discours* they run riot, overflowing normative boundaries, rising into almost mythic stature through the hypnotic spectacle of their social silencing.

The ideological work of each of these texts resides in making silence speak, in charging silence with erotic portent, in immersing us within the all-consuming confines of the socially beleaguered subject. Libidinal energy tends to be drained away in such plots from collective realities, from the larger, systemic pressures and possibilities posed by class, race, and gender. Such texts rarely elaborate or affirm available social alignments. Instead, the irresistible subject dwarfs any actual options. As Terry Eagleton diagnostically puts it, "the very form of our subjection lies in our trust in a subjectivity transcendental of all determinations" ("Subject" 101). Thus private (predication-free) identity is celebrated as a priceless though violated resource, as personal depth, speechlessly resonating. These texts privilege repression because they insist upon the unconscious as that interiority which social codes mangle and despoil. In their will to tragedy – to the spectacle of the gifted individual terrifyingly irreducible to conditions and affiliations – such texts, including *The Sound and the Fury*, cannot afford Pierre Bourdieu's disturbing suggestion that the unconscious is not "in here" but "out there": "The 'unconscious' is never anything other than the forgetting of history which history itself produces" (78).

Failure, finally, cloaks success as cunningly as impotence cloaks power. Foucault has suggested that truth and power interpenetrate rather than serve as each other's opposite, and I think this insight echoes in both the empowerment of Mr. Compson in the book (he who speaks so seductively of impotence) and in the success of the book itself (Faulkner who speaks so stubbornly of failure about a book that – he has to have known – put him beyond the reach of his competitors). This is the text he rode en route to canonical eminence. How better to misrecognize this empowering alignment within a hegemonic interpretive community of New Critics than to insist upon a text written wholly for himself: beyond exchange, radically innocent, satisfyingly failed?

I have dealt so far with the resonance of failure and with the narrative form implicit in psychoanalysis to convey some of the "rituals of truth" – the fantasy of release from ideological harness – that account for *The Sound and the Fury's* canonical status. I turn now to one last psychoanalytic *donnée*, the phenomenon of transference. The subject–object boundary seems to dissolve as we engage the free-floating, unaligned consciousnesses of those opening chapters; in a certain measure we become what we read. All this changes radically when we enter Jason's chapter – indeed Jason never recovers from his placement after Benjy and Quentin – and I would speculate the following: that one reason we assign this book year after year is to reimmerse ourselves in those first two chapters, to reexperience their extraordinary dislocations.

Such reexperiencing is voyeurism of a high order. We seem to escape the culture's maps of maturation, its clichés of project and predication.

Without denying the freshening that comes of such an encounter, I can no longer avoid acknowledging a counterreality: that the experience of reading this book energizes a very powerful act of reorientation. Losing oneself spurs the desire to find oneself. We may lecture all we want about the gaps and discontinuities of *The Sound and the Fury:* our students calmly take this down, secure that such remarks are part of the process of mapping a text at first sight unmappable. Are they wrong? Surely this act of mapping generates a large part of their pleasure in the text, and it raises the following question. How do we square our and their work of mapping the text with the fact that this text attests so eloquently to the catastrophic effects of cultural maps upon its characters' lives?

Until recently I have carefully pieced together the shards of Compson time, have worked out their traumas in the past and their repercussions in the present, and never noticed that this recomposing of their lives into coherently abbreviated narratives embodies a remarkable act of fantasized containment. Peter Brooks tells us that we are always replaying time so as not to lose it, always seeking that transcendent home where our life narrative began. "All we can do," he writes, "is subvert or, perhaps better, pervert time: which is what narrative does" ("Freud's Masterplot" 299). Compson time may be lost for the Compsons, but the reader's acts of transference and memory enable the most splendidly perverse – almost Proustian – experience of temporal recovery. To test this premise, compare the coherence of the patterns that remain in the mind after reading *The Sound and the Fury* with the incoherence of those that remain in the mind after reading Beckett's *Molloy.* In reading the earlier text we engage simultaneously in acts of ideological destabilization and ideological recontainment. But the rhetoric of loss and disorientation, of sublime failure, has concealed these latter acts and made it all seem what on reflection it cannot be: innocent.

I have tried to convey the sense of unmapped liberation that so endears our "heart's darling" to us, and to suggest that, within this illusory escape from ideology, a set of valorizing "rituals of truth" – what Donald Pease has recently referred to as a text's participation within a "field-Imaginary," a disciplinary unconscious (11) – is actively at work, generating canonical status. Appearing to be beyond ideology is ideology's defining move. So let us look, for just a moment, at a few things that such a reading of "innocence" and "failure" necessarily scants. It pays no attention to the by-no-means randomly selective readership of *The Sound and the Fury.* As that student at the University of Virginia stubbornly glimpsed, grammar matters. Only those deeply trained in conventional novelistic language can make their way through Faulkner's experiment. This Modernist text will "make sense" mainly to a college-educated audience; it exploits on every page the cultural training (required to master its *discours*) that it mocks through the unfolding of its *récit*. It also is empowered by a gender hierarchy of the first importance. The questing and troubled subjective spirit is intrinsically male here; the objectified source of trouble is intrinsically female. And, because its figuring of race is everywhere subordinated to the probing of white Compson turmoil, this text cannot compare with *Light in August* and *Absalom, Absalom!* when it comes to articulating the reciprocal nightmare of American race relations.

But its deepest blandishment remains intact: private "depth" itself. It is the Narcissus mirror into which we inexhaustibly peer, searching for that Imaginary core of individual resource not yet besmirched by entry into our culture's Symbolic paradigms. It seems to intimate our inexpressible selves – that in us that is beyond co-opting – and therefore we might best encounter its spell by taking to it Roland Barthes's tonic injunction: that literature does not express the inexpressible, but rather it unexpresses the expressible. Not the depth of individual souls, but the surface of inter-twined cultural codes; not a nature prior to cultural mapping, but a cultural mapping we delight in taking as nature; not beyond ideology but successfully (i.e., invisibly) within ideology. My own ambivalence about rising to such a labor of mapping, my mixed feelings about giving up this Imaginary icon of uncharted subjectivity, my desire to keep the text at all costs "beautiful" and "moving" and "passionate" (Faulkner's terms for excluding Caddy from the narrator's role): all this reveals how much is at stake in those precious and problematic acts of transference that produce the "darlings" of our canonical literature.

᪶

The Sound and the Fury was Faulkner's first canonical masterpiece but hardly his last (even though the writing and the reading experience of the others would never convey to the same extent this exquisite sense of escape from ideological harness). A sense of interiority too rich for nor-mative projects, a psychic urgency destined for failure – these recur in all of his canonical texts between 1929 and 1936, and they limn the crucial ingredient on which his Modernist reputation would be established: the representation of tortured, priceless, defiantly unaligned subjectivity. These *are* (as I see it) Faulkner's masterpieces, in the sense that they explore most compellingly the widest social implications and agony of subject formation. My aim in this book has not been to debunk them but to identify the concealed ideological currents that coil within their pre-cincts, to chart the tensions between, on the one hand, a project (com-mon to writer, character, and reader) to escape conventional confines – to engender or experience a cosmos all one's own – and, on the other, a performance (again, common to writer, character, and reader) that is necessarily caught up within those conventions it would transcend.

The optics employed for carrying out this critical pursuit have changed with each chapter. Imitating *The Sound and the Fury*'s procedure of repercussive revisiting of the same materials, chapter after chapter, my four chapters have each grouped and probed four of the major texts written between 1929 and 1942. I have not gone out of my way to make later observations contest earlier claims, but I have not avoided it either. *Absalom, Absalom!* and *Go Down, Moses* receive, for example, a quite different (and more suspicious) treatment in the diachronic discussions (half of Chapter 3, all of Chapter 4) than in the more synchronic ones I offer in Chapters 1 and 2. This is because these latter texts begin to reveal a different set of rhetorical practices whose implications my later chapters seek to interrogate more critically.

The form of my commentary enacts my conviction that every "take" at these texts is scandalously partial, repressing largely in order to have its little "say." I have chosen instead to return repeatedly, within altered optics that produce readings either slightly or greatly different from each other. No chapter centers on a single Faulkner text, in the illusion that its claims can fix (in both senses) that text. The chapters seek to be both intra- and interdialogical, playing text against text, optic against optic. The fruitfulness of this approach, it seems to me, exceeds any execution of it that I can master, for it allows for (at least it does not punish) an alertness to difference that is potentially infinite. (Though in practice how limited: try as we may, we cannot think the unthought of our thought.) To the extent that I have succeeded, some of the discursive economies that allow Faulkner to become "Faulkner" have emerged into view, as well as an understanding of the constructedness of identity that makes it impossible to see him steady and see him whole.

With few exceptions I have limited my scrutiny to canonical texts. I do this not because I believe his other novels to be inconsequential to our construal of "Faulkner." There is no pretense of completeness here, no attempt to repropose an essential portable Faulkner. Rather, I have wanted a kind of concentration and repercussion possible only within a severe frame of attention. The texts I do examine convey fairly enough the range of his achievement, and with respect to race they are inescapable choices. To consider them is to consider both a writer's visible accomplishment and a culture's invisible complicity therein. For, as Bakhtin has argued, these text objects do not exist unto themselves. We cannot but approach them through the sedimented "say" that has accreted to them over the years. It would require another study to develop fully the problematics of canonicity at issue here. I have examined only *The Sound and the Fury* directly and at length from that perspective. But I have relied in general upon my concern with omnipresent cultural coding to keep this study of the Faulknerian canon from succumbing to canonical reverence.

Light in August, Absalom, Absalom!, and *Go Down, Moses,* I have argued, invite quite different relations with their readers – different from each other, different from the relations proposed by *The Sound and the Fury.* After *Light in August* textual subjectivity becomes increasingly clothed in a hospitable, culturally furnished rhetoric. The voice we like to think of as "Faulkner" is inconceivable without the virtuosity of this new rhetoric. Its flourishes assert the Southern oratorical tradition from which they derive, as its figures rehearse the downfall of the Old South – mangling yet heroic, unavailing yet inescapable – whose mores he saw receding from him. The texts turn toward their nineteenth-century Southern heritage with a critical energy increasingly weighted with nostalgia, as their author begins to write himself out of the shock tactics and alienation of Modernism and into a new form of (if I may be permitted) apocalyptic regionalism.

Absalom emerges as the pivotal text in Faulkner's career, the one in which he first sounded the syntax and vocabulary of "his" magnificent voice, the one in which we first believe ourselves to be hearing *him.* The deliberate treatment of race in this and subsequent texts takes on an unprecedented resonance and power. And the voice(s) that narrate them have proved to be as seductive for many readers as the earlier ventriloquated masterpieces were. As seductive, perhaps, but enabled by (and therefore contained within) a rhetoric of polysyllabic insistence and syntactical extravagance, on the one hand, or a rhetoric of vernacular reasonableness and heightened common sense, on the other. Both rhetorics have tended to produce (and valorize) a subjectivity redolent of man's noble failing/enduring/prevailing. Both tend to refuse an (apparently) unmediated engagement with subjectivities that sound the stark incapacitation of Benjy Compson, the savage misfit of Joe Christmas.

We have gone to Faulkner for many reasons, then, and these will continue to change and be charted as the interpretive climate changes and charts itself. Further commentaries based in cultural studies will uncover a greater textual complicity with ideological practices than we have yet ascertained, and the studies based in gender and racial tropes are likely to find his cosmos even less his own than I have argued here. Indeed, the age of literary heroism has ended (or been suspended), as we read authorial subjectivity as more and more contained within frames of ideological affiliation. Entire books devoted to Faulkner will diminish. The case for individual achievement – a cosmos of one's own – will become harder, if not impossible, to make. The claim of a disinterested aesthetic criterion is already so politically vexed that it barely surfaces in contemporary literary criticism.

In alignment with these developments, and in the face of them (I am not middle-aged for nothing), I have written this book. I believe that these texts, as troubling as we are learning to find them, still embody an extraordinary achievement. The most thoroughgoing New Historicist convictions will not alter the fact that individuals experience their lives through their "own" subjective prisms. However fissured, however mystified, however overdetermined, subjectivity is the Imaginary space through which we uniquely know and feel ourselves, through which we register the Other in all its ramifications. No one has mapped its pathos – its incoherence, its array of fantasies, its contradictory scripting, its preciousness – better than Faulkner. This is, I think, his best claim to the attention he receives and an underlying reason for the novelistic choices I have made.

His great texts not only remind us of what is at stake in our cultural insertions. They recreate in us, within the act of reading, the vertigo of such a ceaseless traffic of failed or achieved accommodations. So much that we might think to be outside finds its way heartbreakingly within. Reading him, we undergo again the strangeness of our being in culture. There can be no agential reshaping of our practices, no refocusing of our optics, until we measure how penetrated we are by arrangements we did not invent and do not control. To engage Faulkner's cosmos is to experience a compelling subjective desire (his, his characters', ours as we read him) for mastery – and to recognize in the fate of that desire a remapping of our place in culture, culture's place in us. His cosmos matters most because no one can possibly own it.

Bibliography

Aiken, Conrad. "William Faulkner: The Novel as Form." In *William Faulkner: Three Decades of Criticism,* Edited by Frederick J. Hoffman and Olga W. Vickery, 135–41. New York: Harcourt, 1960.

Althusser, Louis. "Ideology and Ideological State Apparatuses." In *Lenin and Philosophy, and Other Essays,* 127–86. London: New Left Books, 1971.

Bakhtin, Mikhail. "Discourse in the Novel." In *The Dialogic Imagination,* translated by Caryl Emerson and Michael Holquist, 259–422. Austin: University of Texas Press, 1981.

Baldwin, James. "Stranger in the Village." In *The Price of the Ticket: Collected Nonfiction, 1948–1985,* 79–90. New York: St. Martin's, 1985.

Barthes, Roland. *A Barthes Reader.* Edited by Susan Sontag. New York: Farrar, Straus, & Giroux, 1982.

Mythologies. Translated by Annette Lavers. New York: Farrar, Straus, & Giroux, 1972.

The Pleasure of the Text. Translated by Richard Miller. New York: Farrar, Straus, & Giroux, 1975.

Roland Barthes by Roland Barthes. New York: Farrar, Straus, & Giroux, 1977.

S/Z. Translated by Richard Miller. New York: Farrar, Straus, & Giroux, 1974.

Beauvoir, Simone de. *The Second Sex.* Translated by H. M. Parshley. New York: Knopf, 1968.

Belsey, Catherine. *Critical Practice.* London: Methuen, 1980.

Bennett, Tony. *Formalism and Marxism.* London: Methuen, 1979.

Bernheimer, Charles. *Flaubert and Kafka,* 1–44. New Haven: Yale University Press, 1982.

Bleikasten, André. "Fathers in Faulkner." In *The Fictional Father: Lacanian Readings of the Text,* edited by Robert Con Davis, 115–45. Amherst: University of Massachusetts Press, 1981.

"Faulkner and the Paradoxes of Description." In *Faulkner's Discourse: An International Symposium,* edited by Lothar Hönnighausen, 170–83. Tübingen: Niemeyer, 1989.

Faulkner's "As I Lay Dying." Translated by Roger Little. Bloomington: Indiana University Press, 1973.

"Figures de la mort." *l'Arc: W. Faulkner,* edited by Marc Saporta, 109–22. Paris: Editions le Jas, 1984–85.

"In Praise of Helen." In *Faulkner and Women: Faulkner and Yoknapatawpha 1985,* edited by Doreen Fowler and Ann J. Abadie, 128–43. Jackson: University Press of Mississippi, 1986.

The Ink of Melancholy: Faulkner's Novels from "The Sound and the Fury" to "Light in August." Bloomington: University of Indiana Press, 1990.

"Light in August: The Closed and Its Subjects." In *New Essays on* Light in August, edited by Michael Millgate, 81–102. New York: Cambridge University Press, 1987.

The Most Splendid Failure: Faulkner's "The Sound and the Fury." Bloomington: University of Indiana Press, 1976.

Booth, Wayne. *The Company We Keep: An Ethics of Fiction.* University of California Press, Berkeley: 1988.

Bourdieu, Pierre. *Outline of a Theory of Practice.* Translated by Richard Nice. Cambridge: Cambridge University Press, 1977.

Bove, Paul. *Intellectuals in Power: A Genealogy of Critical Humanism.* New York: Columbia University Press, 1986.

Brooks, Cleanth. Introduction to *Light in August,* v–xxv. New York: Random House, 1968.

Introduction to *Faulkner's Women: Characterization and Meaning,* by Sally R. Page. Deland, Fla.: Everett/Edwards, 1972.

William Faulkner: The Yoknapatawpha Country. New Haven: Yale University Press, 1963.

Brooks, Peter. "Freud's Masterplot." In *Literature and Psychoanalysis: The Question of Reading: Otherwise,* edited by Shoshana Felman, 280–300. Baltimore: Johns Hopkins University Press, 1982.

"'Incredulous Narration': *Absalom, Absalom!*" In *Reading for the Plot,* 286–312. New York: Knopf, 1984.

Cain, William E. *The Crisis in Criticism.* Baltimore: Johns Hopkins University Press, 1984.

Carroll, David. *The Subject in Question: The Languages of Theory and the Strategies of Fiction.* Chicago: University of Chicago Press, 1982.

Cash, W. J. *The Mind of the South.* New York: Knopf, 1941.

Clément, Catherine, and Helene Cixous. *The Newly Born Woman.* Translated by Betsy Wing. Minneapolis: University of Minnesota Press, 1986.

Collins, Carvel. "The Interior Monologues of *The Sound and the Fury.*" In *English Institute Essays,* edited by Alan S. Downer, 29–55. New York: Columbia University Press, 1954.

Cowan, Louise. *The Fugitive Group: A Literary History.* Baton Rouge: Louisiana State University Press, 1959.

Cowley, Malcolm. Introduction to *The Portable Faulkner,* 1–24. New York: Viking, 1946.

Davis, Thadious. *Faulkner's "Negro": Art and the Southern Context*. Baton Rouge: Louisiana State University Press, 1983.

"From Jazz Syncopation to Blues Elegy: Faulkner's Development of Black Characterization." In *Faulkner and Race: Faulkner and Yoknapatawpha 1986*, 70–92. Jackson: University Press of Mississippi, 1987.

Derrida, Jacques. "Force and Signification." In *Writing and Difference*, translated by Alan Bass, 3–30. University of Chicago Press, 1978.

Of Grammatology. Translated by Gayatri Spivak. Baltimore: Johns Hopkins University Press, 1976.

"Racism's Last Word." In *"Race," Writing, and Difference*, edited by Henry Louis Gates, 329–38. Chicago: University of Chicago Press, 1986.

"Structure, Sign, and Play in the Discourse of the Human Sciences." In *Writing and Difference*, translated by Alan Bass, 278–93. Chicago: University of Chicago Press, 1986.

Dowling, William. *Jameson, Althusser, Marx*. Ithaca: Cornell University Press, 1984.

Dreyfus, Hubert L., and Paul Rabinow. *Michel Foucault: Beyond Structuralism and Hermeneutics*. Chicago: University of Chicago Press, 1982.

Duvall, John. "Faulkner's Critics and Women: The Voice of the Community." In *Faulkner and Women: Faulkner and Yoknapatawpha 1985*, edited by Doreen Fowler and Ann J. Abadie, 41–57. Jackson: University Press of Mississippi, 1986.

Faulkner's Marginal Couple: Invisible, Outlaw, and Unspeakable Communities. Austin: University of Texas Press, 1990.

Eagleton, Terry. *Criticism and Ideology*. London: NLB, 1976.

Ideology: An Introduction. London: Verso, 1991.

Literary Theory: An Introduction. Oxford: Blackwell, 1983.

"The Subject of Literature." *Cultural Critique* 2 (1985–6): 95–104.

Early, James. *The Making of Go Down, Moses*. Dallas: Southern Methodist University Press, 1972.

Faulkner, William. *Absalom, Absalom!: The Corrected Text*. New York: Random House, 1986.

As I Lay Dying: The Corrected Text. New York: Random House, 1987.

Collected Stories of William Faulkner. New York: Random House, 1950.

"Evangeline." In *Uncollected Stories of William Faulkner*, edited by Joseph Blotner, 583–609. New York: Random House, 1978.

Faulkner in the University: Class Conferences at the University of Virginia, 1957–58. Edited by Frederick L. Gwynn and Joseph L. Blotner. New York: Random House, 1965.

"Gold Is Not Always." *Atlantic Monthly* (1940). Reprinted in *Uncollected Stories of William Faulkner*, edited by Joseph Blotner, 226–37. New York: Random House, 1981.

Go Down, Moses. New York: Random House, 1942.

The Hamlet. New York: Random House, 1964.

Intruder in the Dust. New York: Random House, 1948.

Light in August: The Corrected Text. New York: Random House, 1987.

"A Point of Law." *Collier's* 105 (1940): 20–1, 30–1. Reprinted in *Uncollected Stories of William Faulkner*, edited by Joseph L. Blotner, 213–25. New York: Random House, 1981.

Sartoris. New York: Signet, 1964.

Selected Letters of William Faulkner. Edited by Joseph Blotner. New York: Random House, 1978.

The Sound and the Fury: The Corrected Text. New York: Random House, 1987.

Foucault, Michel. *The Archaeology of Knowledge*. Translated by A. M. Sheridan Smith. New York: Harper and Row, 1972.

Discipline and Punish. Translated by Alan Sheridan. New York: Random House, 1979.

The History of Sexuality. Vol. 1. Translated by Robert Hurley. New York: Random House, 1980.

"Nietzsche, Genealogy, and History." In *Language, Counter-Memory, Practice: Selected Essays and Interviews of Michel Foucault*, translated by Donald F. Bouchard and Sherry Simon, 139–64. Ithaca: Cornell University Press, 1977.

"What is an Author?" In *Language, Counter-Memory, Practice: Selected Essays and Interviews of Michel Foucault*, translated by Donald F. Bouchard and Sherry Simon, 113–38. Ithaca: Cornell University Press, 1977.

Fowler, Doreen. "Joe Christmas and 'Womanshenegro.'" In *Faulkner and Women: Faulkner and Yoknapatawpha, 1985*, edited by Doreen Fowler and Ann J. Abadie, 144–61. Jackson: University Press of Mississippi, 1986.

Freud, Sigmund. *The Interpretation of Dreams*. In *The Standard Edition of the Complete Psychological Works of Sigmund Freud*, edited and translated by James Strachey, vols. 4–5. London: Hogarth Press, 1953–74.

"Leonardo da Vinci and a Memory of His Childhood." In *The Standard Edition of the Complete Psychological Works of Sigmund Freud*, edited and translated by James Strachey, 11: 63–137. London: Hogarth Press, 1953–74.

"Mourning and Melancholia." In *The Standard Edition of the Complete Psychological Works of Sigmund Freud*, edited and translated by James Strachey, 14: 243–58. London: Hogarth Press, 1953–74.

Gallop, Jane. *The Daughter's Seduction*. Ithaca: Cornell University Press, 1982.

Reading Lacan. Ithaca: Cornell University Press, 1985.

Gardiner, Judith Kegan. "On Female Identity and Writing by Women." *Critical Inquiry* 8 (1981): 347–61.

Gates, Henry Louis. "Dis and Dat: Dialect and the Descent." In *Afro-American Literature: The Reconstruction of Instruction*, edited by Dexter Fisher and Henry Louis Gates, 88–119. New York: MLA, 1979.

The Signifying Monkey: A Theory of African-American Literary Criticism. New York: Oxford University Press, 1988.

"Writing 'Race' and the Difference It Makes." In *"Race," Writing and Difference*, edited by Henry Louis Gates, 1–20. Chicago: University of Chicago Press, 1986.

Genovese, Eugene D. *Roll, Jordan, Roll: The World the Slaves Made*. New York: Random House, 1972.

Godden, Richard. "Iconic Narrative: Or, How Faulkner Fought the Second Civil War." In *Faulkner's Discourse: An International Symposium*, edited by Lothar Hönnighausen, 68–76. Tübingen: Niemeyer, 1989.

Gresset, Michel. *Faulkner ou la fascination: poétique du regard*. Paris: Klingsieck, 1982.

"Faulkner's Voice." In *Faulkner's Discourse: An International Symposium*, edited by Lothar Hönnighausen, 184–94. Tübingen: Niemeyer, 1989.

Grimwood, Michael. *Heart in Conflict: Faulkner's Struggles with Vocation*. Athens: Georgia University Press, 1987.

Gwin, Minrose. *The Feminine and Faulkner*. Knoxville: University of Tennessee Press, 1989.

Howe, Irving. *William Faulkner: A Critical Study*. New York: Random House, 1951.

Irigaray, Luce. *Ce Sexe qui n'en est pas un*. Paris: Editions de Minuit, 1977.

This Sex Which Is Not One. Translated by Catherine Porter and Carolyn Burke. Ithaca: Cornell University Press, 1985.

Irwin, John. *Doubling and Incest, Repetition and Revenge: A Speculative Reading of Faulkner*. Baltimore: Johns Hopkins University Press, 1975.

Jacobus, Mary. "Dora and the Pregnant Madonna." In *Reading Woman: Essays in Feminist Criticism*, 137–93. New York: Columbia University Press, 1986.

Jameson, Fredric. "Imaginary and Symbolic in Lacan." In *Literature and Psychoanalysis: The Question of Reading: Otherwise*, edited by Shoshana Felman, 338–95. Baltimore: Johns Hopkins University Press, 1982.

The Political Unconscious: Narrative as a Socially Symbolic Act. Ithaca: Cornell University Press, 1981.

Jehlen, Myra. *Class and Character in Faulkner's South*. New York: Columbia University Press, 1976.

Jenkins, Lee. *Faulkner and Black-White Relationships*. New York: Columbia University Press, 1981.

Jones, Ann R. "Writing the Body: Towards an Understanding of l'écriture féminine." In *The New Feminist Criticism*, edited by Elaine Showalter, 361–77. New York: Pantheon, 1985.

Jordan, Winthrop D. *White over Black: American Attitudes Toward the Negro, 1550–1812*. Chapel Hill: University of North Carolina Press, 1968.

Kartiganer, Donald M. *The Fragile Thread: The Meaning of Form in Faulkner's Novels*. Amherst: University of Massachusetts Press, 1979.

Kaufmann, Linda S. *Discourses of Desire: Gender, Genre, and Epistolary Fictions*. Ithaca: Cornell University Press, 1986.

Kavanaugh, James. "Marxism's Althusser: Toward a Politics of Literary Theory." In *diacritics* 12 (1982): 25–45.

Kazin, Alfred. "The Stillness of *Light in August*." In *William Faulkner: Three Decades of Criticism*, edited by Frederick J. Hoffman and Olga W. Vickery, 247–65. New York: Harcourt, 1963.

Kenner, Hugh. *A Home-Made World*. New York: Knopf, 1975.

King, Richard. "Memory and Tradition." In *Faulkner and the Southern Renaissance:*

Faulkner and Yoknapatawpha 1981, edited by Doreen Fowler and Ann J. Abadie, 138–57. Jackson: University Press of Mississippi, 1982.

"The South and Cultural Criticism." In *American Literary History* 1 (1989):699–714.

A Southern Renaissance: The Cultural Awakening of the American South 1930–1955. London: Oxford University Press, 1980.

Kovel, Joel. *White Racism: A Psychohistory.* New York: Random House, 1970.

Kreiswirth, Martin. "Overpassing, Transgression, and Auto-Intertextuality: Ways of Reading Yoknapatawpha." Faulkner panel, ALA Conference, June 1990.

Kristeva, Julia. "Stabat Mater." In *The Female Body in Western Culture: Contemporary Perspectives,* edited by Susan R. Suleiman, 99–118. Cambridge: Harvard University Press, 1986.

"The System and the Speaking Subject." In *The Kristeva Reader,* edited by Toril Moi, 24–33. New York: Columbia University Press, 1986.

"Women's Time." In *The Kristeva Reader,* edited by Toril Moi, 187–213. New York: Columbia University Press, 1986.

Kucich, John. *Repression in Victorian Fiction.* Berkeley: University of California Press, 1987.

Lacan, Jacques. "The Agency of the Letter in the Unconscious or Reason since Freud." In *Ecrits: A Selection,* translated by Alan Sheridan, 146–78. New York: Norton, 1977.

"The Mirror Stage as Formative of the Function of the I." In *Ecrits: A Selection,* translated by Alan Sheridan, 1–7. New York: Norton, 1977.

"The Signification of the Phallus." In *Ecrits: A Selection,* translated by Alan Sheridan, 281–91. New York: Norton, 1977.

"The Subversion of the Subject and the Dialectic of Desire in the Freudian Unconscious." In *Ecrits: A Selection,* translated by Alan Sheridan, 292–325. New York: Norton, 1977.

Lacqueur, Thomas. "Orgasm, Generation, and the Politics of Reproductive Biology." *Representations* 4 (1986): 1–41.

Lauretis, Teresa de. *Alice Doesn't: Feminism, Semiotics, Cinema.* Bloomington: Indiana University Press, 1984.

Lemaire, Anika. *Jacques Lacan.* Translated by David Macey. London: Routledge & Kegan Paul, 1977.

Lentricchia, Frank. *After the New Criticism.* Chicago: University of Chicago Press, 1980.

Lester, Cheryl. "To Market, to Market: *The Portable Faulkner.*" *Criticism* 29 (1987):371–92.

Lilly, Paul R. "Caddy and Addie: Speakers of Faulkner's Impeccable Language." *Journal of Narrative Technique* 3 (1973): 170–83.

Lukacs, Georg. "The Ideology of Modernism." In *Realism in Our Time: Literature and the Class Struggle,* translated by John and Necke Mander, 17–46. New York: Harper and Row, 1971.

Macherey, Pierre. *Pour une Théorie de la production littéraire.* Paris: Maspero, 1966.

Martin, Jay. "'The Whole Burden of Man's History of His Impossible Heart's Desire': The Early Life of William Faulkner." *American Literature* 53 (1982): 607–29.

Matthews, John. "Faulkner's Narrative Frames." In *Faulkner and the Craft of Fiction: Faulkner and Yoknapatawpha 1987*, edited by Doreen Fowler and Ann J. Abadie, 71–91. Jackson: University Press of Mississippi, 1989.

"Modernism and Modernization." Faulkner panel. ALA Conference, June 1990.

The Play of Faulkner's Language. Ithaca: Cornell University Press, 1982.

"The Rhetoric of Containment in Faulkner." In *Faulkner's Discourse: An International Symposium*, edited by Lothar Hönnighausen, 55–67. Tübingen: Niemeyer, 1989.

Meats, Stephen. "Who Killed Joanna Burden?" *Mississippi Quarterly* 24 (1971): 271–77.

Miller, J. Hillis. *The Ethics of Reading*. New York: Columbia University Press, 1987.

Miller, Nancy. "Emphasis Added: Plots and Plausibilities in Women's Fiction." In *The New Feminist Criticism*, edited by Elaine Showalter, 339–60. New York: Pantheon, 1985.

Millgate, Michael. *The Achievement of William Faulkner*. New York: Random House, 1963.

Minter, David. *William Faulkner: His Life and Work*. Baltimore: Johns Hopkins University Press, 1980.

Moi, Toril. *Sexual/Textual Politics*. London: Methuen, 1985.

Moreland, Richard C. *Faulkner and Modernism: Rereading and Rewriting*. Madison: University of Wisconsin Press, 1990.

Morris, Wesley, with Barbara Alverson Morris. *Reading Faulkner*. Madison: University of Wisconsin Press, 1989.

Mortimer, Gail. *Faulkner's Rhetoric of Loss*. Austin: University of Texas Press, 1983.

O'Brien, Michael. *The Idea of the American South 1920–1941*. Baltimore: Johns Hopkins University Press, 1979.

O'Donnell, Patrick. "Sub Rosa: Voice, Body, and History in *Absalom, Absalom!*" *College Literature* 16 (1989): 28–47.

Pease, Donald. "New Americanists: Revisionist Interventions into the Canon." *Boundary 2* 17 (1990): 1–37.

Polk, Noel. "The Dungeon Was Mother Herself: William Faulkner: 1927–1931." In *New Directions in Faulkner Studies: Faulkner and Yoknapatawpha 1983*, edited by Doreen Fowler and Ann J. Abadie, 61–93. Jackson: University Press of Mississippi, 1984.

An Editorial Handbook for William Faulkner's The Sound and the Fury. New York: Garland, 1985.

"Man in the Middle: Faulkner and the Southern White Moderate." In *Faulkner and Race: Faulkner and Yoknapatawpha 1986*, edited by Doreen Fowler and Ann J. Abadie, 13–51. Jackson: University of Mississippi Press, 1987.

Porter, Carolyn. *Seeing and Being: The Plight of the Participant Observer in Emerson,*

James, Adams, and Faulkner. Middletown, Conn.: Wesleyan University Press, 1981.

Ragland-Sullivan, Ellie. *Jacques Lacan and the Philosophy of Psychoanalysis*. Urbana: University of Illinois Press, 1986.

Rose, Jacqueline. *Sexuality in the Field of Vision*. London: Verso, 1976.

Ross, Stephen M. *Fiction's Inexhaustible Voice: Speech and Writing in Faulkner*. Athens: University of Georgia Press, 1989.

"The Loud World of Quentin Compson." *Studies in the Novel* 7 (1975): 245–57.

Sartre, Jean-Paul. *The Philosophy of Jean-Paul Sartre*. Edited by Robert D. Cumming. New York: Random House, 1965.

Schwartz, Lawrence H. *Creating Faulkner's Reputation: The Politics of Modern Literary Criticism*. Knoxville: University of Tennessee Press, 1989.

Sensibar, Judith L. "Drowsing Maidenhead Symbol's Self: Faulkner and the Fictions of Love." In *Faulkner and the Craft of Fiction: Faulkner and Yoknapatawpha, 1987*, 124–47. Jackson: University Press of Mississippi, 1989.

Singal, Daniel J. *The War Within: From Victorian to Modernist Thought in the South, 1919–1945*. Chapel Hill: University of North Carolina Press, 1982.

Smith, Paul. *Discerning the Subject*. Minneapolis: University of Minnesota Press, 1988.

Snead, James. *Figures of Division: William Faulkner's Major Novels*. New York: Methuen, 1986.

Stein, Jean. "William Faulkner: An Interview." In *William Faulkner: Three Decades of Criticism*, edited by Frederick J. Hoffman and Olga W. Vickery, 67–82. New York: Harbrace, 1963.

Steinberg, Stephen. "The Reconstruction of Black Servitude." In *The Ethnic Myth*, 173–200. Boston: Beacon, 1982.

Stonum, Gary Lee. *Faulkner's Literary Career: An Internal Literary History*. Ithaca: Cornell University Press, 1979.

Sundquist, Eric. *Faulkner: The House Divided*. Baltimore: Johns Hopkins University Press, 1983.

Swan, Jim. "Mater and Nannies: Freud's Two Mothers and the Discovery of the Oedipus Complex." *American Imago* 31 (1974).

Taylor, Walter. *Faulkner's Search for a South*. Urbana: University of Illinois Press, 1983.

Tindall, George B. *The Emergence of the New South, 1913–1945*. Baton Rouge: Louisiana State University Press, 1967.

Tompkins, Jane, ed. *Reader-Response Criticism: From Formalism to Poststructuralism*. Baltimore: Johns Hopkins University Press, 1980.

Trilling, Lionel. *The Liberal Imagination: Essays on Literature and Society*. Garden City, N.Y.: Doubleday, 1953.

Tucker, John. "William Faulkner's *Light in August*: Towards a Structuralist Reading." *MLQ* 43 (June 1982): 138–55.

Urgo, Joseph R. *Faulkner's Apocrypha*: A Fable, *Snopes, and the Spirit of Human Rebellion*. Jackson: University Press of Mississippi, 1989.

Vickery, Olga W. *The Novels of William Faulkner: A Critical Interpretation*. Baton Rouge: Louisiana State University Press, 1959.

Wadlington, Warwick. *Reading Faulknerian Tragedy*. Ithaca: Cornell University Press, 1987.

Warren, Robert Penn. "William Faulkner." In *Selected Essays*, 59–79. New York: Random House, 1958.

Weinstein, Elizabeth W. *Dimensions and Projections of Identity in Faulkner and Proust*. Senior Thesis. Princeton University, 1989.

Weinstein, Philip M. "Precarious Sanctuaries: Protection and Exposure in Faulkner's Fiction." *Studies in American Fiction* 6 (1977): 38–52.

Werner, Craig. "Tell Old Pharaoh: The Afro-American Response to Faulkner." *Southern Review* 19 (1983): 711–35.

Whorf, Benjamin Lee. *Language, Thought and Reality: Selected Writings of Benjamin Lee Whorf*. Edited by John B. Carroll. Cambridge: MIT Press, 1956.

Wilson, Edmund. *Classics and Commercials*, 460–9. New York: Farrar & Straus, 1950.

Wittenberg, Judith B. "Gender and Linguistic Strategies in *Absalom, Absalom!*" In *Faulkner's Discourse: An International Symposium*, 99–108, edited by Lothar Hönnighausen. Tübingen: Niemeyer, 1989.

"William Faulkner: A Feminist Consideration." In *American Novelists Revisited: Essays in Feminist Criticism*, edited by Fritz Fleischmann. Boston: G. K. Hall, 1982. Reprinted in *Modern Critical Views: William Faulkner*, edited by Harold Bloom, 233–46. New York: Chelsea House, 1986.

"The Women of *Light in August*." In *New Essays on Light in August*, edited by Michael Millgate, 103–22. New York: Cambridge University Press, 1987.

Woodward, C. Vann. *The Burden of Southern History*. Baton Rouge: Louisiana State University Press, 1960.

Origins of the New South, 1877–1913. Baton Rouge: Louisiana State University Press, 1971.

Woolf, Virginia. *A Room of One's Own*. New York: Harbrace, 1957.

Yeats, W. B. *The Collected Poems of W. B. Yeats*. New York: Macmillan, 1956.

Zender, Karl. "Faulkner and the Power of Sound." *PMLA* 99 (1984): 89–108.

Index

Absalom, Absalom!, 3, 8, 63, 80, 89, 122, 144, 148, 163, 164; the body in, 131–5; class in, 136–8; exoticism in, 55–6, 57, 132, 135; gender in, 21–4; and *Gone with the Wind*, 94–7; hysteria in, 22–3; male pairing in, 21, 23–4; oratory in, 141–2; race in, 53–7, 162; subjectivity in, 92–8; time in, 138–9; and tragedy, 140–2; voice in, 135–42
agency, 10, 11, 153; *see also* Smith, Paul
Althusser, Louis, 8, 9, 82; on ideology, 2n, 89–91, 92, 93, 100, 106, 112n, 118; on interpellation, 73–4; *see also* ideology
Anderson, Sherwood, 123
aristocracy, Southern, 16, 120, 146; *see also* South, American
As I Lay Dying, 3n, 58n, 80, 122, 124, 125, 130n, 131
Atlantic Monthly, The, 65, 68

Bakhtin, Mikhail, 106n, 111, 119n, 146, 151, 163; on dialogic, 2n, 100, 136n; on ideology, 9, 66, 107, 112–13, 118, 141; on internally persuasive dicta, 77; on "ventriloquy" and double-voicing, 122, 148n
Baldwin, James, 51

Balibar, Etienne, 98n
Balzac, Honoré, 1
Barthes, Roland, 31, 37n, 89, 119, 130, 159, 162
Bataille, George, 159
"Bear, The," 101, 102, 105, 108, 143, 148
Beauvoir, Simone de, 11, 13n, 20n, 27–8
Beckett, Samuel, 85, 161
Belsey, Catherine, 112n
Bennett, Tony, 89n, 98n
Bernheimer, Charles, 45n, 108n, 114
Bible, the, 74–5, 148–9; *see also* Christianity
Blake, William, 159
Bleikasten, André, 7, 8, 16, 31, 40, 41, 84n, 102n, 103n, 122n, 125n, 127n, 134n, 158
body, the, 110–12, 152; in *Absalom, Absalom!*, 131–5; in *Go Down, Moses*, 58–9, 66, 70–2, 142–6; in *Light in August*, 124–8, 133; in *The Sound and the Fury*, 114–18, 133
Booth, Wayne, 114n
Bourdieu, Pierre, 5, 103, 107–8, 160; on "habitus," 2n, 90, 100, 102
Brooks, Cleanth, 6, 12, 86n, 98, 139n
Brooks, Peter, 57n, 94n, 139n, 161
Brown, Clarence, 80n

Calvinism, 124, 125, 128
Carroll, David, 100n
Christianity, 34, 74–5, 111, 148; *see also* Bible, the
Cixous, Hélène, 12n, 22n, 31n
Clément, Catherine, 22n, 31n
Collier's, 65, 67
Collins, Carvel, 158
conferences, on Faulkner, 30, 82, 83, 87–9, 99
Conrad, Joseph, 123

Darwin, Charles, 65
Da Vinci, Leonardo, 33
Davis, Thadious, 47n, 49, 52n, 60n, 107n
deconstruction, 2n, 43–4, 45n, 101, 141; *see also* Derrida, Jacques
"Delta Autumn," 73, 83, 102, 105, 108, 143, 148
Derrida, Jacques, 1n, 2n, 4, 6, 7, 42, 43, 98, 159; *see also* deconstruction
Donne, John, 98
Dowling, William, 89n
Dreyfus, Herbert L. and Paul Rabinow, 111n
Duvall, John, 107n, 126n

Eagleton, Terry, 2n, 89n 112n, 160
Eliot, T. S., 158
"Evangeline," 136

Fable, A, 80, 125
Faulkner in the Univesity, 12, 15, 157
Faulkner, William, biography of, 40–1, 48, 116, 160; career of, 81, 83, 101, 108–9, 113, 131, 151–3, 162, 164; as "Faulkner," 3–5, 28–9, 83, 98–9, 109, 123, 138, 141, 142, 163, 164; interview with, 101n; juxtapositional talent of, 79–81; racial anxieties of, 16, 42–3, 48; *Selected Letters,* 142; as self-ratifying, 1–2, 140
"Fire and the Hearth, The," 59n, 60, 66, 69–75, 77, 108, 143, 147, 148

Fish, Stanley, 114n
Flags in the Dust, 29
Foucault, Michel, 9, 39n, 66, 116n, 117, 118, 151; on discipline, 2n, 100, 103–4, 111–12; on discourse, 5, 159; on power, 131, 156, 160
Fowler, Doreen, 12n, 155
Francis, Saint, 120
Freud, Sigmund, 7, 40–1, 65, 86, 91–2, 98, 100n, 123, 127, 159; on maternity, 33; *see also* psychoanalysis
Frye, Northrop, 100n

Gallop, Jane, 28n, 37, 91
Gardiner, Judith Kegan, 86n
Gates, Henry Louis, 42, 44n, 74, 154; *see also* "signifying"
gender, 12–13; in *Absalom, Absalom!,* 21–4; in *Go Down, Moses,* 24–7; in *Light in August,* 17–21, 50–1, 126–8; in *The Sound and the Fury,* 13–17, 29–39, 116–17; *see also* virginity
Genet, Jean, 85
Genovese, Eugene D., 45
Godden, Richard, 149n
Go Down, Moses, 3, 6, 8, 9, 55, 65, 77, 80, 81, 82, 113, 123, 163, 164; animals in, 144–5; the body in, 58–9, 66, 70–2, 142–6; exoticism in, 70; gender in, 24–7; male pairings in, 73; oratory in, 150; race in, 26–7, 56, 57–64, 69–75; subjectivity in, 101–9; voice in, 66–7, 146–51
"Gold Is Not Always," 68–9, 71n
Gone with the Wind, 94–6; *see also* Mitchell, Margaret
Gresset, Michel, 141n, 150
Grimwood, Michael, 43n, 69n, 80, 102n, 143
Gwin, Minrose, 8, 12n, 21n, 22, 114n, 155

Hamlet, The, 80, 144
Hemingway, Ernest, 157

homosexuality, 19, 20
Howe, Irving, 6

I'll Take My Stand, 140
ideology, 3, 94, 117, 126, 127, 144,
    152; as Althusserian interpella-
    tion, 2n, 73–4, 89–92, 93, 100,
    106, 112n, 118; of containment,
    75, 147, 150, 153; as critical ap-
    proach, 83, 88, 101; definition
    of, 9n, 112n, 164; escape from,
    130, 131, 151, 158–62; as knowl-
    edge/language, 31, 66, 92, 107,
    113, 118, 123, 141; male-au-
    thored, 32–3; of racism, 54, 71,
    73, 75; and sexuality, 128; as stat-
    ic, 69, 120, 122, 124, 139; work
    of, 54, 68, 75, 113, 159–60; *see
    also* Althusser, Louis, and subjec-
    tivity
Imaginary, 8, 10, 31, 65, 82, 91, 93,
    94, 100, 154, 156, 161, 165; defi-
    nition of, 2n; as fantasy, 99, 104,
    108, 162; *see also* Lacan, Jacques
Intruder in the Dust, 8, 43, 65, 71, 80,
    81, 125, 148, 149; film of, 80n;
    race in, 75–81
Irigaray, Luce, 2n, 11, 36, 37; on
    mimicry, 107
Irwin, John, 4n, 7, 31, 92, 97, 98,
    158
Iser, Wolfgang, 114n

Jacobus, Mary, 34–5
Jakobson, Roman, 122n
James, Henry, 158
Jameson, Fredric, 2n, 85, 89n, 99,
    100, 104n, 112n, 123n, 130, 152
Jehlen, Myra, 70, 78
Jones, Ann, 12n
Jordan, Winthrop, 35n
Joyce, James, 85, 120n, 123

Kartinger, Donald, 158
Kavanaugh, James, 89n
Kazin, Alfred, 17
Kenner, Hugh, 143n
Kovel, Joel, 35n

Kreiswirth, Martin, 1n, 110n
Kristeva, Julia, 2, 11, 34–5, 35n, 40,
    109n, 159; *see also* "semiotic"
Kucich, John, 159

Lacan, Jacques, 8, 9, 89, 108; and the
    Other, 13n, 103, 114n, 159; on
    Symbolic and Imaginary, 2n, 82,
    91–2, 94, 100, 104; *see also*
    other/Other
Laqueur, Thomas, 117n
Lawrence, D. H., 98
Lester, Cheryl, 97n
Light in August, 3, 6, 9, 26, 29, 37,
    43, 80, 82, 122, 135, 144, 158,
    164; the body in, 124–8, 133;
    gender in, 17–21, 50–1, 126–8;
    male pairings in, 19–20, 51; race
    in, 49–53, 107–8, 129, 162; sub-
    jectivity in, 101–9; voice in,
    128–31
Lukacs, Georg, 123n

Macherey, Pierre, 98n; on ideology,
    2n, 112n
male pairings, 155; in *Absalom, Ab-
    salom!,* 23–4; in *Go Down, Moses,*
    73; in *Light in August,* 18–20, 51
Malraux, André, 98, 105
Marcuse, Herbert, 159
Marx, Karl, 65, 98n, 100
Matthews, John, 8, 21n, 49n, 97n,
    98, 113n, 136n, 139n
Miller, J. Hillis, 114n
Milton, John, 98, 127
Minter, David, 48n
miscegenation, 16, 53, 56, 62–3, 85,
    97, 136, 149–50
Mitchell, Margaret, 95, 96; *see also
    Gone with the Wind*
Modernism, 85, 96n, 108, 112n,
    113n, 114n, 118, 119, 159; as
    alienated, 155, 162, 164; as High
    Culture, 120n, 150, 161; ideolog-
    ical orientation of, 123; as shock,
    6, 9, 130–1, 151, 164; as subver-
    sive, 3, 142, 151–3
Molière, Jean-Baptiste, 5

Moreland, Richard C., 8, 22n, 24n, 44, 96n, 114n, 123n, 138n
Morris, Wesley, 8, 42, 79n, 80n, 119, 134n, 136n, 139n
Mortimer, Gail, 84n
Mosquitoes, 128, 132

New Criticism, 7, 82, 98, 154, 160; as universalizing, 28, 42, 86–9, 158
Nietzsche, Friedrich, 7, 98

"Old People, The," 102, 105, 108, 143
other/Other, 8, 12–14, 83, 103n, 149; women as, 13n, 27; *see also* Beauvoir, Simone de, and Lacan, Jacques

"Pantaloon in Black," 58–9, 87–8, 143, 145–6, 147
Pease, Donald, 161
"Point of Law, A," 67–8, 72
Polk, Noel, 32, 79n, 97
Porter, Carolyn, 8, 135n
Postmodernism, 3, 130, 131
Prince, William Meade, 67
Proust, Marcel, 120n
psychoanalysis, 34, 38, 83, 86n, 93, 100, 104, 158–9, 160; *see also* Freud, Sigmund
Pylon, 122, 125, 131

race, 42–6; in *Absalom, Absalom!*, 53–7, 162; in *Go Down, Moses*, 26–7, 56, 57–64, 69–75; in "Gold Is Not Always" and "A Point of Law," 67–9; in *Intruder in the Dust*, 75–81; in *Light in August*, 49–53, 107–8, 129, 162; in *The Sound and the Fury*, 16–17, 46–9, 56
Ragland-Sullivan, Ellie, 91, 104n
Ransom, John Crowe, 86n
Reivers, The, 147n
Rose, Jacqueline, 11, 101
Ross, Stephen, 8, 97n, 113n, 119n, 120n, 128n, 133n, 141n, 150

Sanctuary, 1, 37, 126, 147n
Sartoris, 99, 157
Sartre, Jean-Paul, 13n, 15n, 98, 158
Saussure, Ferdinand de, 100n
Schwartz, Lawrence, 158
Selected Letters of William Faulkner, 142
"semiotic," 2, 35, 40, 83, 155, 159; *see also* Kristeva, Julia
Sensibar, Judith L., 12n, 155
"signifying," 44–5, 60, 68, 72, 155; *see also* Gates, Henry Louis
Singal, Daniel J., 52
Smith, Paul, 2n, 9n, 65, 66, 100n, 101, 153; *see also* agency
Snead, James, 3n, 5–6, 8, 36n, 42, 101n, 107n
Sound and the Fury, The, 3, 6, 7, 8, 11, 26, 29, 51, 58, 63, 71n, 80, 85, 113, 127, 128, 131, 135, 164; Appendix of, 97–8; the body in, 114–18, 133; canonical status of, 4, 156–62, 163; as favorite text, 3, 121, 156–7; gender in, 13–17, 29–39, 116–17; the home in, 117–18; maternity in, 29–39, 116; pastoral in, 48–9, 53, 119; race in, 16–17, 46–9, 56; stream of consciousness in, 83–5, 122; subjectivity in, 83–6; voice in, 116–24
South, the American, codes of, 139; industrialized, 140; and oratory, 133n, 141, 142, 150, 153, 164; and race, 35, 52, 62–3, 103; and women, 134; *see also* aristocracy, Southern
Stein, Jean, 2, 101n
Steinberg, Steven, 62n, 139n
Stonum, Gary, 1, 110n, 123n, 151, 152
subjectivity, 1–4, 6, 8, 11, 57, 63–7, 74, 82–3; in *Absalom, Absalom!*, 92–8; as centered (sutured) identity, 9, 85–9, 106, 108; as decentered (fissured) identity, 2, 10, 96–101, 108–9; and ideology, 89–92, 94, 112–13; in *Light in August* and *Go Down, Moses*,

101–9; psychoanalytic privileging of, 158–60; reader's, 67, 88, 121, 160–1, 165; in *The Sound and the Fury*, 83–6

Sundquist, Eric, 1, 8, 42, 56n, 94n, 157, 158

Swan, Jim, 40

Symbolic, 2, 8, 35, 63, 82, 83, 91–2, 93, 94, 99, 104, 108, 119, 120, 162; definition of, 2n, 65–6n; and Kristeva, Julia, 35; as male, 24, 33, 38, 39–41; and race, 105, 106; as static, 16, 37, 102, 124; *see also* Lacan, Jacques

Tate, Allen, 86n

"That Evening Sun," 88

Tompkins, Jane, 114n

transference, 51, 93, 99, 160–2

Trilling, Lionel, 158

Tucker, John, 50n

Urgo, Joseph, 1n

Vickery, Olga, 6, 98

virginity, 103, 117, 125–7; male lust for, 125–6, 145; in *The Sound and the Fury*, 30–2, 35–9, 85, 115–16

voice, 110–13, 152; in *Absalom, Absalom!*, 135–42; definition of, 113n; in *Go Down, Moses*, 66–7, 146–51; in *Light in August*, 128–31; in *The Sound and the Fury*, 116–24

Wadlington, Warwick, 2n, 8, 96n, 108n, 113n, 114n, 116n, 124n, 129n, 133n, 136n, 137n, 141n, 146n, 155

Warren, Robert Penn, 6

"Was," 25, 143, 144, 147

Werner, Craig, 60n

Whorf, Benjamin Lee, 5–6

Wild Palms, The, 126

Wimsatt, William, 86n

Wittenberg, Judith, 8

Wolfe, Thomas, 157

Woodward, C. Vann, 140n

Woolf, Virginia, 74, 89n, 96n, 120n, 123

Wright, Richard, 64

Yeats, William Butler, 158

Zender, Karl, 150

Cambridge Studies in American Literature and Culture.

Continued from the front of the book

42. Susan K. Harris, *19th-Century American Women's Novels: Interpretive Strategies*
41. Susan Manning, *The Puritan-Provincial Vision: Scottish and American Literature in the Nineteenth Century*
40. Richard Godden, *Fictions of Capital: Essays on the American Novel from James to Mailer*
39. John Limon, *The Place of Fiction in the Time of Science: A Disciplinary History of American Writing*
38. Douglas Anderson, *A House Undivided: Domesticity and Community in American Literature*
37. Charles Altieri, *Painterly Abstraction in Modernist American Poetry: The Contemporaneity of Modernism*
36. John P. McWilliams, Jr., *The American Epic: Transforming a Genre, 1770–1860*
35. Michael Davidson, *The San Francisco Renaissance: Poetics and Community at Mid-century*
34. Eric Sigg, *The American T. S. Eliot*
33. Robert S. Levine, *Conspiracy and Romance: Studies in Brockden Brown, Cooper, Hawthorne, and Melville*
32. Alfred Habegger, *Henry James and the "Woman Business"*
31. Tony Tanner, *Scenes of Nature, Signs of Men*
30. David Halliburton, *The Color of the Sky: A Study of Stephen Crane*
29. Steven Gould Axelrod and Helen Deese (eds.), *Robert Lowell: Essays on the Poetry*
28. Robert Lawson-Peebles, *Landscape and Written Expression in Revolutionary America*
27. Warren Motley, *The American Abraham: James Fenimore Cooper and the Frontier Patriarch*
26. Lynn Keller, *Re-making It New: Contemporary American Poetry and the Modernist Tradition*
25. Margaret Holley, *The Poetry of Marianne Moore: A Study in Voice and Value*
24. Lothar Honnighausen, *William Faulkner: The Art of Stylization in His Early Graphic and Literary Work*
23. George Dekker, *The American Historical Romance*
22. Brenda Murphy, *American Realism and American Drama, 1880–1940*
21. Brook Thomas, *Cross-examinations of Law and Literature: Cooper, Hawthorne, Stowe, and Melville*
20. Jerome Loving, *Emily Dickinson: The Poet on the Second Story*
19. Richard Gray, *Writing the South: Ideas of an American Region*
18. Karen E. Rowe, *Saint and Singer: Edward Taylor's Typology and the Poetics of Meditation*
17. Ann Kibbey, *The Interpretation of Material Shapes in Puritanism: A Study of Rhetoric, Prejudice, and Violence*

16. Sacvan Bercovitch and Myra Jehlen (eds.), *Ideology and Classic American Literature*

15. Lawrence Buell, *New England Literary Culture: From Revolution through Renaissance*

14. Paul Giles, *Hart Crane: The Contexts of "The Bridge"*

13. Albert Gelpi (ed.), *Wallace Stevens: The Poetics of Modernism*

12. Albert J. von Frank, *The Sacred Game: Provincialism and Frontier Consciousness in American Literature, 1630–1860*

11. David Wyatt, *The Fall into Eden: Landscape and Imagination in California*

10. Elizabeth McKinsey, *Niagara Falls: Icon of the American Sublime*

9. Barton Levi St. Armand, *Emily Dickinson and Her Culture: The Soul's Society*

8. Mitchell Breitwieser, *Cotton Mather and Benjamin Franklin: The Price of Representative Personality*

7. Peter Conn, *The Divided Mind: Ideology and Imagination in America, 1898–1917*

6. Marjorie Perloff, *The Dance of the Intellect: Studies in the Poetry of the Pound Tradition*

The following books in the series are out of print

5. Stephen Fredman, *Poet's Prose: The Crisis in American Verse*

4. Patricia Caldwell, *The Puritan Conversion Narrative: The Beginnings of American Expression*

3. John P. McWilliams, Jr., *Hawthorne, Melville, and the American Character: A Looking-glass Business*

2. Charles Altieri, *Self and Sensibility in Contemporary American Poetry*

1. Robert Zaller, *The Cliffs of Solitude: A Reading of Robinson Jeffers*